GEORGIAN COLLEGE LIBRARY 2

250101 (00)

MW01518319

Casting Solutions for the Automotive Industry

SP-1504

Learning Resource Centre
Georgian College
One Georgian Drive
Barrie, ON
L4M 3X9

GLOBAL MOBILITY DATABASE
*All SAE papers, standards, and selected
books are abstracted and indexed in the
Global Mobility Database*

Published by:
Society of Automotive Engineers, Inc.
400 Commonwealth Drive
Warrendale, PA 15096-0001
USA
Phone: (724) 776-4841
Fax: (724) 776-5760
March 2000

TL240 .C38 2000

0134105480377

Casting solutions for
   the automotive industry.
      2000.

2002 09 24

Permission to photocopy for internal or personal use of specific clients, is granted by SAE
for libraries and other users registered with the Copyright Clearance Center (CCC), provided that the base fee of $7.00 per article is paid directly to CCC, 222 Rosewood Drive,
Danvers, MA 01923. Special requests should be addressed to the SAE Publications
Group. 0-7680-0554-X/00$7.00.

Any part of this publication authored solely by one or
more U.S. Government employees in the course of their
employment is considered to be in the public domain,
and is not subject to this copyright.

No part of this publication may be reproduced in any form, in an electronic retrieval system or otherwise, without the prior written permission of the publisher.

ISBN 0-7680-0554-X
SAE/SP-00/1504
Library of Congress Catalog Card Number: N98-42939
Copyright © 2000 Society of Automotive Engineers, Inc.

Positions and opinions advanced in this
paper are those of the author(s) and not
necessarily those of SAE. The author is
solely responsible for the content of the
paper. A process is available by which
the discussions will be printed with the
paper if is is published in SAE Transactions. For permission to publish this paper
in full or in part, contact the SAE Publications Group.

Persons wishing to submit papers to be
considered for presentation or publication
through SAE should send the manuscript
or a 300 word abstract to: Secretary,
Engineering Meetings Board, SAE.

Printed in USA

PREFACE

Technological advances are continually being made within the cast metals industry. In an effort to present the latest developments in casting technology to the automotive community, the "Engineered Casting Solutions" session was organized for the SAE 2000 World Congress. The papers written for this session are contained within this SAE Special Publication, Casting Solutions for the Automotive Industry (SP-1504).

Traditionally, casting related papers have been organized by metal type such as aluminum castings or iron castings. This outdated approach has treated castings as commodities. In reality, cast products offer unique solutions to automotive engineering problems. The papers within this publication are organized into one of five major categories, specifically:

1. New and Emerging Casting Methods,
2. Simulation of the Casting Process,
3. Investigations of Material Property Data,
4. Underhood Applications for Cast Components, and
5. Chassis Applications for Cast Components.

The first three sections focus on new processes for producing castings and assuring sound products. Sections four and five focus on automotive applications for cast products regardless of metal type.

Also contained within this special publication is a section titled "Casting Industry Resources" which is intended to be a reference for automotive product engineers, casting designers, and purchasing representatives. This additional section contains a glossary of metalcasting terms, a listing of casting technical organizations, and a listing of universities engaged in casting technology research.

Edward J. Vinarcik
Navistar International Transportation Corp.

Session Organizer

TABLE OF CONTENTS

NEW AND EMERGING CASTING METHODS

2000-01-0675 Novel Near-Net-Shape Tool-Less Method for Manufacturing of Cast Metal Matrix Composites: Three-Dimensional Printing (3DP) of Ceramic Preforms Combined with Investment Casting Technology 3
Maxim Seleznev, Brett Shulz, James Cornie and Shiyu Zhang
Metal Matrix Cast Composites, Inc.
Eli Sachs, James Serdy and Michael Cima
Massachusetts Institute of Technology

2000-01-1384 The Freeze Cast Process...11
Arnie Yodice
Freeze Cast Engineering-Duramax Co.

2000-01-0676 Semisolid Metal Processing: A New Paradigm in Automotive Part Design 15
Andreas N. Alexandrou and Gilmer R. Burgos
Semisolid Metal Processing Laboratory,
Metal Processing Institute, WPI
Vladimir M. Entov
Institute for Problems in Mechanics of the Russian Academy of Science

2000-01-0677 Advanced Rehocasting Process Improves Quality and Competitiveness 21
Mitsuru Adachi and Satoru Sato
UBE Industries Ltd.

2000-01-0678 Automotive Applications Using Advanced Aluminum Die Casting Processes 39
Rathindra DasGupta and Dayne Killingsworth
SPX Corporation CONTECH Division

2000-01-0679 Lightweight Iron and Steel Castings for Automotive Applications 55
Alan P. Druschitz and David C. Fitzgerald
Intermet Corporation

SIMULATION OF THE CASTING PROCESS

2000-01-0754 Concurrent Product and Process Development Using Casting Process Simulation 67
Jiten V. Shah
K+P Agile, Inc.

2000-01-0755 Flow Modeling of Casting Processes 71
Ken A. Williams
Flow Simulation Services, Inc.

2000-01-0756 Ensuring Castable Designs with Casting Process Simulation 79
Christopher Rosbrook and Ralf Kind
MAGMA Foundry Technologies, Inc.

2000-01-0757 Automotive Casting Defect Reduction by Process Simulation 85
Yun Xia
K + P Agile, Inc.
TingXu Hou
Citation Corporation

INVESTIGATIONS OF MATERIAL PROPERTY DATA

**2000-01-0758 Monotonic and Cyclic Property Design Data for Ductile
Iron Castings** 95
John M. Tartaglia, Paige E. Ritter and Richard B. Gundlach
Climax Research Services
Lyle Jenkins
Ductile Iron Society

**2000-01-0759 The Effect of Copper Level and Solidification Rate on the
Aging Behavior of a 319-Type Cast Aluminum Alloy** 115
Carla A. Cloutier and J. Wayne Jones
University of Michigan,
Department of Materials Science & Engineering
John E. Allison
Ford Motor Company, Ford Research Laboratories

UNDERHOOD APPLICATIONS FOR CAST COMPONENTS

**2000-01-0760 High Integrity Structural Aluminum Casting Process
Selection** 129
Robert Wolfe and Rob Bailey
Madison-Kipp Corporation

**2000-01-0761 Design Review of Cast Aluminum Scroll Compressor
Components** 141
David T. Gerken
Casting Technology Company
John Calhoun
Sanden International (U.S.A.), Inc.

**2000-01-0763 Dissimilar Welding of Si-Mo Ductile Iron Exhaust Manifold
Welded to Stainless Steel Catalytic Converter using NI-ROD
Filler Metal 44HT** 147
Brian Baker and Samuel Kiser
Special Metals Corporation
Peter Chen
Ford Motor Company
Brian Skinn and Rick Williams
Wescast Foundries, Ltd.

2000-01-0764 Automotive Applications of Austempered Ductile Iron (ADI): A Critical Review 159
John R. Keoug and Kathy L. Hayrynen
Applied Process Inc., Technologies Div.

CHASSIS APPLICATIONS FOR CAST COMPONENTS

2000-01-1290 Austempered Ductile Iron Castings for Chassis Applications 173
Robert J. Warrick, Paul Althoff, Alan P. Druschitz,
Jeffrey P. Lemke and Kevin Zimmerman
Intermet Corporation
P. H. Mani
Research Consultant, Ductile Iron Society
Mitchell L. Rackers
Caterpillar Corporation

2000-01-1291 Aluminum Alloys for Automotive Knuckle Castings 181
Gangalore Keshavaram, David Seiler and Dave DeWitt
Amcast Automotive

CASTING INDUSTRY RESOURCES

Metalcasting Technology Nomenclature 203
Michael J. Lessiter, Ross Foti
The American Foundrymen's Society

Metalcasting Industry Organizations 207
Michael J. Lessiter, Ross Foti
The American Foundrymen's Society

Metalcasting University Programs 213
Bill W. Sorenson
The Foundry Education Foundation

NEW AND EMERGING CASTING METHODS

2000-01-0675

Novel Near-Net-Shape Tool-Less Method for Manufacturing of Cast Metal Matrix Composites: Three-Dimensional Printing (3DP) of Ceramic Preforms Combined with Investment Casting Technology

Maxim Seleznev, Brett Shulz, James Cornie and Shiyu Zhang
Metal Matrix Cast Composites, Inc.

Eli Sachs, James Serdy and Michael Cima
Massachusetts Institute of Technology

Copyright © 2000 Society of Automotive Engineers, Inc.

ABSTRACT

New three-dimensional printing technology (3DP) developed at MIT was tried as a manufacturing method to fabricate ceramic preforms for a discontinuously reinforced metal matrix composites. Minor modifications to the "legacy" 3DP technology allowed to produce such preforms successfully. Preforms were then infiltrated with liquid aluminum resulting in composite materials as strong as produced via conventional methods. Net shape connecting rod preforms were 3D-printed and used to produce composite connecting rods without building any molds or tooling using novel Tool-less Mold™ technology.

INTRODUCTION

Industrial designers, purchasing agents and military SPO's have three wishes: high quality, low cost, and quick delivery. Rarely are all three attainable at the same time, and almost never when selecting metal matrix composites. Conventional materials, like monolithic aluminum and steel, have well established manufacturing technologies. Their mechanical behavior is well understood by industrial designers and manufacturing engineers alike. However today's markets are demanding better performance at a lower cost, driving the need for continued development of materials and manufacturing technologies to satisfy these requirements. Discontinuously reinforced metal matrix composites (DRMMC's) are beginning to find their way into many of today's demanding applications due to the wide range of desired material properties that can be obtained, including low weight, high stiffness, controlled expansion, fatigue and wear resistance to name a few. To date, metal composites have been cost prohibitive, only utilized in expensive systems such as aerospace and high end automotive applications. It is imperative to break this cost barrier by developing highly loaded aluminum and copper MMC's which require no physical tooling for making either the porous ceramic preform or the metal infiltrated composite component.

One of the most critical steps in manufacturing metal matrix composites is fabrication of a uniformly porous ceramic preform, which is an exact dimensional replica of the final cast component. Ceramic preforms can be made many ways including slurry forming, injection molding, and powder compaction. All of these methods require a hard tool or pattern to define the shape and the results for complex shapes is poor leading to low yield counts. The tooling is usually made of hardened steel or aluminum, which can take months to machine costing thousands of dollars, and since the preforms are made with highly abrasive ceramic particles the tool pattern eventually loses dimensional accuracy and must be replaced. Moreover, design changes and/or new product concepts require a completely new set of tooling or modifications to existing tooling (if applicable). This situation does not fit well with today's quick paced market conditions where delays in new product introductions and high manufacturing costs can thwart production efforts.

To overcome these challenges, feasibility study of manufacturing ceramic preforms by a process called three-dimensional printing (3DP™) for making complex, porous ceramic shapes for liquid metal infiltration was conducted. The method is inherently flexible and extremely cost effective since it relies on computer generated CAD models to switch from one shape to another and does not require any investment in tooling to make the preform. Ceramic shapes printed by this method have very uniform properties and complex shapes are easily manufactured without the design limitations associated with conventional methods. Present study showed that after some modifications aimed at maximizing composite's properties the 3DP process can be successfully used to make robust preforms for metal matrix composites. In parallel, a Tool-less Mold™ investment casting approach to direct manufacturing pressure infiltration cast composite parts is being developed. Parts made using by this process are also discussed.

EXPERIMENTAL METHODS AND MATERIALS

MANUFACTURING OF CERAMIC PREFORMS.

The process flow for the 3D-printing process as conceived at MIT in late 80's is presented in Figure 1. Later in the paper we refer to it as "legacy" approach. A polymer or silica binder is printed into a bed of ceramic powder layer by layer. After the printing process is complete the binder is set at an elevated temperature and the ready preform is separated from the rest of the loose powder bed by shaking or ultrasonic vibration in water. Often the preform is subjected to additional sintering. This is particularly necessary if polymer binder is used since at high process temperature it burns off, and one has to rely on particle to particle sintering for preform support.

Other preforms used in the work were produced using a water-based slurry casting technique.

ALUMINUM MATRIX ALLOY

Aluminum 2214 alloy (Al-4.5%Cu-0.85%Si-0.5%Mg-0.8%Mn) [1] was used as a matrix material in the present work.

MANUFACTURING OF COMPOSITES

Most composites made in the course of the program were produced using the Advanced Pressure Infiltration Casting (APIC^{TM}) process [2] -Figure 2, which relies on graphite molds to define the shape of the final composite part. Graphite molds were machined with dimensions to accommodate ceramic preforms. Preforms were placed in the molds and the mold assemblies were placed into a steel mold vessel. The preheated to 700C molds and preforms were then infiltrated with liquid aluminum alloy at 725C under 7 MPa pressure.

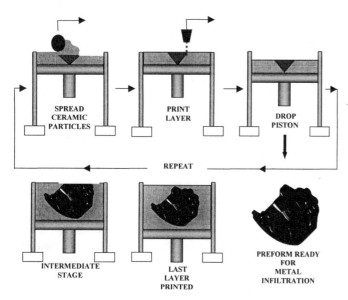

Figure 1. Schematic of MIT Three Dimensional Printing (3DP^{TM}) process.

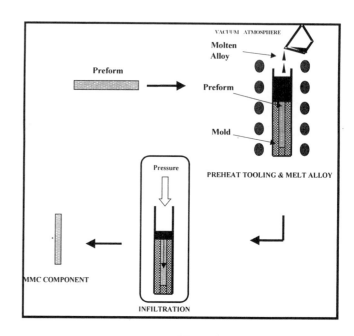

Figure 2. Schematic of APIC^{TM} processes.

HEAT TREATMENT OF COMPOSITES

Composite panels extracted from the molds after infiltration were subjected to homogenization and aging T6 heat treatment. The purpose of the heat treatment was to maximize yield strength of the matrix alloy and bring composite to the same reference condition as for previously databased composite mechanical properties. Homogenization of composites was done at 493C for 12 hours followed by quenching of the parts in the water. Aging was done at 170C for 6 hours followed by cooling in still air.

MECHANICAL TESTS OF COMPOSITES

Mechanical testing of composite specimens was done in tension. A universal testing Instron machine with 10-ton load cell was used for the testing. In most cases, test specimens were cut out of 2.5 mm thick composite plate with a diamond saw. Specimens width was 12 mm. Grinding with a diamond disk on both sides insured that the surfaces of the specimen were parallel to each other. Gauge length during testing was maintained at 25 mm. Crosshead speed during testing was 1.27 mm per minute.

COMPOSITES MICROSTRUCTURE CHARACTERIZATION

Composite microstructures were studied on metallographically polished specimen crossections in an AMRAY 1200B SEM equipped with a EDS detector. Backscattered and secondary electron contrast was employed for imaging. EDS spectroscopy was used to characterize phases of interest in the microstructure.

RESULTS AND DISCUSSION.

CHARACTERIZATION OF COMPOSITES WITH
PREFORMS PRINTED USING MIT'S 3DP LEGACY
APPROACH.

Three-dimensional printing (3DP) of ceramics, which
originated at MIT in the late 80's, was not specifically tailored
to manufacturing preforms for metal matrix composites.
Therefore it was important to characterize composites
produced using preforms which were printed by that
technology and identify problems which should be resolved
before it could be successfully used for making MMCs.
Initially, composites with alumina preforms that were printed
using 30-micron alumina particles and silica binder were
characterized. Silica binder was set after printing at 900°C and
the specimens were then removed from the ceramic bed and
infiltrated with 2214 alloy.
Testing of the specimens in tension showed very low strength
values – 180 MPa (Table 1) compared to 350 MPa routinely
achieved on alumina reinforced composites produced using
APIC[TM] technology.

Table 1. Mechanical properties of alumina reinforced
composites with preforms printed by MIT legacy 3DP
technology.

Preform Particulate	Preform Binder	Particulate Size (Volume Fraction)	Composite UTS, MPa
Alumina	SiO2	30 micron (30%)	180
Alumina	SiO2	13 micron (32%)	160

Examination of the microstructure showed that layers of silica
binder, which apparently did not react with aluminum
surrounded the alumina particles – Figure 3. These layers were
obviously full of defects, weak and probably the reason for
low mechanical strength.
Another possible reason for low strength could be the large
particle size used in the printing of preforms. Usually
composites produced via APIC[TM] have 13 micron alumina
particles as preform for it since a study done earlier [3]
indicated that composites reinforced with larger particles show
lower strength – Figure 4.
Therefore, MIT investigated whether it would be possible to
print ceramic preforms using 13-micron alumina powder.
After some experimentation with printing parameters, a 13-
micron alumina particulate preform with silica binder was
printed and then infiltrated with 2214 alloy. However, tensile
testing of the specimens showed low strength again – Table 1.
The specimens printed using much smaller particles contained
excess binder around reinforcement particles, similar to that
shown in composites with larger particles– Figure 5.
The amount of binder in both studied preforms was obviously
excessive. Therefore, investigation was conducted whether
there is a safe amount of silica binder which could be used in
preforms for alumina reinforced composites. The study was
performed on slurry cast preforms. Varying amounts of silica
were added to the preforms. The amount was measured to
produce increasing Si concentrations in the composite matrix
alloy assuming the silica would react with aluminum fully to
form aluminum oxide and free silicon. The amount varied

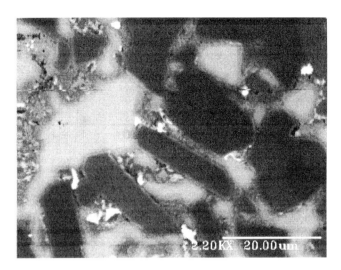

Figure 3. Microstructure of composite with 30 micron alumina
preform printed at Specific Surfaces Corp. using MIT legacy
3DP technology.

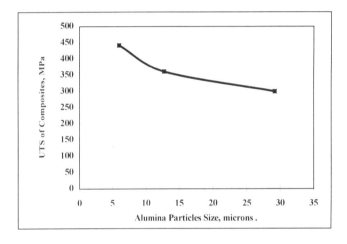

Figure 4. Tensile strength of alumina particulate reinforced
2214 alloy vs. reinforcement particle size

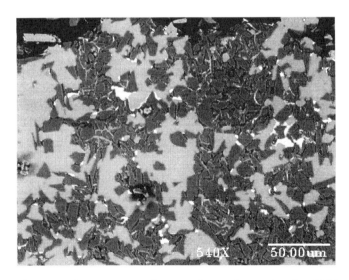

Figure 5. Microstructure of composite preform printed at MIT
using 13-micron alumina particulate and silica binder.

from 0.4 to 6% by weight of Si from silica binder as compared to the weight of the matrix alloy. The preforms were then infiltrated and tensile specimens sliced from composite panels. Results of the study are presented in Table 2.

Table 2. Mechanical properties of composites with increasing silica binder content.

Si from binder as % of matrix weight	Heat Treatment	UTS, MPa	St. Dev. MPa
0.4	T6	369	32
0.675	T6	336	26
1.028	T6	313	30
2.151	T6	281	9
3.076	T6	168	25
6.086	T6	234	11

As one may see, the strength of composites drops dramatically with increased binder content – Figure 6. Therefore, the conclusion was made that printing preforms with silica binder should be avoided to preserve composite strength.

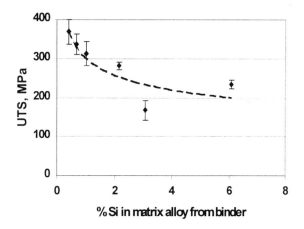

Figure 6. Tensile strength of composite versus Si content in the binder.

Another problem identified upon characterization of "legacy" preforms was low reinforcement volume fraction – Table 1. Lower volume fraction of ceramic particles in composite results in reduced composite stiffness – an extremely valuable mechanical property.

The study also called for the solution to yet another technological problem. To be truly flexible, 3DP technology, which does not require making of expensive dies or molds, should be used in conjunction with a similarly mold-less pressure infiltration process.

PROBLEMS WITH USING 3DP "LEGACY" TECHNOLOGY IDENTIFIED AS A RESULT OF THE STUDY.

Four problems to overcome were identified as a result of characterization of the MIT 3DP legacy approach:

➢ A new 3DP process which does not rely on silica binder should be developed
➢ Smaller particles should be used for printing preforms

➢ A way to increase preform volume fraction should be identified.
➢ A moldless investment process for pressure infiltration casting should be demonstrated on 3DP preforms.

The following sections of the paper will describe how these challenges were overcome.

3DP "LEGACY" APPROACH PROBLEM RESOLVED: PRINTING WITH SMALLER PARTICLES.

As mentioned earlier, "legacy" 3DP technology relied on larger particle sizes to print ceramic shapes. The larger reinforcement particle size is detrimental to the strength of metal matrix composites. The reason is that larger particles are more likely to contain larger flaws, which initiate fractures at lower loads [4]. Therefore, an experimental run using 13-micron alumina particles was conducted.

At first, MIT experienced significant problems with splashing of the powder upon binder droplet impact. Since the 13-micron particles are much lighter than 30-micron particles, they are ejected upon impact of a printer droplet more readily. The problem was resolved by means of blowing humid water vapor on the surface of the powder bed during printing. This procedure prevented particulate ejection upon binder impact. However, that breakthrough in itself did not bring any improvements to the mechanical properties of 3DP composites since large amounts of silica binder were used, keeping the volume fraction of ceramic reinforcement low.

3DP "LEGACY" APPROACH PROBLEM RESOLVED: PRINTING WITHOUT SILICA BINDER.

Since it was established that the presence of silica binder even in small quantities reduces composite strength, another way of binding the 3DP preform together had to be found.

One of the possible solutions was to print order of magnitude smaller alumina particles in-between larger 13-micron particles and then sinter the particulate bed. Then, the areas where the smaller particles are present would be sintered preferentially, defining the shape of the 3DP part. The part could then be removed from the rest of the printing bed through ultrasonic vibration in water or by mechanical brushing.

This suggested solution to the binder problem, if successful, could also eliminate another drawback of 3DP "legacy" preforms by increasing the volume fraction of reinforcement in the preform since the smaller particles would be introduced into the gaps between the larger ones.

Before that path could be taken, a fundamental question had to be answered: would it be possible to infiltrate such a fine powder mix? Pressure infiltration casting relies on relatively low pressures (7-10 MPa) to overcome capillary forces and drive liquid metal in-between the reinforcement particles. The threshold beyond which aluminum could not be infiltrated into alumina lies somewhere close to 1-micron pore size if model for spherical particles is used [5].

Therefore, a composite preform was made by mixing together 13-micron and 1-micron powders, ball-milling the mix in slurry form and then casting the slurry into panel-shaped preforms. Some of the preforms were then subjected to pressure infiltration APIC™ process in a just dried condition and some preforms were infiltrated after being sintered at 1300 C.

Upon testing it was determined that the properties of the composites with preforms which were sintered were much higher than of the non-sintered ones – Table 3.

Table 3. Mechanical properties of bimodal (13-micron + 1-micron) particulate alumina preforms infiltrated with 2214 alloy.

Preform Sintering Regime	UTS, MPa
none	190
1300C for 4h	428

Upon examination of the microstructure of these composites it became apparent that the composite with a non-sintered bi-modal preform was only partially infiltrated, but the bi-modal preform of the composite subjected to sintering was infiltrated completely – Figure 7.

Next, an attempt was made to 3D-print a 1-micron particle slurry in-between the 13-micron particles in the dry powder bed. The successful run resulted in printing of a series of 6 x 8 x 110 mm bars which were then removed from powder bed after sintering at 1300C for 4 hours. Measured volume fraction of alumina in the printed bi-modal preform was 37% - much higher than 30% for the monomodal 3D-printed preforms.

After the printing the preforms were infiltrated with 2214 matrix alloy and the resulting composite evaluated under SEM – Figure 8. Evaluation clearly showed that the preforms were infiltrated completely and 1-micron particles were evenly distributed in-between larger alumina particles.

3DP "LEGACY" APPROACH PROBLEM RESOLVED: LOW DENSITY OF THE PREFORM.

The next step in developing acceptable (from the point of view of composite properties) 3DP preforms was to achieve higher particulate volume fraction. As mentioned earlier, printing of bimodal instead of mono-modal preforms substantially increased the particulate volume fraction in the preform (from 30 to 37%); however it was still lower than the 55% volume fraction of composites produced using slurry cast preforms. To achieve higher particulate volume fraction an attempt was made to increase the flow rate at which the fine particulate slurry is printed into a coarser powder bed. This goal proved to be difficult to achieve. When the flow rate was increased without changing other parameters of the printing process, the integrity of the printed droplets was compromised and they began to break down, which resulted in formation of tiny satellite slurry droplets that were difficult to control. Only after considerable experimentation was stable printing achieved. The printhead nozzles had to be increased from 50 to 70 micron to sustain the 2.25 cc/min flow rate of slurry, which contained 20% of 1-micron alumina particles by volume. As a result preforms containing 52% volume fraction of alumina were printed and then sintered at 1300C for 4h.

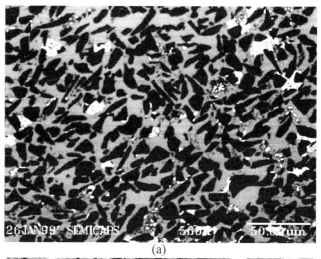
(a)

(b)

Figure 7. Microstructures of composites with sintered (a) and non-sintered (b) preforms. The composite with the sintered preform is infiltrated completely. The composite with non-sintered preform is infiltrated only partially.

The printed preforms were then infiltrated with 2214 alloy. Resulting composite was studied under the SEM. The microstructure of the bimodal composite reinforced with 52% volume fraction of alumina is presented in Figure 9. It is clear from the micrographs that larger particles are uniformly surrounded by smaller particles. High magnification observations of the microstructure confirmed that the composite is fully infiltrated. After the bimodal preforms were infiltrated and their microstructure characterized, a study of mechanical properties was performed on these composites. The results of the study are presented in Table 4.

Table 4. Mechanical properties of composites with bimodal (13+1 micron) 37% and 52% volume fraction preforms.

Composite Preform	UTS, MPa
3DP 13+1 micron, 37% dense	362.4
3DP 13+1 micron, 52% dense	225.96
Slurry cast 13-micron alumina, 55% dense	388

As one may see, a composite with a 37% volume fraction particulate preform has a strength that is close to the level measured for the slurry cast 13-micron alumina preform composite. The reason why the composite with 52% dense preform showed lower strength is not clear. It is possible that slight variations in deflocculating additions to the fine slurry during printing played a negative role. This inconsistency definitely points out to the necessity of a much more detailed study and characterization of 3DP composites. However, we believe that by reaching a strength of 362 MPa, the potential of the technology was proven.

DEMONSTRATION OF MOLDLESS INVESTMENT TECHNOLOGY IN COMBINATION WITH 3D-PRINTING OF COMPOSITE PREFORMS AND ADVANCED PRESSURE INFILTRATION CASTING PROCESS

One of the main goals of the study was to demonstrate that 3D-printing of composite preforms could be combined with moldless investment technology for pressure infiltration casting.
If this idea was proven, the resulting process for manufacturing composite materials would become truly flexible and robust. At no stage of the process would it be necessary to design and machine molds or other expensive tooling. Instead, the design process could concentrate on the composite part itself, exploiting the unique mechanical properties of the composite to the maximum performance benefit of the component.
A schematic illustration of proposed investment casting process is presented in Figure 10. Challenging shape for the demonstration of the technology was used – a connecting rod. Preforms in the shape of the connecting rod were 3D-printed at Specific Surfaces Corporation using the MIT legacy approach, since at that early stage of development new bimodal printing technology did not yet provide the same definition of the 3DP parts. The preforms were then sealed and coated with parting agents and invested with proprietary Tool-less Mold™ compound. Following this, the parts were pressure infiltrated using the APIC™ process. Figure 11 shows a metal matrix composite connecting rod that was processed by the 3DP™/Tool-less Mold™/APIC™ process. Also shown is an un-infiltrated preform. These objects are practically indistinguishable.
As shown, it was demonstrated that 3D-printing of preforms can be successfully used in conjunction with the Tool-less Mold™ and APIC™ processes to provide a qualitatively new level of flexibility for composite manufacturing technology.

CONCLUSIONS

As a result of the present work the following conclusions and recommendations for future work can be made:

1. 13-micron ceramic particles can be used to 3D-print preforms for composite materials.
2. Silica binder used in 3D-printing of composite preforms degrades composite properties.
3. 3D-printing of composite preforms can be done without the use of silica binder. Preforms can be defined by printing fine ceramic particles into the bed of coarser grit followed by preferential sintering.
4. Volume fractions of up to 52% of ceramic particles were achieved by jetting slurries loaded with fine particles in-between the coarser ones.

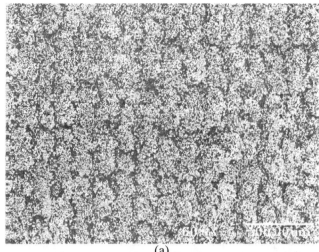

(a)

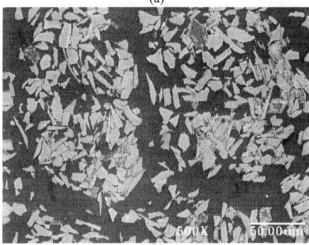

(b)

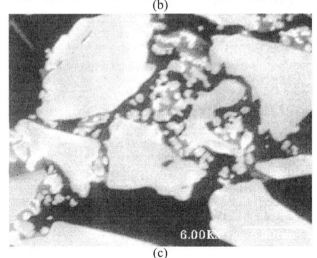

(c)

Figure 8. Microstructure of bimodal 13+1 micron alumina preform infiltrated with 2214 alloy at low (a), intermediate (b) and high (c) magnifications.

Composites with bi-modal 37% particulate volume fraction preform demonstrated the same level of mechanical strength as composites produced using slurry casting of preforms.
5. 3D-printing of preforms can be successfully used in conjunction with the Tool-less Mold™/APIC™ process.

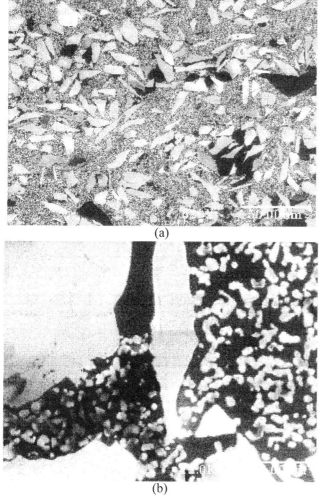

(a)

(b)

Figure 9. Microstructure of 3DP bimodal (13+1micron) 52% dense preform infiltrated with 2214 Al alloy at low (a) and high (b) magnifications.

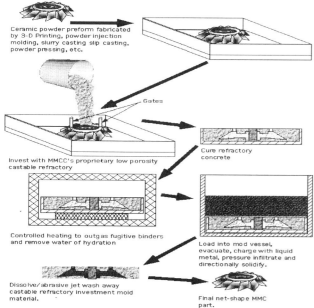

Ceramic powder preform fabricated by 3-D Printing, powder injection molding, slurry casting slip casting, powder pressing, etc.

Gates

Invest with MMCC's proprietary low porosity castable refractory

Cure refractory concrete

Controlled heating to outgas fugitive binders and remove water of hydration

Load into mod vessel, evacuate, charge with liquid metal, pressure infiltrate and directionally solidify.

Dissolve/abrasive jet wash away castable refractory investment mold material.

Final net-shape MMC part.

Figure 10. Schematic of Tool-less Mold™/APIC™ process for pressure infiltration casting

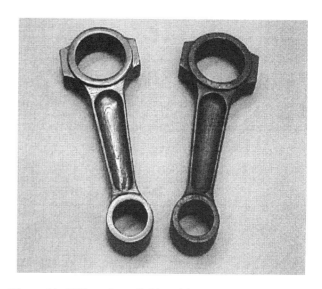

Figure 11. 3DP preform (left) and investment pressure cast connecting rod (right)

ACKNOWLEDGMENTS

Support from the Ballistic Missile Defense Organization (BMDO) is gratefully acknowledged. We appreciate the continuing interest of Mr. Albert Bertram (BMDO) in new manufacturing technologies for advanced materials.

REFERENCES

1. *Metals handbook*, vol.2, ASM International, 1990.
2. US Patent #5322109, June 21, 1994
3. M. L. Seleznev et al. *SAE Transactions-Journal of Materials and Manufacturing*, 1998
4. Llorca J. et al, *Acta Metallurgica et Materiala*. v.43, 1995, pp. 181-192, 1995.
5. A. Mortensen and J.A. Cornie, *Metallurgical Transactions A*, Volume 18A, p 1160.

CONTACT

Dr. Maxim L. Seleznev can be contacted at the following address:
MMCC, Inc.
101 Clematis Avenue
Waltham, MA 02453
Phone: (781)893-4449 ext.12
Fax: (781)893-7230
E-mail: mseleznev@mmccinc.com
Web: www.mmccinc.com

The Freeze Cast Process

Arnie Yodice
Freeze Cast Engineering-Duramax Co.

Copyright © 2000 Society of Automotive Engineers, Inc.

ABSTRACT

The Freeze Cast Process (FCP) for casting precision automotive and other parts, freezes water in rubber molds to make temporary ice patterns that can be invested in ceramic slurries to make a shell that can be filled with any molten metal. The resulting precision casting will be of tight dimensional tolerance, exhibit excellent surface finish and reproduce intricate detail so that parts obtained will require little or no machining.

Parts can be produced at 35-50% of the cost of competing precision casting processes such as Lost Wax and Lost Foam, competing in price with sand castings.

INTRODUCTION

The process, presented in U.S. Patent #5,072,770 has many advantages over other precision casting processes. These advantages are:

It cuts cost by 50%, improves quality, is EPA friendly and lends itself very well to rapid prototyping. It uses 35-65% less labor and capital equipment than competing investment casting processes.

THE PROCESS

1. A solid master pattern is produced.
2. Rubber molds are made from the master pattern with one or more part cavities. Gating can be included or not.
3. The rubber mold is filled with water and frozen.
4. The rubber mold is stripped from the frozen pattern.
5. The ice pattern or tree is then invested in a refrigerated slurry.
6. The slurry-coated pattern/tree is stuccoed with powdered ceramics.
7. The coated pattern/tree is then hung to dry in a refrigerated room where temperature is kept below zero degrees Centigrade.
8. Steps 5, 6, 7 are repeated as many times as necessary to build a strong enough shell to withstand the hydrostatic pressure of the molten metal.
9. The shell is then put into a low temperature oven to melt the ice patterns and the water is poured out of the shell.
10. The empty shell is then fired in a furnace prior to pouring the molten metal into it.

Advantages Over Lost Wax

- It is not necessary to inject wax into metal molds. No presses, ducting, or tempering of wax needed.

- It does not require gluing and assembly of individual patterns into clusters or washing of the pattern clusters prior to investing them in the slurry.

- Autoclaves to wash out wax are not necessary, nor high temperature furnaces for the burning of wax residues, a source of pollution of water and air.

All that labor and equipment are not required!

Advantages Over Lost Foam

- No polystyrene beads are used; therefore, they don't show on the surface of the castings.

- Molds don't have to be heated.

- No foam-blowing equipment required.

- No steam generating equipment required.

- No gluing of patterns and gating required.

- No flasks and vibrating equipment required.

A lot of savings in labor and equipment!

Advantages Over Sand Casting

Sand/Metal Ratio:

Vertical Molding (Disamatic)... 12:1 Approx.

Cope & Drage & Squeezer..... 15:1 Approx.

Large Mold (no-bake)......... 20:1 Approx.

The move and mix an average of 7.27 Kgs. (16 Lbs.) of sand to obtain .45 Kgs. (1.0 Lbs.) of castings.

Freeze Cast Process (FCP):

Moves and mixes .45 Kgs. (1.0 Lbs.) of sand (ceramics) to obtain 3.18 Kgs. (7.0 Lbs.) of castings!

To cast the same weight of castings:

Sand Castings require: .51 Kgs. (112.0 Lbs.) of sand

Freeze Cast require: .45 Kgs. (1.0 Lbs.) of sand (ceramics)

Tooling Advantages

The cost of FCP tooling is a fraction of that of metal dies for Lost Wax and Lost Foam.

Example: Impeller Casting for Trim & Drain pump for Trident and Seawolf submarines.

Lost Wax	Lost Foam	Freeze Cast
$15,000	$20,000	$4,500

Die Casting	Freeze Cast
$50,000*	$4,000**

*4-cavity water cooled aluminum die with ejector pins.

**1-Master pattern-10 rubber molds.

Quality Advantages

Dimensional linear tolerance over 254mm (10.0 in):

Sand Castings	Lost Wax-Lost Foam	Freeze Cast
+/- 2.54mm(.100in)	+/- 1.95mm(.077in)	+/- .94mm(.037in)

Draft:

Sand Castings	Lost Wax - Lost Foam	Freeze Cast
1.0%	No draft.	Negative draft possible due to use of rubber molds.

Surface Finish:

Sand Castings	Lost Wax - Lost Foam*	Freeze Cast
6RA(600 micro in)	2RA(125 micro in)	2RA(125 Micro in)

*L.F. Beaded texture visible.

Casting defects, blow holes, inclusions, skin blemishes, Scale: 1-10

Sand Castings	Lost Wax - Lost Foam	Freeze Cast
10	5	3
.		

Fabrication Avoided

Since ice patterns do not have the "fabricated" or glued as much as in lost wax-lost foam, shells are cleaner which minimizes inclusions in the castings. When gluing is necessary it is done by wetting the contact surface on the gating with water which is sucked in by capillarity between the two opposite surfaces.

Ferrous Cooling

The FCP allows the control of carbide formation as well as any other microstructure desired in the metal matrix. This is done by pouring the shells at 1093°C (2000°F) as they come out of the furnace, at room temperature or chilled. In cast irons by pouring the shells at high temperature, chilled edges and hard spots are absent and Brinell hardness more predictable, since the iron will cool slowly.

Defects Avoided

No lustrous carbon is deposited on the casting surface, as in the case with lost foam. The chemical composition of the casting is not changed, and very low carbon content stainless steel (.02%C) can be cast as is required for weldable grade CF3M and CN7M (Carpenter 20 Austenitic Steel) for instance.

Flexibility

All metals used for casting can be poured with the FCP, including Ductile and Austempered Ductile Iron. If we add to this the ability to control the microstructure of the castings, and; therefore, their mechanical properties, the FCP offers a whole range of possibilities for automotive castings applications, part design, and reduction of weight.

Environmental Advantages

Compared to sand foundries a FCP foundry does not require dusty shakeout operations, sand systems, or backhouses. Operations are not noisy.

It is also not necessary to dispose of large volumes of sand and there is no contamination of the air with chemical additives.

Compared with Lost Foam, the FCP has no contaminants such as, pentane, soot, benzene. No PNA (Polynuclear Aromatic Hydrocarbons) measurements are required. The small amounts of VOC's (Volatile Organic Compounds) generated from alcohol used in the slurries, are confined to the cold rooms exhaust manifolds and eliminated before they are released to the atmosphere.

In contrast with Lost Foam the FCP does not produce smoke from burning wax nor the smells associated with it, and there is no contaminated water from wax washout in autoclaves to dispose of.

Rapid Prototyping

Metal cast prototypes can be cast in 24-36 hrs. when master patterns are made by Stereo Lithography, SLS, LOM, SLA or other desktop manufacturing methods.

The cost of master patterns are the same as for those from use in other processes.

The big advantage for the FCP is that it can produce, in a short time, many, say 50 or 100 prototypes, not just one like all other precision casting processes, since we do not need to burn out the master pattern like they do.

We make a rubber mold from the master pattern and can produce as many ice patterns as needed from it. This is a valuable attribute of the FCP for controlling dimensional repeatability, machining tests, interaction with mating parts, etc. Better data is obtained from testing 100 parts than just one.

Tooling

The rubber molds used in the FCP have the advantage of being an off the shelf technology, well known to pattern makers and people in the precision casting industry.

They are inexpensive, $3-5 for materials and about $50-100 labor cost for a multiple cavity mold. They are easy to make (mix and pour the liquid rubber and wait for it to cure, then strip it from the master pattern). It takes anywhere between 12-24 hrs. to cure.

As previously mentioned, master patterns cost the same as those used for other precision cast processes.

The materials used are:

Urethane Polysulphide (resin & hardener) and Silicon Rubber.

Accuracy: .127mm per 25.4mm (.001-.005 in/in)
Thickness: 1.60-3.18mm (1/16-3/8 in.)

For short runs, the rubber mold must be supported by a contoured backup plate made of any castable plastic material. For long runs, the plastic backup plate can be used as a pattern to cast it in aluminum.

Rubber molds can be used to -65°C without shrinking or expanding. Compare this to expandable polystyrene patterns used in the lost foam process, which grow .2-.3% in a few hours, then shrink .7-.8% over the next 30 days.

Ice Patterns

Ice patterns are very predictable due to the fact that the ice always exhibits the same linear expansion when frozen at the same temperature.

Temperature (°C)	Volume Increase (frozen)
-1.0	1.0002
-2.0	1.0003
-3.0	1.0004
-4.0	1.0006
-5.0	1.0007
-6.0	1.0009
-7.0	1.0011
-8.0	1.0013
-9.0	1.0016
-10.0	1.0019

Following are some examples of **dimensional** tolerances obtained with the FCP:

Step Bar Casting

Master	Ice Pattern	Growth
180mm(7.089in)	180.08mm(7.090in)	.08mm(.001in)
30.023mm(1.182in)	30.0253mm(1.1821in)	.0023mm(.0001in)
12.49mm(.492059in)	12.498mm(.492059in)	.0010mm(.000059in)

Ice temperature was measured with contact thermometer.
Length was measured with height gage at room temperature.
Width and thickness with an electronic comparator at room temperature.

Starting with a master pattern, a rubber mold was made from which ice patterns were obtained for a GEOMETRICAL FEATURES casting. This was used to study the ability of ice to be able to reproduce sharp features and dimensional tolerance of features with different casting modules (ratio of volume over casting cooling surface). Several Austempered ductile iron castings were poured, these are the results:

Geometrical Features Casting

Length 83.82mm(3.300in)	+/- .076mm(.003in) max. deviation
Boss diam. 19.380mm(.763in)	+/- .25mm(.001in) max. deviation
Boss thickness 12.827mm(.505in)	+/- .050mm(.002in) max. deviation
Boss I.D. 9.398mm(.370in)	+/- .025mm(.001in) max. deviation

Process Production Capability

We have designed FCP plants for the production of shells that can produce 100 net tons of castings in eight hours with twelve people using only off the shelve technology, methods and machines.

We have also designed systems that can be retrofitted to existing Cope and Drag horizontal green sand molding lines as well as vertical green sand molding lines (Disamatic) to be able to produce precision castings, using FCP shells, at the same production rate as with green sand molds.

SUMMARY

There is no single casting process that is universally used to comply with every casting specification. However, the Freeze Cast Process was developed for industries that would like to have precision castings, at a reasonable cost that require little or not machining; attributes that we are sure, are desired by the automotive industry.

REFERENCES

1. Yodice A. April 1999. Freeze Process Cuts Castings Costs. Tech Spotlight, Advance Materials & Processes, Volume 1555, No. 4. ASM International.
2. Martin Leland D. December 1998. Freeze Cast Process Ready for Licensing, Incast Magazine, Volume XI, No. 12. Investment Casting Institute.
3. Yodice A. October 1998. The Freeze Cast Process, Paper No. 27, 46th Annual Technical Meeting. Investment Casting Institute.
4. Peters Dean M. August 1995. Patterns in Ice, Foundry Management & Technology.
5. Heine Hans J. International Editor, November 1992, Casting with Ice Patterns Technical Developments, Foundry Management & Technology

CONTACT

Arnie Yodice, Freeze Cast Engineering-Duramax Co., 240 Barber Ave., Worcester, MA 01606, USA. Telephone: 508-854-0600, Fax No.: 508-854-0369. E-mail: Yodicea@javanet.com

2000-01-0676

Semisolid Metal Processing:
A New Paradigm in Automotive Part Design

Andreas N. Alexandrou and Gilmer R. Burgos
Semisolid Metal Processing Laboratory, Metal Processing Institute, WPI

Vladimir M. Entov
Institute for Problems in Mechanics of the Russian Academy of Science

Copyright © 2000 Society of Automotive Engineers, Inc.

ABSTRACT

Processing of metal alloys in their mushy state represent a new trend in metal processing. The process produces components with low porosity, high crack resistance along with fine microstructure and mechanical properties that are better than those produced by casting and comparable to those of forged alloys. In the present work, a summary of the current understanding on the rheology of semisolid slurries is presented. This is followed by an overview of the different mathematical models proposed by the authors to describe the experimentally observed behavior of the material and salient numerical results including die filling.

INTRODUCTION

Traditionally metals are cast in liquid state using various methods. Sand casting produces parts with inferior strength due to porosity caused by gas entrapment, and it encounters difficulties in manufacturing of thin-wall parts. High-pressure casting is used to produce thinner parts, but the ductility of the parts tends to be low. Heat treatment to improve ductility is not possible due to blistering caused by entrapped gases. Squeeze casting is designed to operate at higher-than-usual pressures. The increased pressure reduces porosity, however, tool wear and manufacturing costs are higher.

For years, metallurgists and scientists are looking for a process that produces parts with better mechanical properties or looking for new alloys with improved characteristics. However, the discovering of the processing of metal alloys in their semisolid state was almost accidentally. In the early 70's, Flemings and co-workers at MIT, while working on the hot tearing in alloy castings [Spencer et al., 1972], envisioned that the rheological properties of vigorously stirred tin-lead slurries offered potential advantages over processing metal alloys in liquid phase. In the last few years, the interest in the process has increased rapidly. This is

evidenced by the incidence of five bi-annual international conferences devoted to the subject in the last eight years. Currently, a number of automotive components are being produced using semisolid metal (SSM) processing technology.

THE SSM PROCESS

The processing of metal alloys in semisolid state can be divided into: (a) a pre- and (b) a processing stage. During preprocessing, the raw material is melted and allowed to cool while growing dendrites are broken up using mechanical or electromagnetic stirring. The resultant slurry has an equiaxed microstructure made up of round, rosette-like crystals mixed in eutectic liquid. The specially preprocessed material is either immediately injected into a die (rheocasting) or solidified in billet forms for later processing (thixoforming). In the last process, the billets are reheated to a temperature in the mushy zone, and then injected into a die (thixocasting) or shaped between closed dies (thixoforging). The process is called rheocasting in that the melt is rheologically manipulated during the liquid solid transformation.

In thixoforming, the preprocessing of the raw material can be alternatively performed using a process called Strain Induced Melt Activated (SIMA). This consists in deforming the billet at a temperature above the recristallization temperature (hot working) followed by cold work at room temperature.

The preprocessing of the raw material plays a very important role. Figure 1 shows the microstructure of an A357 aluminum alloy obtained by classical casting and by electromagnetic stirring (MHD). In conventional casting, the nuclei formed during solidification grow and become coarse, heavily branched dendrites as depicted in Figure 1a. In contrast, when continuous electromagnetic stirring is used, the microstructure is extremely fine, composed of coarsened dendrite fragments as shown in Figure 1b.

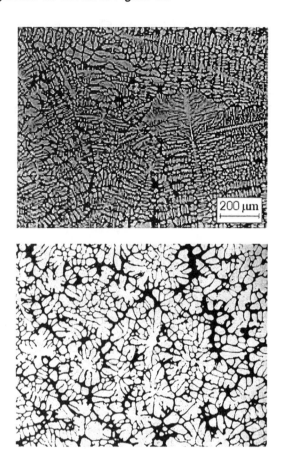

Figure 1. Dendritic and equiaxed microstructure

The desired morphology in the solid phase is obtained only after reheating the billet into the semisolid state just before injection. Figure 2 shows that the microstructure of the electromagnetically stirred alloy, after a holding time of 10 min at 580 °C, evolves to a more spheroidal microstructure. The reheating time is long enough to allow a minimum degree of spheroidization, but it has to be limited to avoid excessive ripening for thin section castability.

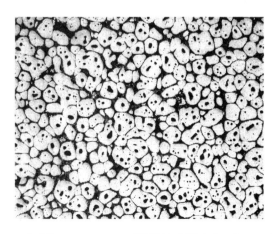

Figure 2. Microstructure of MHD A356 aluminum alloy after reheating to 580 °C and 10 min holding time

ADVANTAGES OF THE PROCESS

The processing of materials in semisolid state offers distinct advantages over other near-net shape manufacturing processes. Upon reheating the semisolid billet to the mushy zone, the material exhibits solid-like and liquid-like behavior. It maintains its structural integrity and it can be easily handled. And due to its higher than liquid viscosity, the flow remains mostly laminar minimizing the possibility for gas entrapment, thus allowing heat treatment to obtain superior mechanical properties.

The process can be used to produce parts with complicated geometry and close dimensional tolerances. The process is performed at a lower temperature, resulting in shorter solidification times, less shrinkage and increased productivity. The lower temperature also results in longer die life, and lower energy requirement than in other traditional casting methods. Products made using the process also have high strength and integrity with improved surface finish. The process can be also used to produce composite materials with enhanced properties. For instance, beryllium-reinforced aluminum alloys have increased elasticity, while the density and thermal expansion decrease with beryllium content.

RHEOLOGY OF SSM

The theoretical understanding of SSM materials during shape making operations is still under development. Most systematic studies of SSM relate to equilibrium steady-state shear flow experiments [Spencer et al. (1972), Joly and Mehrabian (1976), Charreyron and Flemings (1985), Kattamis and Piccone (1991), Turng and Wang (1991), Flemings (1991), Kumar et al. (1994)]. In these experiments, the SSM samples were cooled continuously to a given solid fraction while sheared at a constant shear-rate. Under these conditions, SSM's behave as shear thinning (pseudoplastic) fluids with effective viscosity decreasing with increasing shear rate. However, available experimental data on transient flows show a shear-thickening behavior, i.e., increasing effective viscosity with increasing shear rate [Kumar et al. (1994), Martin et al. (1994), Modigell et al. (1998)]. In constant shear-rate experiments, the structure of the material is allowed to evolve to a new steady state corresponding to the imposed shear field. On the other hand, in rapid transients, the structure of the material does not have enough time to adjust to the new conditions. Additionally, experimental results by Kumar et al. (1994) show that these materials resist finite shear stresses before deformation begins, thus behaving like Bingham fluids.

The difference in behavior under steady and unsteady deformation is due to the complex rheology of the slurry. In the mushy state, the slurry is a dense suspension made up of eutectic liquid and alpha phase particles. The average solid volume fraction is a function of the

16

bulk temperature of the suspension that as the temperature varies from the liquidus to the solidus limits, changes from zero to unity. During processing, the applied forces are transmitted throughout the bulk of the mixture, thus squeezing the liquid out of the solid matrix. As the liquid is squeezed out, and the local volume fraction changes, the viscosity of the mixture also varies.

The kinetic nature of the skeleton, breakdown/restoration process, is manifested in step-shear-rate experiments. It was found that he breakdown of the network formed by the solid metal particles in the slurry is faster than the restructuring [Mada and Ajersch (1990), Peng and Wang (1996), Kumar et al. (1994), Modigell et al. (1998)]. The characteristic time for the stress evolution was estimated to be about 10 s. Also, in an early work, Joly (1974) conducted hysteresis-loop tests for the Sn-15%Pb SSM and concluded that the SSM's are thixotropic. Peng and Wang (1996) using shear-rate step experiments after different rest times confirmed this behavior. The most plausible explanation for this behavior is that at high solid fractions, the particles form a skeleton, and the apparent mechanical behavior of the system is determined primarily by the structure and properties of the skeleton. The structure is almost never at equilibrium, it depends on the mechanical and thermal history of the material, and its evolution is governed by a number of kinetic phenomena of different characteristic time-scales. As a result of these kinetic processes, the rheological properties of the material, such as effective viscosity and yield stress, decrease with structure breakdown and increase with its development.

The dynamic response of the material under net-shape forming conditions is the result of the combined effects of liquid-solid and solid-solid interactions. Unlike most conventional materials, the geometry of the flow also affects the rheological behavior of the slurry: solid walls and geometric details of the die can induce relative motion between the solid matrix and the liquid phase, thus leading to phase separation and particle crowding. Moreover, the material response is different depending on the nature of the applied forces. For instance, pure shear can cause particle migration that produces variable density. The material under extensional shear conditions however, results in a more uniform microstructure. It is important to note that most real flows are a combination of the above two extremes. The resultant material microstructure and its response to processing variables are needless to say complicated.

Figure (2) summarizes the current understanding of the behavior of semisolid slurries: (a) under steady shear conditions the micro-structure evolves exhibiting shear-thinning behavior, (b) under rapid transients the material structure remains constant thus exhibiting shear thickening behavior, (c) at low shear rates the material shows a finite yield stress. This implies that the material will not deform unless a stress level is exceeded. Note, also that the above behavior depends also on time and temperature.

IMPLICATIONS FOR AUTOMOTIVE PART DESIGN

Given the complex rheology of the SSM slurries, i.e. nonlinear stress-shear rate relationship, finite yield stress, thixotropic behavior, and temperature and shear rate dependent properties, the filling of complex geometries is significantly different from that of liquid casting of melt aluminum. Moreover, the mechanical properties of the final part will depend on the deformation history of each part. This is both an advantage and a disadvantage for the design of automotive parts where property consistency is essential. While the disadvantages are obvious, the time dependency of the properties can be made into an advantage by exploiting this fact through proper die design. For instance, dies can be designed to fill so that the final parts have non-homogeneous mechanical properties that meet performance requirements. Through proper design then, parts can be made with less material (hence, less weight) and of course less cost. In order to develop a better understanding of the process and to optimize the operation, it is important to gain a deep insight into the underlying theoretical and physical concepts associated with this novel family of materials. Mathematical and computational models then are essential tools for the further development and application of the process.

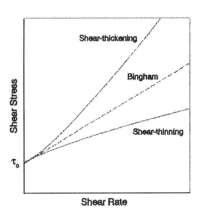

Figure 3. Behavior of SSM: shear thinning in steady flow and shear thickening in rapid transient flow.

MODELING SSM

BULK MODELS

Semisolid materials are two-phase mixtures of liquid and solid particles. Therefore, a complete mathematical model should involve a complete description of both phases. However, it is possible to capture the bulk behavior of the slurry by using average models.

Model with constant structure

Bulk models that ignore the evolution of the microstructure attempt to reproduce the experimentally observed behavior that SSM slurries exhibit shear-thinning and shear-thickening behaviors under steady-shear and rapid transients, respectively. Therefore, the majority of such constitutive models are based on power-law type fluid models (e.g. Turng and Wang, 1991). These models are valid to the extent of the underlying assumptions, i.e. shear thinning models are only valid for steady processes (not representative of fast filling processes). Similarly, shear-thickening models are valid under the assumption of constant microstructure, characteristic of rapid transient response. Alexandrou (1996) used a phenomenological constitutive equation based on a Herschel-Bulkley fluid that fits both shear-thinning and shear-thickening behaviors. The finite yield stress implicit in the model accounts for the existence of finite yield stress,

$$\tau = \tau_o + K\dot{\gamma}^n \qquad (1)$$

where τ is the shear stress tensor, $\dot{\gamma}$ the shear rate tensor, τ_o the yield stress, K the consistency index, and n the power law index. Indeed, numerical results in a sudden 3-d square expansion by Burgos and Alexandrou (1998) show that this model predicts the time evolution of yielded/unyielded regions (Figure 4). In unyielded zones, the material does not deform, and hence it remains stagnant or flows like a solid body.

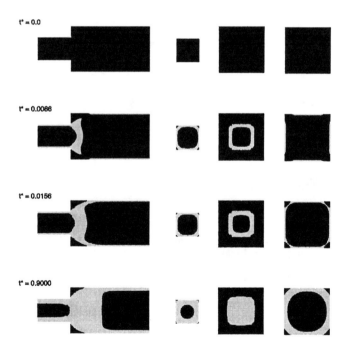

Figure 4. Evolution of yielded (gray) and unyielded zones (black) in a sudden 3-D square expansion.

Model with variable structure

The time-dependent rheological behavior is modeled using a non-dimensional structural parameter λ, similar to the one introduced by Mada and Ajersch (1990) and Kumar et al. (1994). This parameter characterizes the state of the structure of the solid particles in the slurry. In a fully structured state i.e. when all the particles are connected, λ is assumed to be unity. In a fully broken state, when none of the particles are connected, λ is assumed to be zero. The evolution of this structural parameter is defined by a first-order rate equation, similar to the approach in chemical reaction kinetics (Moore, 1959). Typically, it is assumed that the rate of breakdown depends on the fraction of links existing at any instant and on the deformation rate. Similarly, the rate of build-up is assumed to be proportional to the fraction of links remained to be formed,

$$\frac{\partial \lambda}{\partial t} + u \cdot \nabla \lambda = a(1-\lambda) - b\lambda|\dot{\gamma}|e^{c|\dot{\gamma}|} \qquad (2)$$

where the recovery parameter a, and the breakdown parameters b and c are empirical constants. $|\dot{\gamma}|$ is the second invariant of the rate of strain tensor. The exponential dependence on the deformation rate, in the rate of break-down term of Equation (2) is included to account for the fact that the shear stress evolution for the shear-rate step-up experiment is faster than for the step-down case [Mada an Ajersch (1990), Kumar et al. (1993), and Peng and Wang (1996)]. At equilibrium, the rate of breakdown is the same as the rate of recovery.

Consistent with the experimental evidence, the rheological constants are assumed to depend on λ and volume fraction s (hence, temperature),

$$\tau = \tau_o(\lambda,s) + K(\lambda,s)\dot{\gamma}^{n(\lambda,s)} \qquad (3)$$

Experimental data then are analyzed for the actual dependence of the material parameters by using various assumptions concerning the initial state of the microstructure. For instance, it can be assumed that, starting from the same steady state shear stress, immediately after the shear-rate step-up and step-down experiments the structure remain the same (and hence λ) (Burgos et al. 1998). The assumption is based on the fact that in shear-rate step experiments, there is not enough time for the structure to change. Currently, complete sets of such experimental data are not available to determine the material properties and therefore, more experimental data are needed.

The constitutive model presented above is used to simulate the filling of a tensile bar cavity against gravity. This simple cavity is chosen in order to demonstrate the importance of the thixotropic behavior of SSM slurries. The evolution of the filling process with a gate velocity equal to 1 m/s is presented in Figure 5. The corresponding Reynolds and Bingham numbers are respectively, Re = 195 and Bi = 0.12. For the simulated conditions, the middle section is filled first, and then, the two end sections. A back-flow pattern in the lower section is generated due to the stepped change in cross section. High shear rates are generated close to the walls and specially in the lower end section of the tensile bar due to the change in direction of the flow. In these regions a breakdown of the structure is predicted. Only a small core region penetrating the bar remains almost undeformed at the end of the filling process.

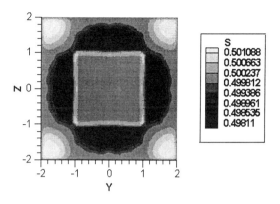

Figure 6. Solid fraction distribution at the sudden expansion section of a 3-D square expansion

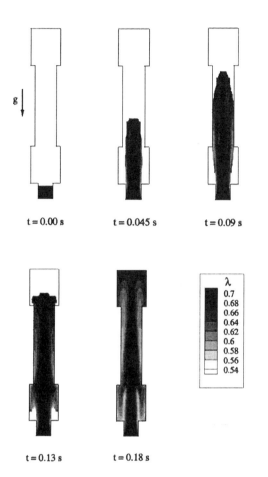

Figure 5. Evolution of the structural parameter λ in the filling of a tensile bar cavity in the direction of gravity (Re =195, Bi = 0.12)

Two-Phase Models

Alexandrou et al. (1997) proposed a two-phase model based on transport phenomena ideas. In this model, the deformation of the solid matrix was assumed to follow the behavior of an incompressible Herschel-Bulkley fluid while the liquid phase is assumed to behave as a Newtonian fluid. Numerical simulations by Alexandrou et al. (1998) and Burgos et al. (1998) predicted relative motion and particle crowding. The development of conservation laws for such two-phase theory is rather straightforward; however, the main issues are the appropriate constitutive models and material parameters that must be obtained through extensive experiments.

Figure 6 shows the distribution of solid fraction at the sudden expansion section of a 3-D square expansion. Di-agglomeration of solid particles are predicted close to the inlet channel wall due to the high shear rates encountered in this region while particle crowding is predicted at the corners.

CONCLUSIONS

Processing metal alloys in their semisolid state has distinct advantages over similar near-net shape manufacturing processes. The process can be used to produce parts with improved mechanical properties compared to parts produced by conventional processes. However, the effective use of the process requires a good understanding of the physics of the process. Several issues remain to be understood before the potential of the process can be fully realized such as: (a) the effect of processing pre-history on microstructure development, (b) the re-heating of the material, (c) the rheology during processing, (d) solid/liquid phase separation etc. A complete understanding of the process can be achieved through simultaneous experimentation and mathematical/numerical modeling.

REFERENCES

1. Alexandrou A. N., "Three Dimensional Flow of Thixotropic Materials in a Channel with a Sudden Expansion Using a Phenomenological Constitutive Relation," Light Metals 96 Symposium Proceedings, edit. W. Hale, TMS, Warrendale, PA 15086, pp. 807-811, 1996.
2. Alexandrou A. N. and Entov V. M., "Two-Phase Rheological Model for Semisolid Material Behavior," Journal of Rheology, 1997.
3. Alexandrou A. N., Burgos G. R., and Entov V. M., "Two-Phase Model for Processing Materials in Semisolid State," Light Metals 98, TMS, Warrendale, PA 15086, ISBN 0873393902, 1081-1086, 1998.
4. Burgos, G. R., Alexandrou, A. N., and Entov, V. M., "Two-Phase Model of Flow of Semi-solid Materials," 5th International Conference on Semi-Solid Processing of Alloys and Composites, Edited by A. Bashin, J. Moore, K. Young, and S. Midson, Colorado School of Mines, June 23-25, ISBN 0918062985, 217-224, 1998.
5. Burgos G.R., Alexandrou A. N., and Entov V. M., "Time Dependent Rheology of Semisolid Metal Suspensions," Symposium Synthesis of Light Metals III, Edited by F. Froes, C. Ward-Close, P. McCormick, and D. Eliezer, San Diego, California, Feb 28-March 4, 1999. Also published in Light Metals 1999, TMS, Edited by C. Eckert, San Diego, California, Feb 28-March 4, 1999.

6. Burgos G. R. and Alexandrou A. N., "Flow development of Herschel-Bulkley Fluids in a sudden 3-D expansion," J. of Rheology, 43(3), 485-498, 1999.
7. Charreyron P. O. and Flemings M. C., " Rheology of Semi-Solid Dendritic Sn-Pb Alloys at Low Strain Rates: Application to Forming Processes", International Journal of Mechanical Science, 27, pp. 781-791, 1985.
8. Flemings M. C., "Behavior of Metal Alloys in the Semisolid State," Metall. Trans., 22A, 957-981, 1991.
9. Joly P. A, "Rheological Properties and Structure of a Semi-Solid Tin-Lead Alloy," Ph. D. Dissertation, Massachusetts Institute of Technology, Cambridge, Massachusetts, 1974.
10. Joly P. and Mehrabian R., "The Rheology of a Partially Solid Alloy", Journal of Material Science, 11 pp. 1393-1418, 1976.
11. Kattamis T. Z. and Piccone T. J., " Rheology of Semi-Solid Al-4.5 %Cu-1.5%Mg Alloy", Materials Science and Engineering A, 131, pp. 265-272, 1991.
12. Kumar P., Martin C. L., and Brown S., "Shear Rate Thickening Flow Behavior of Semi-Solid Slurries," Met. Trans., Vol. 24A, pp. 1107-1116, 1993.
13. Kumar P., Martin C. L., and Brown S., "Constitutive Modeling and Characterization of the Flow Behavior of Semi-Solid Metal Alloy Slurries - I. The Flow Response," Acta Met. et Mater., Vol. 42, 11, pp. 3595-3602, 1994.
14. Mada M. and Ajersch F., "Thixotropic Effects in Semi-Solid Al-6% Si Alloy Reinforced with SiC particles," in Bhagat R. B. et al. (Ed.), Metal & Ceramic Matrix Composites: Processing Modeling & Mechanical Behavior, The Minerals, Metals & Materials Society, pp. 337-350, 1990.
15. Martin C. L., Kumar P., "Constitutive Modeling and Characterization of the Flow Behavior of Semi-Solid Metal Alloy Slurries - II. Structural Evolution under Shear Deformation," Acta Met. et Mater., Vol. 42, 11, pp. 3603-3614, 1994.
16. Modigell M., Koke J.., Petera J., "Two-Phase Model for Metal Alloys in the Semi-Solid State," 5th International Conference on Semi-Solid Processing of Alloys and Composites, Edited by A. Bashin, J. Moore, K. Young, and S. Midson, Colorado School of Mines, June 23-25, ISBN 0918062985, 1998.
17. Moore F., "The rheology of Ceramic slips and bodies," Trans. Brit. Ceramic Soc. 58, pp. 470-494, 1959.
18. Peng H. and Wang K.K, "Steady State and Transient Rheological Behavior of a Semisolid Tin-Led Alloy in Simple Shear," 4th International Conference on Semi-Solid Processing of Alloys and Composites (ed. D. H. Kirkwood and P. Kapranos), University of Sheffield, pp. 2-9, 1996.
19. Spencer, D. B., Mehrabian, R. and Flemings, M. C., "Rheological Behavior of Sn-15%Pb in the Crystallization Range," Metall. Trans., 3, 1925-1932 (1972).
20. Turng L. S. and Wang K. K., " Rheological Behavior and Modeling of Semi-Solid Sn-15%Pb Alloy", Journal materials Science, 26, pp. 2173-2183, 1991.

2000-01-0677

Advanced Rehocasting Process Improves Quality and Competitiveness

Mitsuru Adachi and Satoru Sato
UBE Industries Ltd.

Copyright © 2000 Society of Automotive Engineers, Inc.

ABSTRACT

The New Rheocasting process will provide excellent mechanical properties with a positive solution for the cost of material that has been the weakness of the semi-solid casting process. The process is a kind of batch system. It uses a cup for each shot and a conventional automatic ladling system, which pours molten metal into the cup. This process produces semi-liquid slurry including globular crystals directly from molten metal without a stirring technique. The products made by this process have shown good mechanical properties. The solidification rate of a rheocasting sample is so high that the microstructures of the products are uniform and fine.

INTRODUCTION

Recently material conversion of plastics or cast iron to aluminum or magnesium alloys has been a major issue in automotive industries for weight reduction and material recycling. For these purposes, thixocast a semi-solid casting process (1,2) from heated billet is watched by the entire world with interest. Because their process imparts good qualities to castings that are difficult to achieve with permanent mold casting and traditional high pressure die casting. But there are several weak points, for example, higher material cost for billet in the thixocast process. To reduce material cost, a simple rheocasting process was developed. This process produces semi-liquid slurry including globular crystals directly from molten.metal. This system is designed to utilize Ube squeeze casting machine, therefore it will provide the optimum choice of process, i.e. according to the products either squeeze or rheocasting can be selected without major system change.

In this study, the basic process procedure and system configuration of Ube's rheocasting is presented. The microstructure, mechanical properties and fluidity of the rheocasting process is compared with squeeze casting process, which is considered a high grade aluminum casting process.

EXPERIMENTAL PROCEDURE

RHEOCAST SYSTEM

This system consists of a melting/holding furnace & ladling device, slurry making device, handling robot, high pressure casting machine (HVSC machine) and cup cleaning/coating device. A schematic layout of a system is shown in Fig.1. Melting/holding furnace supplies clean melt continuously and holds the melt in a relatively lower temperature compared to conventional casting process. The ladling device delivers the melt to the slurry making device with the rheocasting process, and delivers to shot sleeve of casting machine directly in case of squeeze casting process. Slurry making device makes rheocasting slurry from the melt one by one. Handling robot transfers the slurry held in the cup from slurry making device to shot sleeve of the casting machine. High pressure casting machine makes products with applying over 100MPa pressure to the slurry in high cycle. Cup cleaning/coating device maintains the cup with cooling down its temperature, removing remain and spraying lubricant to inner surface of the cup. The external appearance of slurry making device is shown in Fig.2. The turntable of this device rotates at a constant cycle time determined by the casting cycle. Each slurry is cooled through cooling section by controlled air blowing and, at the final stage, adjusted temperature distribution by high frequency induction heater. A high pressure casting machine for rheocasting is shown in Fig.3. This machine has a larger injection force than the conventional squeeze casting machine (HVSC machine). The typical features of this machine are outlined below.

1. Horizontal die clamping; Die clamping force 350 ton

2. Vertical, high pressure injection system Injection force: 66 ton (metal pressure:120MPa/80□shot sleeve)

Fig.4 indicates UBE New Rheocasting process flow. First of all, molten metal temperature controlled just above the melting point is poured gently into the cup. After pouring, the semi-liquid metal is cooled down to the target casting temperature by controlled air blowing. Each cup is heat insulated at the top and the bottom with ceramic covers to prevent over cooling at the area of the slurry. And temperature gradient of the slurry is adjusted by heating from outside of the cup with high frequency induction heater. This rheocasting slurry with prepared stably in the casting cycle is poured into the injection sleeve by turning the cup upside down so that oxide layer formed at the top surface of the slurry remains at the injection tip surface. It prevents including the oxide layer in the product. This rheocasting slurry is injected directly into the die cavity. The schematic drawing of 3 steps plate cast on the high pressure casting machine is shown in Fig.5.

ALLOY

99.85%Al, Al-25%Si alloy, Al-40%Cu alloy, Al-10%Mg Alloy, Al-5%Ti alloy and 99.9%Zn were selected to prepare the alloys (Table 1) used in this investigation. Commercial A356 ingots were also used. These alloys were grain refined with about 0.15% titanium. These alloys were melted in graphite crucible in an electric resistance furnace. After melting, argon degassing treatment was performed with the standard impeller technique.

HEAT TREATMENT

To get good mechanical properties, T6 heat treatment was done after rheocasting. Samples were solution treated at various temperatures in an air circulation furnace for various times. They were then quenched into water at room temperature and they were artificially aged to develop mechanical properties except A514 alloy. A514 alloy samples were T4 heat treated without artificial aging.

FLUIDITY

It is a general concern about the fluidity of rheocast metal because semi-liquid state is considered to show higher viscosity than completely liquid state. Fig. 6 shows a schematic drawing of mold for fluidity test. The casting temperature at rheocasting process and squeeze casting process are 580 °C and 720 °C respectively. The mold temperature is about 200 °C.

RESULTS

CHARACTERISTICS OF RHEOCASTING SLURRY

First, a 1.5 kg molten A356 alloy (AlSi7Mg alloy) containing 0.15% Ti which was held 5 °C above the melting point was poured directly into a cup. Second, the melt was cooled at a certain cooling rate to the casting temperature where a specified liquid fraction was established. The slurry was extracted by a stainless pipe (inside diameter was 15 mm) and quenched into water directly to fix the microstructure at that temperature.

Fig. 7 shows typical microstructures of the slurry quenched in water at 580 °C after cooled with cooling rate of 0.2 °C/s. The primary crystals were globular and fine (average diameter of primary crystal; about 100 μm). With a smaller cooling rate they were globular but

grew larger. With larger cooling rate they grew finer but were dendritic. There became dendrite crystals instead of globular crystals when the melt poured into the cup at 50 °C or more above the melting point.

The effects of ceramics covers made with calcium silicate for heat insulator and high frequency induction heater on the distribution of temperature were also investigated by setting six thermocouples in the slurry. Fig. 8 shows the temperature control effect on temperature distribution of the slurry during cooling. In the case of no temperature control after pouring, temperature differences between six positions were wider. It was difficult to discharge such slurry from the cup because some portion of the slurry becomes hard. On the other hand, temperature differences were minimal with proper temperature control by ceramics cover and induction heater, and it was easy to discharge such slurry from the cup.

CHARACTERISTIC OF RHEOCASTING PRODUCTS

Fig. 9 shows mechanical properties of rheocast and squeeze cast A356 (AlSi7Mg), A206 (AlCu4TiMg), 514 (AlMg5), 7075 (AlZnMgCu1.5) and 6061 (AlMg1SiCu) alloys. Hatched bars and plain bars show data of rheocasting and squeeze casting respectively. The plates were T6 heat treated (T4 for AlMg5 alloy) and mechanical properties were investigated at 15 mm thickness. Ultimate tensile strength of rheocasting was almost the same as that of squeeze casting. But rheocasting showed 5 - 10 % better elongation than squeeze casting. It was thought to be related with size and morphology of eutectic Si, segregation and so on. For example, rheocast 7075 alloy showed good elongation because the amount of segregation and shrinkage was smaller than squeeze cast 7075 alloy. This result indicates possibility of applying 7075 rheocasting to automobile parts that need large elongation such as suspension arms. Fig. 10 shows cooling curves of AlSi7Mg four step plate (6 / 12 / 18 / 24 mm thickness, shown in Fig. 11) directly measured at two point's in the die cavity. One measurement point is center of 12 mm thickness part, and the other point is center of the biscuit that acts as head of casting and solidify lastly. It took about 15 seconds for the squeeze casting biscuit to solidify completely, but only 2 seconds in the case of a rheocasting biscuit. This indicates the rheocasting process realizes a faster cycle time than the squeeze casting process.

Fig. 12 and Fig. 13 show microstructures and mechanical properties at 18 mm thickness part of A356 alloy four steps plate respectively. Rheocasting showed larger elongation than squeeze casting because of finer eutectic Si. Therefore rheocasting does not require modification treatment, which is necessary for thick squeeze casting. Modification treatment is usually done by adding 0.1 to 0.2 % strontium to the melt, but it needs some equipment and manpower to maintain proper strontium content. So elimination of modification treatment means cost reduction. And the rheocasting sample had no shrinkage porosity even at maximum 24 mm thickness area.

Table 2 shows the effect of casting process on fatigue strength of T6 heat treated A356 alloy. Rheocasting and squeeze casting samples were cut from 15 mm portion of 3 steps plate cast with high pressure casting machine. And gravity casting samples were cut from block using permanent mold defined in Japanese Industrial Standard H5202. The test is performed by using a rotating bending machine. The fatigue strength of rheocast alloy is equal to that of squeeze casting.

Table 3 shows the effect of casting process and shot velocity on flow length of A356 alloy. The fluidity of squeeze casting process is 2.6 to 4 times higher than that of rheocasting process. These results suggest that either squeeze casting or rheocasting should be selected according to the shape and size of products. For example, the parts having under 5 mm average wall thickness are suitable for squeeze casting process. On the other hand, tough parts having over 20 mm thickness portion are suitable for rheocasting process.

1. When a molten metal temperature controlled just above the melting point is poured gently into the cup and cooled down to the target casting temperature by controlled air blowing and with high frequency induction heater, rheocasting slurry including globular crystal can be prepared stably.

2. The mechanical properties of rheocast alloys were investigated at 15 mm thickness. Ultimate tensile strength of rheocasting is almost the same as that of squeeze casting. But rheocasting shows 5 - 10 % better elongation than squeeze casting. It was thought to be related with size and morphology of eutectic Si, segregation, and other microstructural defects.

REFERENCES

1. K. P. Young: The 3rd INTL CONF. ON SEMI-SOLID PROCESSING OF ALLOYS AND COMPOSITIES (1994) 155
2. M. C. Flemings: Metall. Trans.22B(1991)269

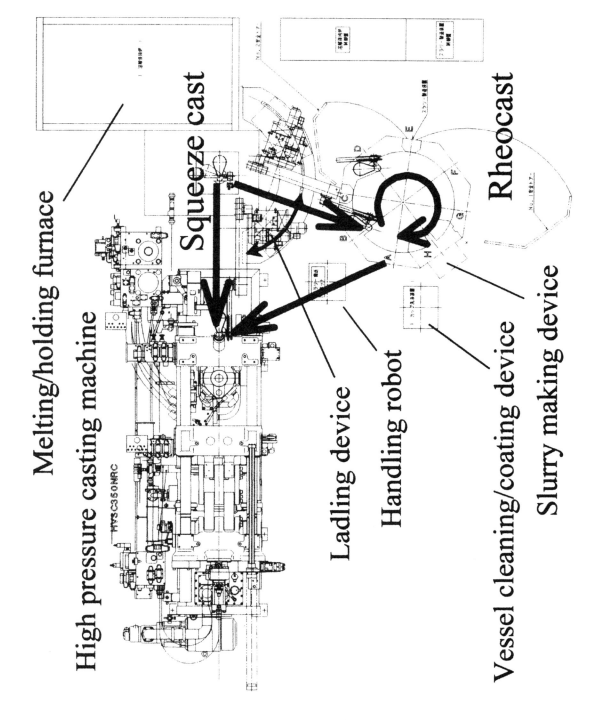

Melting/holding furnace

High pressure casting machine

HVSC350NRC

Squeeze cast

Rheocast

Ladling device

Handling robot

Vessel cleaning/coating device

Slurry making device

Fig. 1.Layout of the UBE New Rheocasting system

Fig. 2 External apperance of slurry making device

Fig. 3 High pressure casting machine for Rheocasting

26

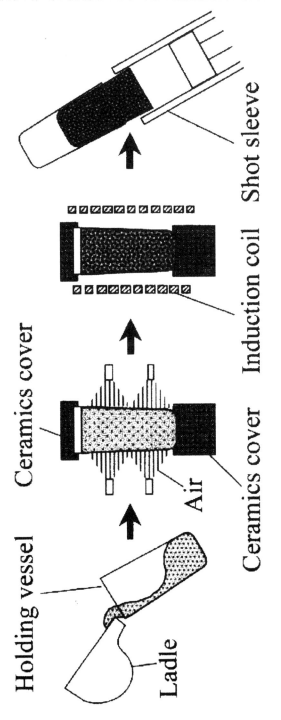

Fig. 4 UBE New Rheocasting process flow

Holding vessel

Ceramics cover

Ladle

Air

Ceramics cover

Induction coil

Shot sleeve

27

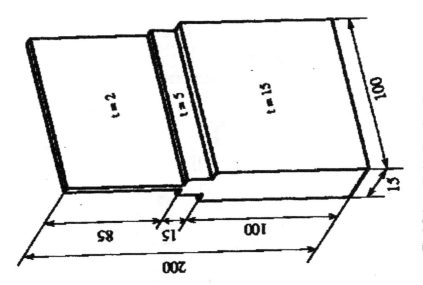

Fig.5 Schematic drawing of the 3 steps plate

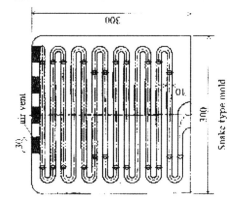

Fig.6 Schematic drawing of mold for fluidity

29

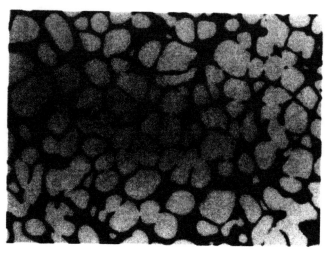

Cooling rate
0.2 °C/s

100 μ m

Fig.7 Typical microstructures of the slurry (AlSi7Mg , Quenched at 580)

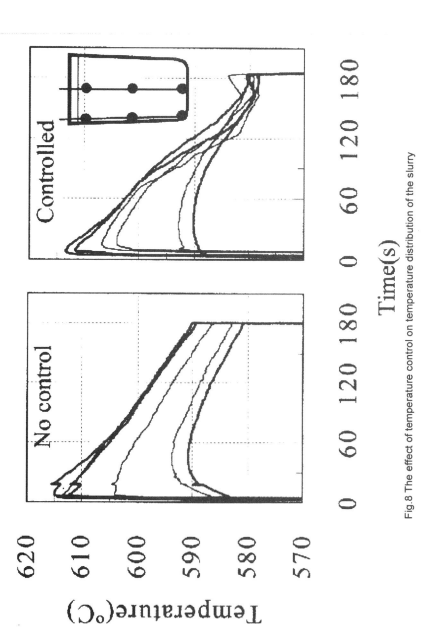

Fig.8 The effect of temperature control on temperature distribution of the slurry

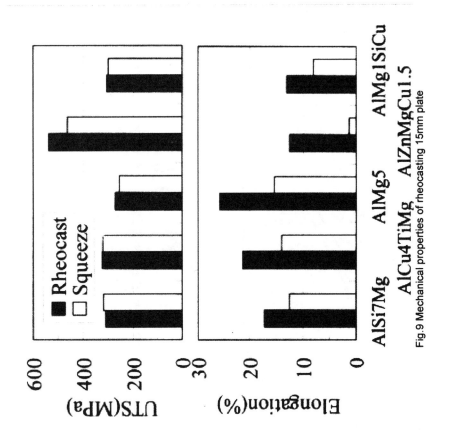

Fig.9 Mechanical properties of rheocasting 15mm plate

32

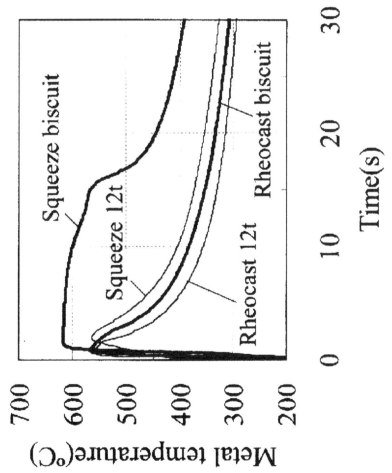

Fig.10 Cooling curves of AlSi7Mg four steps plate directly measured in die cavity

33

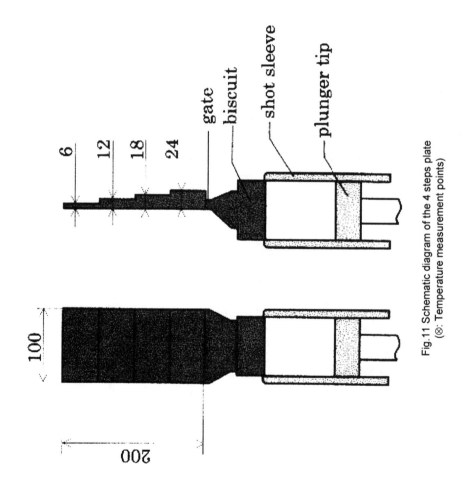

Fig.11 Schematic diagram of the 4 steps plate
(⊗: Temperature measurement points)

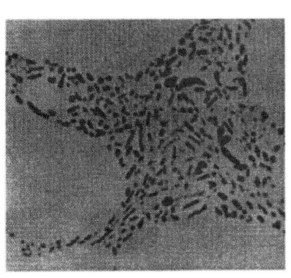

Rheocast 25 μm

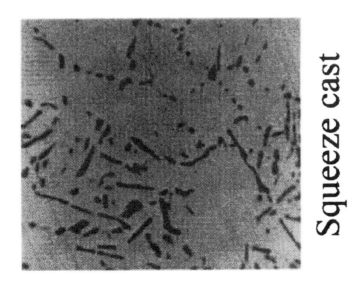

Squeeze cast

Fig.12 Mechanical properties of AlSi7Mg thick plate

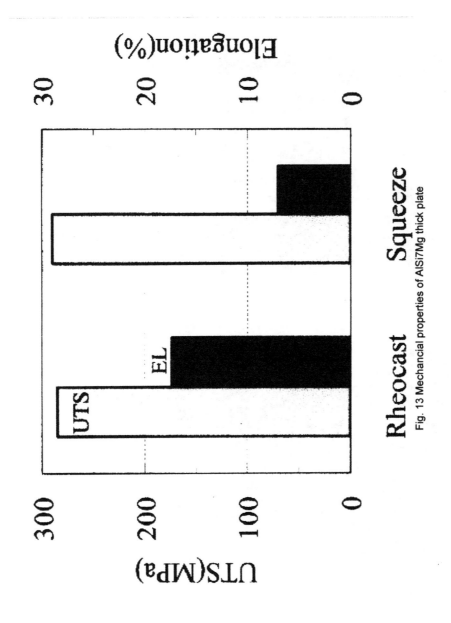

Fig. 13 Mechancial properties of AlSi7Mg thick plate

36

Table1 Chemical composition of alloys (mass %)

Alloy	Cu	Si	Mg	Zn	Fe	Mn	Ti	Al
A356		7.0	0.35		0.13		0.14	rem.
A206	4.6		0.25		0.15		0.15	rem.
A514			4.5		0.15	0.40	0.15	rem.
7075	1.6		2.5	5.5	0.15		0.15	rem.
6061	0.28	0.60	1.0		0.16		0.15	rem.

* Cr is not added to 7075 and 6061.

Table2 Effect of casting process on fatigue properties of T6 treated A356 alloy

Casting process	Sr modification	Fatigue strength (MPa)
Gravity casting	Yes	90
Squeeze casting	No	130
Rheocasting	No	130

Table3 Effect of casting process and shot velocity on flow length of A356 alloy.

Casting process	Flow length velocity (0.2m/s)	Flow length velocity (1.0m/s)
Squeeze casting	1600	2500
Rheocasting	400	950

Automotive Applications Using Advanced Aluminum Die Casting Processes

Rathindra DasGupta and Dayne Killingsworth
SPX Corporation CONTECH Division

Copyright © 2000 Society of Automotive Engineers, Inc.

ABSTRACT

This paper provides a description of commercially available die casting processes including conventional die casting process (high pressure, high velocity), squeeze casting (high pressure, controlled cavity fill rate), semi-solid metal casting, and Vacural™ (a variation of the conventional die casting process). The various automotive products made using these processes are also reported in the study.

In this study, the mechanical (tensile, impact, fatigue strength and fracture toughness) and wear properties are compared among the above processes. Results indicate that mechanical and wear properties of aluminum alloys made using the "high integrity" casting processes (squeeze, semi-solid metal casting and Vacural™) are superior to those of conventional die castings.

Finally, cavitation erosion (mechanical degradation of materials caused by cavitation in liquids) data for select aluminum alloys commonly used in squeeze casting and semi-solid metal casting processes are reported in this study. Results show that the type of casting process used, surface finish and alloy chemistry are key factors influencing erosion wear.

INTRODUCTION

The high pressure, high velocity cold chamber aluminum die casting process is widely used for manufacturing various automotive components including rack and pinion housings, air conditioning compressor units, and transmission components. However, with increasing focus on high product integrity (refined microstructure, reduced or absence of porosity, higher ductility, improved wear resistance, and the ability to heat treat); squeeze casting, semi-solid metal (SSM) and Vacural™ have emerged in recent years as the "high integrity" die casting processes.

Various automotive components made using the new die casting techniques include: master cylinders, steering knuckles, control arms, space frame nodes, wheels, rocker arms, connecting rods, air conditioning compressor units, and steering column components. These products compete well on product performance with gravity permanent mold (GPM), sand cast iron/aluminum, and conventional die castings.

This paper describes each of the commercially available die casting processes for various aluminum alloys and provides examples of automotive components made using these processes.

In this study, microstructures, mechanical and wear properties of conventional die castings are compared with those of the "high integrity" die casting processes. Attempts have also been made to compare cavitation erosion data for select aluminum alloys used in squeeze casting and SSM casting processes.

CONVENTIONAL (HIGH PRESSURE, HIGH VELOCITY) DIE CASTING PROCESS

A schematic of a typical conventional die cast machine (cold chamber) for aluminum alloys is shown in Figure 1.

The die-casting cycle consists of the following steps:

1. Closing and locking the dies

2. Ladling the molten metal into the cold chamber

3. Injecting the molten metal into the die and maintaining the pressure

4. Permitting the molten metal to solidify

5. Opening the die, and ejecting the casting

6. Spraying the die

Because of the combination of metal molds or dies, and pressure, thin sections and excellent detail can be achieved with the above process.

CASTING/TOOLING DESIGN FOR CONVENTIONAL DIE CASTING PROCESS

In regard to casting or tooling design for conventional die casting process, considerations are given to the following:

1. Placement of cooling channels in the tool to remove heat from the tool

2. Location and size of gate inlets to assure "atomized" metal flow

3. Use of separate squeeze pins to eliminate shrinkage porosity in regions otherwise difficult to feed.

4. Use of heat treated, premium grade H13 steel for die cavities

5. Avoidance of undercuts

6. Parting line placement

FACTORS AFFECTING CONVENTIONAL DIE CASTINGS

Key process variables influencing the soundness of conventional die cast products include:

1. Metal temperature

   Control of metal temperature to less than +/-5^{0}C of the set temperature helps minimize "sludge" formation and/or oxidation of metal; thereby reducing the occurrence of inclusions in castings.

2. Die filling conditions including gate velocity, final metal pressure and cavity fill time.

   a). Too low a gate velocity (<30 m/s) promotes poor fill and gate porosity [1].

   b). Too high a gate velocity (>60 m/s) may contribute to gate erosion and vortexing [1].

   c). The final metal pressure helps "densify" the casting by feeding molten metal to voids produced as liquid-to-solid shrinkage occurs [1].

   d). Long cavity fill times promote "cold shut" defect [1].

3. Die temperature

   Control of die temperature is necessary to minimize or prevent "hot spots" (regions susceptible to shrink porosity) and soldering.

4. Lubricant

   Gas entrapment in castings may be reduced via use of appropriate lube and dilution ratio.

CONVENTIONAL DIE CASTING APPLICATIONS

A few examples of components produced using the conventional die casting process for the automotive industry include steering housing, compact variable compressor cylinders for air conditioning compressors, and end plugs (Figure 2) for reciprocal ball power steering gear housings. Each of these components has different expected functional requirements.

A. Customer expectations of Steering Housing

Pressure tight (must not leak when pressurized at 0.55 Mpa)

Wear resistance (<1000 x 10^{-12} m^3)

High burst strength (>36 Mpa)

B. Customer expectations of CVC cylinder

Wear resistance (<100 x 10^{-12} m^3)

Uniform distribution of primary silicon particles

C. Customer expectations of End Plugs

Pressure tight (must not leak when pressurized at 11 Mpa)

High burst strength (>21 Mpa)

SQUEEZE CASTING PROCESS

Two types of casting machines are available for use in squeeze casting: vertical squeeze cast (VSC) and horizontal vertical squeeze cast (HVSC). Figure 3 shows the schematic of a typical HVSC machine [2].

The typical features of the HVSC machine include [3]:

1. Horizontal die clamping

2. A vertical, high pressure delivery system

3. Tilt-docking injection unit; Figure 4

4. Separated sleeve for cooling and transfer

With the exception of the die clamping unit (vertical die clamping), other features of the VSC machine are similar to those of the HVSC machine.

CASTING/TOOLING DESIGN FOR HVSC

The casting/tooling design for HVSC follows much the same rules as for conventional die casting process. However, certain significant differences do exist between the two processes. For example, the HVSC process requires [3]:

1. Larger runner and gate to promote planar cavity fill and to aid in directional solidification.

2. Flat area for gate preferred since the gate must be sawed off and not trimmed.

3. Thicker walls (>2.5 mm) to allow adequate pressure during solidification

FACTORS AFFECTING SQUEEZE CAST PRODUCTS

Key process characteristics [4] impacting the soundness of squeeze cast products include metal temperature, melt cleanliness, cavity pressure (70 Mpa to 100 Mpa), gate placement (normally at the thickest part of the component), gate velocity (<500 mm/sec), sleeve solidification layer, heat treatment, and porosity. These factors have been discussed in detail in an earlier paper by one of the authors [3].

SQUEEZE CASTING APPLICATIONS

Products produced by squeeze casting worldwide include cross members (VSC), control arms (HVSC), steering knuckles (VSC and HVSC), pistons (VSC), engine mount (HVSC), scroll compressors (VSC, HVSC), and wheels (VSC).

This section also provides examples of select automotive components including steering column housings (standard housing, Figure 5), valve housing (Figure 6), steering housing, bearing cap, and differential carrier.

A. Steering Column Housing

1. *Reasons for selecting squeeze casting:*

   Near-net shape (0.023 kg of metal removed after casting)

   High strength (>280 Mpa yield strength)

   Reduced porosity

2. *Customer expectations of castings:*

   No blisters after heat treatment

   No distortion

   Consistent mechanical properties

B. Valve Housing

1. *Reasons for selecting squeeze casting:*

Near-net shape (0.136 kg of metal removed after casting

Pressure tight (must not leak when pressurized at 10.69 Mpa)

High burst strength (>20.69 Mpa)

2. *Customer expectations of castings:*

No blisters after heat treatment

No distortion

Consistent mechanical properties

Ease of machinability

C. Steering Housing

1. *Reasons for selecting squeeze casting:*

High strength (>350 Mpa tensile strength)

High wear resistance (<200 x 10^{-12} m^3)

2. *Customer expectations of castings:*

No blisters after heat treatment

Ease of machinability

No distortion

D. Bearing Cap

1. *Reasons for selecting squeeze casting:*

Near-net shape (0.025 kg of metal removed after casting)

High strength (>350 Mpa tensile strength)

2. *Customer expectations of castings:*

No blisters after heat treatment

Consistent mechanical properties

No distortion

Ease of machinability

E. Differential Carrier

1. *Reasons for selecting squeeze casting:*

Near-net shape

High strength (>280 Mpa yield strength)

2. *Customer expectations of castings:*

No distortion

Pressure tight

High stiffness

Elevated temperature strength

Ease of machinability

SEMI-SOLID METAL CASTING PROCESS

The semi-solid metal (SSM) casting process involves the following:

1. Blanking billets (solid feedstock with diameter of 75 mm or more) to part-size pieces commonly referred to as slugs. The length of the slugs corresponds to the total weight of the component to be made, plus the biscuit and the gating system [4]. The billets can be purchased either electro-magnetically (EM) stirred or grain-refined. The intent of EM stirring or grain-refining is to produce billets with a fine-grained equiaxed structure. It should be noted; however, that EM-stirred billets (because of the vigorous motion associated with stirring and breaking up of the dendritic structure) have a finer microstructure than grain-refined billets; Figures 7 and 8.

2. Heating slugs to semi-solid temperature range in an induction furnace. During heating, the primary phase (α-aluminum) of the billet microstructure becomes globular. The extent of spheroidization of the primary phase is influenced by several factors including the type of billet used. For example, grain-refined billets are known to undergo less spheroidization of the α-aluminum than EM-stirred billets during heating; see Figures 9 and 10.

3. Transfer of heated slug to shot sleeve and injection into the die cavity. The machine is, in many respects, like that employed in conventional die casting. As the slug is injected through the gate, material flow into the cavity is more like plastic than liquid [4].

4. Ejection of casting from the die and cooling. The casting is typically quenched in water following removal from the cavity.

5. Spraying of die and shot sleeve

CASTING/TOOLING DESIGN FOR SEMI-SOLID METAL (SSM) CASTING PROCESS

Casting/tooling design features for SSM are comparable to those in squeeze casting. For example, larger gate and runners are required to promote planar cavity fill and to aid in directional solidification. Also, as in squeeze casting, gates must be sawed off and not trimmed. The SSM casting process may, however, necessitate the use of a stripper ring to remove oxide from the heated slug during injection into the cavity.

FACTORS AFFECTING SSM CAST PRODUCTS

Key process characteristics affecting the integrity of SSM cast components include:

1. Alloy chemistry

An alloy exhibiting a wide freezing range is preferred so that the slug may be heated to the semi-solid state, thereby, achieving the desired microstructure and solid fraction (for flow into the cavity).

2. Billet heating

The billet heating time has to be long enough to promote spheroidization of the α-aluminum primary phase, and to assure complete and homogeneous remelting of the eutectic phase [5]. Incomplete remelting of the eutectic phase may result in the occurrence of "free" silicon in the microstructure, thereby lowering mechanical properties of the aluminum alloy.

3. Oxide skin

Oxide skin may form during die filling and/or transported into the part from the skin of the slug [5]. Regardless of its source, oxide skin in a casting lowers its mechanical properties, especially elongation. Oxide skins may be eliminated through use of stripper rings and/or well-positioned over-flows [5].

4. Injection speed

Too slow an injection speed may contribute to eutectic segregation in the casting, whereas too high an injection speed may result in entrapped air or oxide skin [5].

5. Porosity

a). Gas porosity in SSM cast components may be reduced via proper vent design/location, use of appropriate lube and dilution ratio, and attention to injection velocity.

b). Elimination of shrink porosity in SSM cast parts requires focus on die temperature and injection speed (too low a speed is undesirable).

SSM APPLICATIONS

In recent years, SSM casting process has been used in manufacturing brake master cylinders, suspension components (control arms, multi-link), fuel rails, and steering column components.

The authors' development work in the area of SSM is currently focussed on select steering column, brake and suspension components.

FEATURES AND BENEFITS: CONVENTIONAL DIE CASTING VS SQUEEZE CASTING VS SSM

Table 1 shows the features and benefits of conventional die casting (CDC), squeeze casting and SSM. The rating system (+ indicates favorable rating) is based on comparable part geometries and alloys. The choice of a particular process for manufacturing a certain automotive component will be influenced by numerous factors including plant layout, manpower, energy requirements, maintenance, process security, etc.

TENSILE PROPERTIES: CONVENTIONAL DIE CASTING VS SQUEEZE CASTING VS SSM

Tensile properties of the various aluminum alloys used in this study are shown in Table 2. All tensile data with the exception of those for 319 aluminum alloy are based on samples machined from actual castings.

Key observations from Table 2 are:

1. Squeeze cast 380-F ("F" denotes as-cast) aluminum alloy exhibits higher physical properties (particularly ductility) than conventional 380 alloy die casting. The improvement in ductility is due to reduced porosity and a more refined microstructure [3,6].

2. For a given alloy (A356.2 or 357) and heat treatment, squeeze cast aluminum alloy components exhibit properties comparable to those of SSM cast components. It should be noted, however, that for comparable strength and hardness of either of these two alloys, both squeeze casting and SSM casting processes yield higher ductility than does gravity permanent mold [3].

3. Squeeze cast 390-T6 ("T6" denotes solution treatment, quenched and artificially aged) and SSM 390-T6 aluminum alloys exhibit similar tensile properties.

4. Because of artificial aging, SSM 319-T6 (EM-stirred alloy) yields higher strength than SSM 319-T4 ("T4" denotes solution treatment and quenched).

IMPACT PROPERTIES: CONVENTIONAL DIE CASTING VS SQUEEZE CASTING VS SSM

Impact strength is a property required of aluminum alloys used for automotive steering and suspension components. It was of interest, therefore, to compare impact properties for select conventional die cast, squeeze cast and SSM aluminum alloys; see Table 3.

Key observations from Table 3 are:

1. Conventional die cast 380 aluminum alloy aluminum alloy exhibits lower impact strength than squeeze cast 380 aluminum alloy. Lower ductility of the conventional die cast alloy (associated with a coarser microstructure and higher level of porosity) is a factor responsible for the lower impact strength.

2. Impact strengths of squeeze cast A356.2-T6 and 357-T6 aluminum alloys are comparable to those of SSM A356.2-T6 and 357-T6 aluminum alloys.

3. Like conventional die castings, squeeze cast 390-T6 and SSM 390-T6 aluminum alloys also reveal poor impact strength (<1J). The lack of ductility, associated with the presence of primary silicon in 390 aluminum alloy, is a major factor contributing to their poor impact strength.

4. SSM 319-T4 aluminum alloy (EM-stirred) yields higher impact strength than SSM 319-T6 alloy. This behavior can be attributed to the higher ductility of SSM 319-T4 aluminum alloy (see Table 2).

FRACTURE TOUGHNESS: CONVENTIONAL DIE CASTING VS SQUEEZE CASTING VS SSM

Because of poor strength and/or ductility of conventional die cast aluminum alloys, fracture toughness data for commonly used conventional die cast alloys were not determined in this study. Thus, Table 4 shows the conditional fracture toughness (K_Q) data for select squeeze cast and SSM aluminum alloys.

Fracture toughness specimens [C(T) samples] for A356.2 aluminum alloy were machined from actual castings; whereas those for 319 aluminum alloy were machined from plates [7]. Following machining, the samples were pre-cracked, and tested at 24^{0}C per ASTM E399-90 and ASTM B645.

Key observations from Table 4 are:

1. Fracture toughness of squeeze cast A356.2-T6 aluminum alloy is comparable to that of SSM A356.2-T6 aluminum alloy (this can be attributed to their comparable tensile properties, Table 2)

2. For a given SSM billet source, no significant difference in fracture toughness can be observed between T4 and T6 heat treat tempers

FATIGUE PROPERTIES: CONVENTIONAL DIE CASTING VS SQUEEZE CASTING VS SSM

Fatigue strength is required of automotive brake and suspension components. Unfortunately, very little information on fatigue strength of aluminum alloys (especially for those used in conjunction with squeeze casting and SSM) is documented in literature. It was of interest, therefore, to generate fatigue data for commonly used aluminum alloys in squeeze casting and SSM casting processes; see Table 5.

Key observations from Table 5 are:

1. The fatigue strength for SSM A356.2-T6 aluminum alloy is greater than squeeze cast A356.2-T6 aluminum alloy by approximately 10%. The higher fatigue strength for SSM A356.2-T6 aluminum alloy may be due to reduced porosity and the presence of a globular α-aluminum primary phase in the alloy microstructure.

2. SSM 319-T6 aluminum alloy exhibits the highest fatigue strength. This behavior may be due to the fact that fatigue samples were machined from plates and **not** actual castings. The plates, having virtually no porosity, are expected to yield better mechanical properties.

WEAR AND CAVITATION EROSION PROPERTIES: CONVENTIONAL DIE CASTING VS SQUEEZE CASTING VS SSM

High wear resistance (reduced material volume loss) is a characteristic necessary of automotive brake cylinders, calipers and steering gear housings. High cavitation erosion resistance (reduced weight loss or volume loss of material caused by cavitation in liquids) is a property required of certain transmission components. However, little information on wear and/or erosion of the various alloys used for the above automotive parts is available in literature. It was of interest, therefore, to compare wear and cavitation erosion data for select conventional die cast, squeeze cast and SSM aluminum alloys; see Table 6.

Wear characteristics were measured using the LFW-1 wear tester [4]. The testing for erosion consisted of a single 30 minute exposure of each sample (35 x 35 x1.5 mm) to a 12.7mm tip of an ultrasonic "horn" operating at 20 kHz. The vibrating horn tip was located 0.5mm above the sample that was submerged in a beaker of water at room temperature. Tip amplitude (peak-to-peak) was 45 microns. The cavitation erosion data shown in Table 6 are based on volume loss of material.

Key observations from Table 6 are:

1. Material volume loss for conventional die 380 aluminum alloy is the highest (lowest wear resistance). Porosity and coarser microstructure (plate-like silicon particles) are factors contributing to the lower wear resistance of this alloy [3].

2. Material volume loss (wear resistance) for squeeze cast A356.2-T6 and SSM cast A356.2-T6 aluminum alloys is comparable.

3. Squeeze cast and SSM 357-T6 aluminum alloys reveal higher wear resistance than A356.2-T6 alloy. This is due primarily to the higher magnesium content of 357 alloy. Also to be noted is the fact that squeeze cast 357-T6 and SSM 357-T6 exhibit comparable wear properties.

4. Squeeze cast and SSM 390-T6 aluminum alloys exhibit the highest wear resistance. Reduced porosity in the castings, high silicon and magnesium content of the alloy are factors responsible for the high wear resistance [3]. Also to be noted is the fact that squeeze cast 390-T6 and SSM 390-T6 aluminum alloys reveal comparable wear properties.

5. For a given process (squeeze casting or SSM) and alloy, machined surfaces exhibit higher erosion cavitation resistance than as-cast surfaces. This behavior may be attributed to the fact that the improved surface finish of machined castings delays nucleation of "bubbles" that eventually impinge upon the surface and collapse resulting in erosion.

VACURAL™ DIE CASTING: APPLICATIONS AND ALLOY PROPERTIES

Muller-Weingarten's Vacural™ die casting process is similar to conventional die casting in many respects. However, certain features of the Vacural™ process do set it apart from conventional die casting. For example, in the Vacural™ process:

1. Degassed metal is drawn into the shot chamber through a suction tube under vacuum.

2. Vacuum system is also applied to the die (cavity). Thus, air/gas entrapment in the casting is minimized or eliminated, thereby, enabling the castings to be heat treated for enhanced strength and ductility.

3. Die faces are sealed in order to prevent air from entering the cavity.

The Vacural™ process is reported by Muller-Weingarten to be used in manufacturing space frame nodes, automotive front cross members, suspension arm axles, connecting rod and rocker arms. The wall thickness for many of these components, especially for space frame nodes, ranges from 2 to 5mm [8]

The alloys preferred for the Vacural™ process are Aluminum Rheinfelden's Silafont-36™ and Magsimal-59™. Key elements in Silafont-36™ are: 9.5 to 11.5% silicon, <0.12% iron, 0.5 to 0.8% manganese, 0.15 to 0.5% magnesium, and 0.01 to 0.02% strontium. This low-iron aluminum alloy is used in manufacturing automotive components requiring high ductility (suspension arm axle, space frame nodes); see Table 7.

Magsimal-59™ consists essentially of 1.8 to 2.5% silicon, 0.5 to 0.8% manganese, and 5.0 to 5.5% magnesium, and is reported [9] to be used for automotive components **not** requiring heat treatment (cross member, steering wheel). Mechanical properties of Magsimal-59 aluminum alloy [9] as a function of wall thickness are also shown in Table 7.

SUMMARY

1. With increasing focus on high product integrity, squeeze casting, SSM and Vacural™ have emerged as the "high integrity" die casting processes.

2. Automotive components made using these "high integrity" casting processes include brake cylinders, steering knuckles, control arms, space frame nodes, wheels, rocker arms, connecting rods, air conditioning compressor units, and steering column components.

3. Results from this study show that mechanical and wear properties of aluminum alloys made using the above processes are superior to those of conventional (high pressure, high velocity) die casting process.

4. For a given alloy and heat treat temper, mechanical or wear properties of squeeze castings are comparable with those of SSM castings.

5. Silafont-36™ and Magsimal-59™ aluminum alloys are preferred for use with the Vacural™ die casting process.

REFERENCES

1. Shot Monitoring-Understanding and Applications, Eastern Alloys, Inc, 1988.

2. Theory of Squeeze Casting, Manual from UBE Industries, UBE, Japan, 1993

3. S. Corbit and R. DasGupta, "Squeeze Cast Automotive Applications and Squeeze Cast Aluminum Alloy Properties," presented at 1999 SAE Congress (paper # 1999-01-0343)

4. K. Young, "Semi-Solid Metal Cast Automotive Components: New Markets for Die Casting," NADCA Transactions, 17th International Die Casting Congress and Exposition, 1993, pp 387 – 393

5. W.R. Loue and et al, "Metallurgical Aspects of Thixoforming of A356.0 and 357.0 Alloys," NADCA Transactions, 18th International Die Casting Congress and Exposition, 1995, pp 389 – 396

6. R. DasGupta, "A Comparison of Properties of Common Aluminum Alloy Casting Processes," NADCA Transactions, 18th International Die Casting Congress and Exposition, 1995, pp 237 – 243

7. R. DasGupta, "Characterization of SSM 319 Aluminum Alloy Castings Made Using EM-Stirred and Grain-Refined Billets," to be presented at the 20th International Die Casting Congress and Exposition, November 1999

8. Horst Sternau et al, "Producing Low-Iron Ductile Aluminum Die Castings," NADCA Transactions, 18th International Die Casting Congress and Exposition, November 1995, pp 245 – 249

9. A. J. Franke, "Experience of Three Years Producing Low Iron Ductile Pressure Die Castings," NADCA Transactions, 19th International Die Casting Congress and Exposition 1997, pp 199 - 203

Table 1: Features and benefits of conventional die casting, squeeze casting and SSM

Feature	CDC	Squeeze Casting	SSM
Near-net shape	++	+	+
Metal temperature	-	-	+
Cycle time	+	-	++
Cavity life	-	-	+
# of cavities	+	+	+
Alloy flexibility	+	+	-
Shrink porosity	-	+	++
Oxide entrapment	-	+	+
Equipment cost	++	+	-
Automation	++	+	-
Metal cost	+	+	-
Recycling	+	+	-
Metal heating	+	+	-
Metal loss	+	+	-

Table 2: Tensile properties comparison

Alloy	Process	Yield strength (Mpa)	Tensile strength (Mpa)	Elongation (%)
380[1]-T5	CDC**	NA	152 - 165	1.2 – 1.4
380[1]-F	Squeeze	NA	214 - 234	2 - 3
A356.2[2]-T6	Squeeze	145 – 165	255 - 276	13 - 17
A356.2-T6	SSM	152 – 168	261 - 284	16 - 20
357[2]-T6	Squeeze	241 – 262	324 - 338	8 – 10
357-T6	SSM	237 – 257	315 - 330	7 - 9
390[2]-F	CDC**	241	279	<1
390[2]-T6	Squeeze	NA	352 - 392	<1
390-T6	SSM	NA	341 - 386	<1
319[3]-T4	SSM	182	308	7.3
319[3]-T6	SSM	293	361	3.7

Legend:

** = conventional die casting

1 = data from reference [6]

2 = data from reference [3]

3 = EM-stirred alloy; data from reference [7]

Table 3: Impact strength comparison

Alloy	Process	Temper	Elongation (%)	Impact strength (J)
380	CDC[**]	T5	1.2 – 1.4	<1
380	Squeeze	F	2 – 3	1 – 3
A356.2[1]	Squeeze	T6	13 – 17	14 – 18
A356.2	SSM	T6	16 – 20	17 - 20
357[1]	Squeeze	T6	8 – 10	10 - 13
357	SSM	T6	7 – 9	9 - 11
390[1]	CDC[**]	F	<1	<1
390[1]	Squeeze	T6	<1	<1
390	SSM	T6	<1	<1
319[2]	SSM	T4	7.3	26
319[2]	SSM	T6	3.7	19

Legend:

** = conventional die casting

1 = data from reference [3]

2 = EM-stirred billet; data from reference [7]

Table 4: Fracture toughness comparison

Alloy	Process	% Elongation	K_Q $Mpa(m)^{1/2}$
A356.2-T6	Squeeze[1]	13 – 17	18.7 – 22.5
A356.2-T6	SSM	16 – 20	19.5 – 23.5
319-T4[2]	SSM (EM-stirred)	7.3	22.8
319-T6[2]	SSM (EM-stirred)	3.7	22.9

Legend:

1 = data from reference [3]

2 = data from reference [7]

Table 5: Fatigue properties comparison

Alloy	Process	Fatigue Strength (Mpa)
A356.2-T6[1]	Squeeze	106
A356.2-T6[2]	SSM	117
319-T6[3]	SSM (EM-stirred)	164

Legend:

1 = mean fatigue strength based on "staircase" method at 10^7 cycles; axial loading; R = -1.0; samples machined from actual castings

2 = fatigue strength at 10^7 cycles from S-N curve; samples machined from actual castings; axial loading; R = -1.0

3 = mean fatigue strength based on "staircase" method at 10^7 cycles; axial loading; R = -1.0; samples machined from plates; data from reference [7]

Table 6: Wear and cavitation erosion properties

Alloy	Wear $(m)^3 \times 10^{-12}$	Cavitation Erosion $(m)^3 \times 10^{-10}$
CDC** 380-F	462 – 16,000	NA
A356.2-T6[1]	173 – 434	NA
A356.2-T6[2]	180 – 455	13.5 (machined) 21.8 (as-cast)
357-T6[2]	166 - 347	NA
357-T6[3]	140 - 363	NA
CDC** 390-F	125 - 234	NA
390-T6[2]	55 - 97	NA
390-T6[3]	50 – 100	NA

Legend:

** = conventional die casting

1 = squeeze casting; data from reference [3]

2 = SSM casting process

3 = squeeze casting; data from reference [3]

Table 7: Silafont-36 and Magsimal-59 aluminum alloy properties

Alloy	Yield strength (Mpa)	Tensile strength (Mpa)	% elong.	Impact Strength (J)
Silafont-36™-T6[1]	143	276	12.5	14
Magsimal-59 (F)[2]	~165	~285	~16	NA
Magsimal-59 (F)[3]	~110	~250	~8	NA

Legend:

1 = Properties shown are an average of two tensile bars and two unnotched impact specimens (10mm x 3.3mm cross-section) machined from actual castings

2 = Properties based on 4 mm wall thickness [9]

3 = Properties based on 12 mm wall thickness [9]

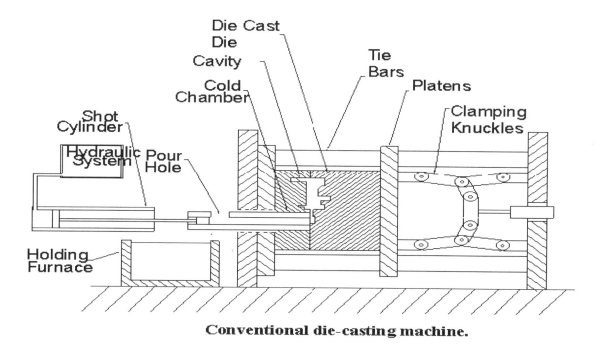

Conventional die-casting machine.

Figure 1. Schematic of a typical conventional die cast machine

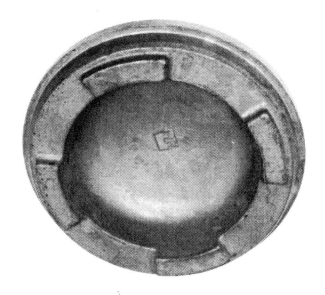

Figure 2. Conventional die cast end plug

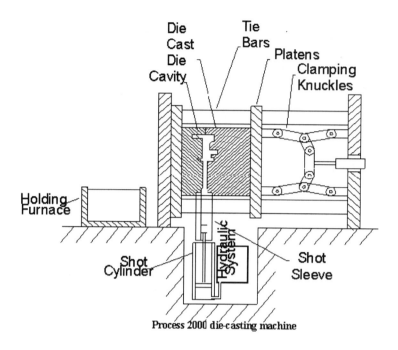

Process 2000 die-casting machine

Figure 3. Schematic of a typical HVSC machine

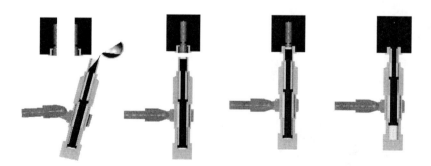

Figure 4. Tilt-docking injection unit

Figure 5. Squeeze cast standard housing

Figure 6. Squeeze cast valve housing

51

Figure 7. Microstructure of EM-stirred billet; 500X

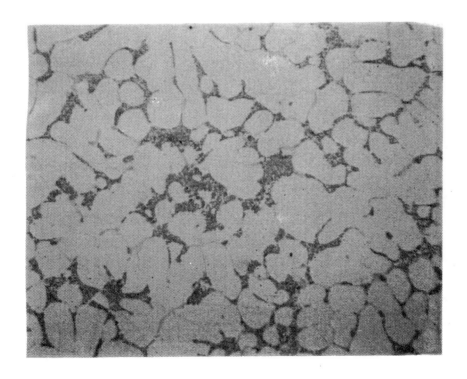

Figure 8. Microstructure of grain-refined billet; 500X

Figure 9. Microstructure of casting made using EM-stirred billet; 100X

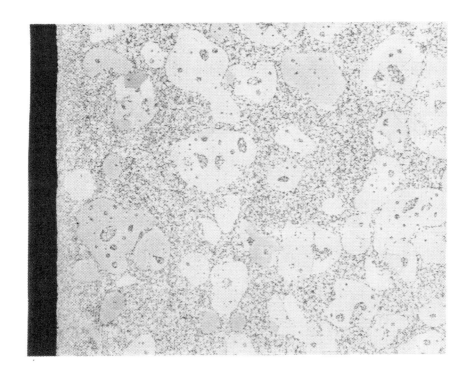

Figure 10. Microstructure of casting made using grain-refined billet; 100X

2000-01-0679

Lightweight Iron and Steel Castings for Automotive Applications

Alan P. Druschitz and David C. Fitzgerald
Intermet Corporation

Copyright © 2000 Society of Automotive Engineers, Inc.

ABSTRACT

The use of aluminum to produce lightweight automotive castings has gained wide acceptance despite significant cost penalties. Lightweight iron and steel casting designs have been largely ignored despite their obvious cost and property advantages.

This paper reviews and discusses the following: 1) various processes for producing lightweight iron and steel castings, 2) examples of lightweight components in high-volume production, 3) examples of conversions from aluminum to iron, 4) material properties of interest to designers, 5) examples of concept components and 6) efforts to improve the design and manufacturing processes for lightweight iron and steel castings.

In summary, the potential for low-cost, lightweight iron and steel castings to aid the automotive industry in achieving both cost and weight objectives has been demonstrated and continues to expand. In general, however, automotive designers and engineers have not yet fully taken advantage of these technologies.

INTRODUCTION

Due to fierce global competition, the automotive industry is forcing the rapid advancement of technology. Today's cars are significantly safer, cleaner and more fuel efficient than those of only a few years ago – and the rate of improvement is increasing. There are many factors that the automotive industry must consider. Four of these factors are: fuel economy, emissions, safety and cost. Fuel economy, emissions and safety are government mandated; cost (or value) is customer mandated. Constantly changing political focus and global regulations cause the automotive companies to constantly reassess the relative importance of each of these areas and consequently the amount of research effort applied to them.

Currently, fuel economy is an area of high interest in the United States. The US Government has promoted the development of a "Supercar" – an environmentally friendly car with up to triple the fuel efficiency of today's midsize cars – without sacrificing affordability, performance, or safety (1). To achieve the fuel economy goal, reducing vehicle weight has been a major research area. The industry trend has been to substitute low density materials (aluminum, magnesium and composites) for iron and steel. Drawbacks to this approach are reduced material strength, ductility and stiffness, a larger product envelope and/or higher cost. An alternative approach, which has not been widely publicized or promoted by the US Government, is the use of lightweight iron and steel design. A notable exception is the Ultra-Light Steel Vehicle program financed by the wrought steel industry (2). This paper describes the little known efforts of the iron and steel foundry industry.

Specifically, this paper describes 1) various processes for producing lightweight iron and steel castings, 2) examples of lightweight components in high-volume production, 3) examples of conversions from aluminum to iron, 4) material properties of interest to designers, 5) examples of concept components and 6) efforts to improve the design and manufacturing processes for lightweight iron and steel castings.

CASTING PROCESSES

The requirements for a casting process to be capable of producing lightweight components are 1) dimensional accuracy, 2) ability to fill thin-sections and 3) consistent metal quality. Processes that have been shown to be capable of meeting these requirements are investment casting, counter-gravity casting, low-pressure bottom-fill, shell, chemically-bonded sand and green sand. New products and product concepts are now possible due to advances in the above listed processes coupled with 1) continuous improvement in the production of clean steel, 2) improved understanding and control of gray, compacted and ductile iron microstructures and 3) reasonably good mathematical models for mold filling and solidification.

Investment casting is the premier process for producing complex, thin-wall castings. Advantages of the investment casting process are highly accurate patterns, strong and stable refractory molds, hot molds and gravity pouring. A hot mold makes filling thin-sections easy (down to 0.4 mm) and gravity pouring is simple. Typically, a hot mold means slow cooling rates, which are beneficial for cast iron since this inhibits carbide formation, but are detrimental for cast steel since this promotes a large grain size. Although gravity pouring is advantageous from a simplicity viewpoint, low casting yield and turbulence during filling are disadvantages. Figure 1 is a schematic showing the pouring of an investment casting.

Hitchiner Manufacturing Co. and General Motors pioneered the development of the counter-gravity process (3) and applied this technology to both investment and sand casting (4-6). In counter-gravity casting, a vacuum is used to draw metal up into the mold as opposed to gravity pulling metal down into the mold, as shown in Figures 2 and 3. Counter-gravity or vacuum assisted casting (VAC) is a more complex process in high volume production (requires unique equipment), but the process yields the benefits of improved metal cleanliness by reduced turbulence during mold filling and improved casting yield (ratio of the amount of saleable metal divided by the amount of metal poured in the mold). A variation, the loose sand VAC process (7), minimizes the thickness of the ceramic or bonded sand molds and uses loose (unbonded) sand to back-up the fragile mold. Using this technique, production costs are reduced by minimizing the use of expensive refractory coatings or chemically bonded sand. The VAC process is applicable to steel (air melt) and nickel-based or titanium-based (inert or vacuum melt) but is not readily applicable to ductile iron due to magnesium fade. A small amount of magnesium dissolved in iron is required to form ductile (or nodular) iron. However, dissolved magnesium slowly reacts with air (oxygen), dissolved sulfur and furnace and ladle linings, thus its "nodularizing" effect fades slowly with time.

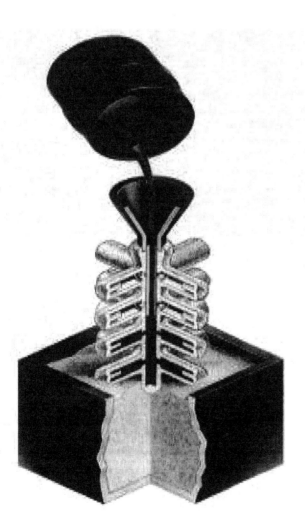

Figure 1. Schematic of Investment Casting Process.

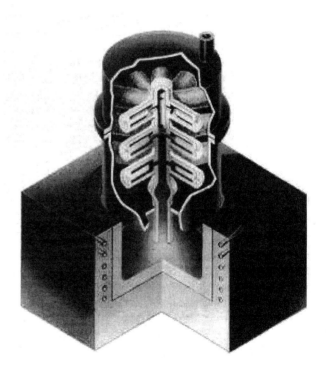

Figure 2. Schematic of Counter-Gravity Casting Process Using a Single Sprue (CLA process).

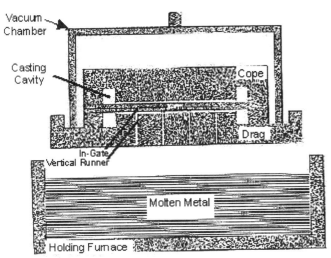

Figure 3. Schematic of Counter-Gravity Casting Process Using a Bonded Sand Mold with Multiple In-Gates (VAC process).

Figure 5. Forty-On Casting Cluster of Gray Iron, Pump Bodies Produced Using the SlimCast Process.

The "SlimCast" process invented by General Motors in 1993 coupled the mold filling technology of the counter-gravity process with the simplicity of gravity pouring (8). Although never used in production, the "SlimCast" process has been used to produce many one-of-a-kind concept castings; including 300 mm long tubes with 1 mm wall thickness, exhaust manifolds in stainless steel and ductile iron with 2 mm wall thickness, differential carriers with 3 mm wall thickness and cylinder blocks with 3 mm wall thickness. A schematic of the SlimCast mold is shown in Figure 4 and an example of a casting cluster produced using the SlimCast process is shown in Figure 5.

The Sadefa FM ("Fonte Mince" or thin-wall iron) process (9) invented by Groupe Valfonde in 1976 and commercialized in 1982 uses low-pressure, bottom-fill to push metal into chemically bonded sand molds. This process provides high casting yield, good dimensional accuracy and the ability to fill relatively thin (2.8 mm) sections. By 1993, Sadefa had supplied GM Cadillac, Renault, Peugeot and Opel with over 2,000,000 thin-wall, ductile iron exhaust manifolds.

The shell process has been used since the 50's to produce "thin-wall" castings in gray and ductile iron and still is today. The high hardness and good dimensional accuracy of the shell mold makes this feasible. Since the 50's, great strides in understanding mold filling have significantly improved casting quality. Figure 6 shows stacked shell molds used to produce thin-wall, ductile iron, rocker arm castings in 1954 (10).

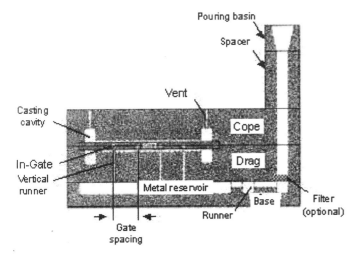

Figure 4. Schematic of SlimCast Mold.

Figure 6. 208-on Casting Cluster of Thin-Wall, Ductile Iron, Rocker Arms Made by Ford Dearborn Specialty Foundry in 1954 Using Stacked Shell Molds.

Figure 7. Thin-Wall, Ductile Iron Castings Made Using the Green Sand Process by Various Intermet Foundries.

The green sand process has been largely overlooked for the production of thin wall, lightweight castings but recently interest has been expanding. One published report described the production of exhaust manifolds with 2.8 +/- 0.65 mm walls (11). The primary dimensional problem with green sand molding has traditionally been cope-to-drag shift. However, new developments in vertically parted machines have recently claimed to reduce mold-to-mold shift to 0.1 mm (12). Further, thoughtful component design can also minimize the effects of this problem in older mold lines. The introduction of low-pressure, bottom-fill, vertically-parted mold lines (13) also provides the potential for significantly improved part quality and reduced part cost.

Minimum wall thickness is an important characteristic of a "lightweight-capable" process, but the ability to make hollow sections and to "core-out" thick sections is even more important. Hollow and cored-out features distinguish castings from forgings and sand castings from most low cost die castings. By cleverly taking advantage of the unique abilities of the various sand casting processes, significant weight savings, with little cost penalty, are possible.

PRODUCTION COMPONENTS

Numerous examples of lightweight iron and steel cast components currently in production are available for review. Some notable examples include exhaust manifolds, rocker arms, pump bodies, control arms, steering knuckles, mounts and brackets. Figure 7 shows a variety of examples of lightweight iron castings currently made using the green sand process.

Exhaust manifolds, Figure 8, have been favorites for thin-wall casting development because 1) castings provide better flow than fabrications (smooth, no abrupt transitions at welds, unlimited cross sectional geometry), 2) thin-walls reduce heat-up time, which speeds catalytic converter light-off and therefore reduces emissions and 3) better durability than fabrications (no welds).

High-silicon, high-silicon moly (Si-Mo) and Ni-Resist ductile irons have been very successful but stainless steel (for >900°C applications) has proven to be a manufacturing challenge due to high pouring temperatures. The green sand process is widely used to produce ductile iron exhaust manifolds with wall thicknesses of 4.0 mm or less by Wescast, Citation-Marion and Georg Fischer AG. The Sadefa FM process produced up to 6000 thin-wall ductile iron castings per day in 1994. The Sadefa FM process provided prototypes in ferritic stainless steel in 1995. The counter-gravity process is currently used for low volume production of stainless steel exhaust manifolds by Alloy Engineering, Wescast, Infun and Daido.

Figure 8. An Example of a Thin-Wall (3 mm) Exhaust Manifold Cast Using 1) the SlimCast Process in Ferritic Stainless Steel or Ni-Resist D5S Ductile Iron and 2) the VAC Process in Austenitic Stainless Steel (current production at Alloy Engineering is 700 per day).

A very high volume application of a thin-wall steel casting is the rocker arm for the General Motors 3800 engine, Figure 9. This casting is made using the process shown in Figure 2 with the addition of sand to support the shell mold (supported-shell or SSCLA process). At present, rocker arm production for all customers is 130,000 per day. The material is a low-alloy steel (AISI 8620).

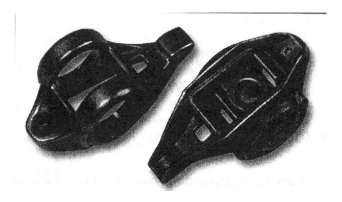

Figure 9. Thin-Wall, Low-Alloy Steel, Rocker Arms Produced for General Motors by Hitchiner Manufacturing Using the SSCLA Process.

General Motors produces the primary pump body for Northstar engine, Figure 10, using the multiple in-gate VAC process. Production rates for this casting are approximately 1000 per day. The sand cores are stacked five-high and designed to form the top of one casting and bottom of the next. The material is a high silicon, gray iron that produces carbide free parts as-cast. Walls thicknesses are as thin as 2.5 mm. All of the critical dimensions are in-the-mold, so cope-to-drag shift is not an issue.

Figure 10. Thin-Wall, Gray Iron, Primary Pump Produced by General Motors Using the VAC Process.

A large number of mounts and brackets are cast using the green sand process. The advantages of cast mounts and brackets are 1) reduced part count, 2) improved strength and stiffness and 3) reduced weight. The design flexibility of castings allows material to be placed where it is most needed to absorb the applied load or redistribute the applied load, unlike stampings that are required to have uniform wall thickness and have limited shape flexibility. Further, castings can have additional material located in corners and junctions to reduce stress and prevent unwanted deflection. Mounts and brackets produced from gray and ductile iron have excellent vibration damping abilities, whereas mounts and brackets produced from low carbon steel are readily welded. Both iron and steel easily handle the underhood temperatures of today's cars and trucks. Numerous examples of automotive mounts and brackets are shown in Appendix I.

CONVERSION OF ALUMINUM TO IRON

Numerous examples of converting aluminum to iron or steel exist. In 1992, CWC Textron described a 1.54 kg (3.4 lbs) cast steel lower control arm produced for a concept vehicle using vacuum casting technology (14). The thin-wall steel casting was 39% lighter than an aluminum alloy forging. The replacement of a wrought aluminum fuel tank spacer with a lightweight ductile iron casting is shown in Figure 11.

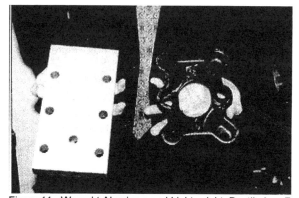

Figure 11. Wrought Aluminum and Lightweight, Ductile Iron Fuel Tank Spacer Produced by Intermet Wagner Foundry.

Production aluminum and prototype lightweight iron designs for a steering knuckle casting are shown in Figure 12. The lightweight iron design was 0.9 kg (2 lbs) heavier than the aluminum design but approximately half the cost. Anticipated benefits of the lightweight iron design are 1) longer life due to reduced bearing and bushing distortion and wear (ductile iron is harder and more wear resistant than aluminum) and 2) improved NVH (ductile iron has better damping properties than aluminum).

Figure 12. Aluminum and Lightweight Iron Steering Knuckles for the Ford Taurus. Current Production is Cast Aluminum.

Table I. Comparison of Tensile Properties of Various Cast Metals (15,16).

Material	Elastic Modulus (GPa)	Minimum* Tensile Strength (MPa)	Minimum* Yield Strength (MPa)	Minimum* Elongation (%)
Gray Iron				
Class 30	90-113	207		
Class 40	110-138	276		
Ductile Iron				
SAE J434 D4018	162-170	414	276	18
SAE J434 D4512	162-170	448	310	12
SAE J434 D5506	162-170	552	379	6
SAE J434 D7003	162-170	690	483	3
ADI grade 1	----------	850	550	10
Steel				
SAE J435c 0025	200	415	207	22
SAE J435c 080	200	550	345	22
SAE J435c 0050B	200	690	485	10
Aluminum				
sand cast				
319 T6	71	250	164	2.0
356 T6	72	228	164	3.5
A356 T6	72	278	207	6.0
permanent mold				
319 T6	71	280	185	3.0
356 T6	72	262	185	5.0
A356 T61	72	283	207	10.0

*Properties for aluminum are "typical", not "minimum"

MATERIAL PROPERTIES OF INTEREST TO DESIGNERS

Iron and steel have many material characteristics that aluminum, magnesium and composites simply cannot duplicate. Aluminum and magnesium are heat treated to achieve peak strength by quenching followed by aging. Prolonged use at temperatures near or above the aging temperature (typically 150-175°C) result in dimensional distortion and strength reduction. Cast iron and steel are both mechanically and dimensionally stable to much higher temperatures. Iron and steel are often used in the as-cast condition or can be heat treated to a wide variety of properties. Table I is a comparison of tensile properties of various cast metals.

A unique feature of cast iron and steel is the ability to harden surfaces – that is, produce a hard wear resistance surface and a tough, ductile core. This is not possible with aluminum or magnesium without costly secondary coating processes

Other material properties of interest to automotive engineers are damping capacity (the ability to suppress vibration), coefficient of thermal expansion, coefficient of thermal conductivity, creep resistance, work hardening or softening and damage tolerance. Table II is a comparison of relative damping capacity for various metals and Table III is a comparison of thermal conductivity and thermal expansion for various metals.

Table II. Comparison of Relative Damping Capacity for Various Metals (17).

Material	Relative Damping Capacity
Gray Iron, coarse flake	100-500
Gray Iron, fine flake	20-100
Ductile Iron	5-20
Pure Iron	5
Eutectoid Steel	4
Aluminum	0.4

Table III. Comparison of Thermal Expansion and Thermal Conductivity for Various Metals (15,16,18).

Material	Coefficient of Thermal Expansion μm/m X °K	Coefficient of Thermal Conductivity W/m X °K
Gray Iron	10.5	48.5-57.1
Ductile Iron	10.6-11.2	26.0-41.5
Compacted Graphite Iron	- - -	38-52
Low Carbon Steel	12.1	97
Aluminum Alloy 319	21.5	109
Aluminum Alloy 356	21.5	151-159

LIGHTWEIGHT IRON AND STEEL CONCEPTS

Once a design engineer understands the abilities of the casting process and the specific characteristics of a material, there is no limit to the unique designs that can be created.

Compacted graphite iron is now in high-volume production at the Intermet Ironton Iron Foundry for bedplates (19) and low-volume production at Halberg Guss for cylinder blocks (Audi V-8 TDI). The bedplate application (DaimlerChrysler 4.7 Liter V-8) demonstrated improved "noise quality" and durability over gray iron.

Experimental programs have repeatedly demonstrated the potential for lightweight iron. Examples of these programs are:

- General Motors 2.5 liter, 3 mm wall, gray iron block (20% weight savings) produced using the VAC process

- Adam Opel AG's 2.5 liter, compacted graphite, V-6 Calibra (20.4% weight reduction)

- Adam Opel AG's 1.6 liter, compacted graphite, Family I cylinder block (29.4% weight reduction after machining)

Weight reductions of 10-25% compared to gray iron are anticipated when using compacted graphite iron (20) if the higher strength and toughness of the compacted graphite iron are properly utilized.

Also, high-specific output diesel engines are being designed using lightweight, compacted graphite iron, cylinder blocks in Europe. Aluminum is not strong enough for these applications.

Crankshafts are typically machined from alloy steel billet stock (highest strength, highest cost), forged from microalloyed steel (medium strength, medium cost) or cast in ductile iron (lowest strength, lowest cost). Regardless of material or manufacturing process, the weight is similar. However, mass can be significantly reduced by using the flexibility of the sand casting process to develop a crankshaft that optimizes the location of the counterweight mass and reduces mass in areas not needed for structural integrity, Figure 13. Lightweight crankshaft designs can easily provide 15-25% weight savings and aggressive designs can provide 45-50% weight savings (as much as 20.5 kg in V-10 applications) by hollowing-out main and pin bearings, coring-out counterweights and using grade 1 austempered ductile iron.

Figure 13. Example of Concept Lightweight Crankshaft.

The use of hydroformed steel for primary body structures and components provides unique opportunities for castings. An iron or steel casting is ideally suited for attachment to a hydroformed rail section by stud welding or MIG welding. A casting can reduce part count by integrating features, such as multiple attachment or mounting points and can provide unique features, such as vibration damping/isolation and controlled crush. An integrated front shock tower and lower control arm mount is shown in Figure 14. The advantages of this design are improved stiffness for ride and handling and reduced part count compared to a stamped steel fabrication.

Figure 14. Thin-wall Ductile Iron and Steel Concept Castings Produced by General Motors Research Laboratories Using the SlimCast Process. Steel: engine mounts, exhaust manifolds, lower control arm/front shock tower mount, lower control arm, torque converter cover. Ductile Iron: exhaust manifold, differential carrier, power steering gear housing. Gray Iron: cylinder block, primary pump body.

Hydroformed, rolled or extruded body structures also rely on nodes (the point where various linear components come together). Nodes tend to be complex, three-dimensional structures that are typically cast. Methods of reliably joining the structures together at the nodes are still a major issue.

EFFORTS TO IMPROVE DESIGN AND MANUFACTURING

The foundry industry has internally produced 1) significant improvements in the ability to design castings and tooling and 2) manufacturing enhancements. Mathematical modeling has become commonplace and current efforts are aimed at fine tuning models for specific plants, processes and materials. Whereas the US Government has supplied tremendous amounts of resources for the development of aluminum and magnesium, the iron and steel foundry industries have developed their own programs.

As one example, the Ductile Iron Society has undertaken the task of generating strain life fatigue data, which are the inputs for finite element stress analysis, for ductile iron. This data is freely distributed by way of their website (www.ductile.org) and at the SAE 2000 Congress.

Also, the Thin-Wall Iron Group (TWIG), a consortium of industry (users, producers and suppliers), universities (University of Alabama and University of North Carolina at Charlotte) and a national lab (Albany Research Center) was independently established in 1998 to 1) develop materials and methods for producing thin-wall iron castings and 2) characterize thin-wall casting properties. The results of this group will be forthcoming. The American Foundrymen's Society can provide more information on TWIG.

ACKNOWLEDGMENTS

The authors would like to thank Dick Chandley of Metal Casting Technology, Inc. (Hitchiner--General Motors joint venture) for allowing the use of their process and product photographs and for helpful comments made during the review of this paper. Tony Thoma of Wescast, the SAE reviewers and Edward Vinarcik (Session Organizer) are also thanked and complimented for their helpful comments and suggestions made during the review of this paper.

CONTACT

Dr. Alan P. Druschitz received his PhD in Metallurgical Engineering in 1982 from the Illinois Institute of Technology, Chicago IL. He is currently the Chairman of TWIG (Thin-Wall Iron Group) and is the Director of Materials Development for Intermet Corporation. He is located at the Intermet Product Design and Technical Center, 939 Airport Road, Lynchburg VA 24502. He can be reached at adruschitz@notes.intermet.com or (804) 237-8749. He has been a member of the American Foundrymen's Society for eleven years, the Society of Automotive Engineers for eighteen years and ASM International for twenty-three years.

REFERENCES

1. From the Partnership for a New Generation of Vehicles website (www.ta.doc.gov/pngv/introduction).
2. K. Buchholz, "ULSAB proves lighter is stronger," Automotive Engineering International, Vol. 106, No. 5, May 1988, pp. 36-38.
3. G.D. Chandley and R.L. Sharkey, "Method of Casting Metal in Sand Mold Using Reduced Pressure," U.S. Patent No. 4,340,108, July 20, 1982.
4. G.D. Chandley, "Making Castings Without Ladles or Sprues – The CLA Process," AFS Transactions, Vol. 84 (1976) pp. 37-42.
5. G.D. Chandley, "Countergravity Low-Pressure Casting, " Metals Handbook, Vol. 15, "Casting," ASM International, (1988) pp. 317-319.
6. A.T. Spada, "Hitchiner Manufacturing Co. – Turning the Casting World Upside Down," Modern Casting, Vol. 88, No. 7, July 1998, pp. 39-43.
7. G.D. Chandley, "Countergravity Casting Apparatus and Method," U.S. Patent No. 4,957,153, September 18, 1990.
8. A.P. Druschitz, et al, "Mold for Producing Thin Wall Castings by Gravity Pouring," U.S. Patent No. 5,263,533, November 23, 1993.
9. "High Integrity Thin Wall Castings, Major Advance for Automotive Industry," Metallurgia, Vol. 59, No. 1, January 1992.
10. Source Book on Ductile Iron, American Society for Metals, (1977) p. 260.
11. K. Hornung, "Thin Section Ductile Iron Castings," 61st World Foundry Congress (Technical Forum) Beijing, 1995, pp. 75-83.
12. Georg Fischer Disa 230 Product Literature.
13. Lambert, Guy R., "Low-Pressure, Green Sand Process Produces Thin-Walled Castings," Modern Casting, August 1999, pp. 72-73.
14. P. Warren, "Vacuum casting advances create new design options," Automotive Engineering, Vol. 100, No. 2, February 1992, pp. 12-15.
15. Metals Handbook 10th Edition, "Properties and Selection: Irons, Steels and High-Performance Alloys," ASM International (1990) pp. 18-60, 365-374.
16. Metals Handbook 10th Edition, "Properties and Selection: Non-ferrous Alloys and Special-Purpose Materials," ASM International (1990) pp. 143-165.
17. Metals Handbook 10th Edition, "Properties and Selection: Irons, Steels and High-Performance Alloys," ASM International (1990) p. 31.
18. Handbook of Chemistry and Physics 71st Edition, CRC Press (1990) p. 12-122.
19. R.J. Warrick, et al, "Development and Application of Enhanced Compacted Graphite Iron for the Bedplate of the New Chrysler 4.7 Liter V-8 Engine," SAE Technical Paper No. 1999-01-0325, 1999.
20. SinterCast Product Literature, SinterCast Inc., Auburn Hills, MI.

FORD MOTOR COMPANY'S WORLD CAR CDW - 27 PROGRAM
MONDEO ~ CONTOUR ~ MYSTIQUE

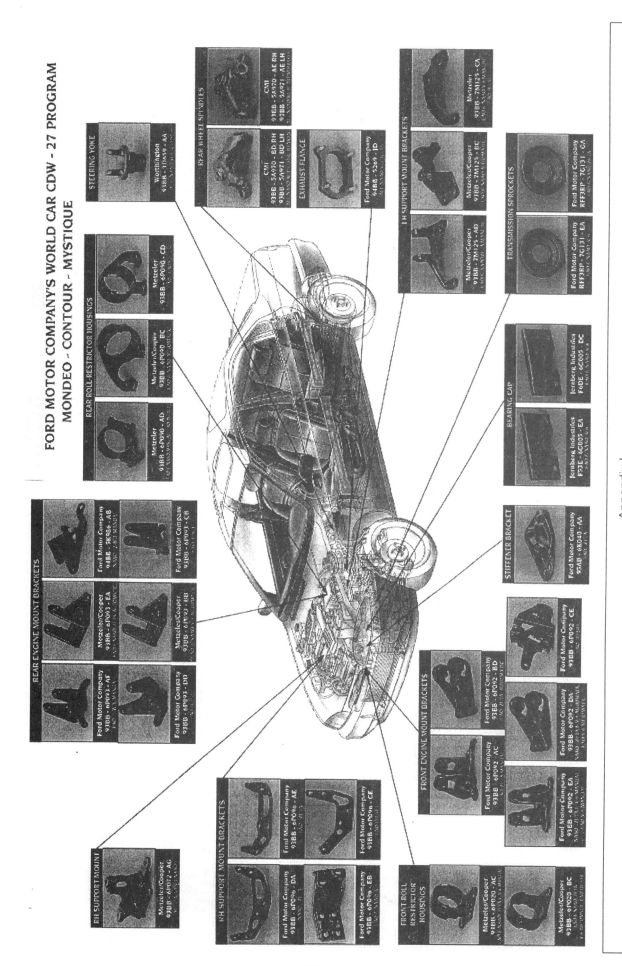

Appendix I.

Examples of Lightweight, Ductile Iron, Mounts and Brackets Made for Ford by Intermet Wagner Foundry Using the Green Sand Process.

SIMULATION OF THE CASTING PROCESS

2000-01-0754

Concurrent Product and Process Development Using Casting Process Simulation

Jiten V. Shah
K+P Agile, Inc.

Copyright © 2000 Society of Automotive Engineers, Inc.

ABSTRACT

In today's global competitive environment, the OEMs (original equipment manufacturers) are forced to introduce new products in a relatively short turnaround time and the products are required to be custom designs and developed in a concurrent engineering environment. Concurrent Product and Process Development (CPPD) using Casting Process Simulation brings agility to new product and process design and development.

The current computer aided technologies have enabled metal casters to understand and apply physics behind mold filling, solidification, and microstructure evolution. The commercially available tools allow to simulate most of the conventional casting processes such as sand, plaster molded, investment, permanent mold and die casting. Using this technology, castings are virtually made on computer before any hard tooling is made. Case study on cast component product development is presented. A brief description about the use and effectiveness of Casting Process Modeling for the development of the new casting processes such as Semi Solid Molding is discussed.

NOMENCLATURE

CAD – Computer Aided Design
CIM – Computer Integrated Manufacturing
CAE – Computer Aided Engineering
CPPD – Concurrent Product and Process Development
CNC – Computer Numerically Controlled
RP – Rapid Prototyping
OEMs – Original Equipment Manufacturers

INTRODUCTION

A key to manufacture a sound cast component is to design the component geometry, rigging system and process parameters in such a way that directional solidification is achieved. By utilizing cost-effective Casting Process Modeling tool, design engineers can inspect and validate their casting components before any hard tooling is made and any metal is poured.

Global competition in the manufacturing industry demands continued improvement in the cost of manufacturing and quality with quick turn around time. The OEMs are forced to introduce new products in a relatively short turnaround time and the products are required to be custom designs and developed in a concurrent engineering environment. A traditional trial and error approach is found to be uneconomical and ineffective to satisfy today's customer demands. The manufacturing process development portion is the most time-consuming and costly part of the product development cycle. This phase covers all the necessary work to reach a stage at which production can begin. This is the phase of product development that must be targeted for time and cost reduction. The current technology allows design engineers to develop manufacturing process simultaneous to the product geometry. CPPD using computer aided engineering tools along with Internet bring agility to new product design, development and manufacturing; thereby enabling faster new product developments, product redesigns and conversions. Computer Aided Engineering (CAE) tool kit consists of Computer Aided Design (CAD) / Three-Dimensional (3D) solid model building; casting process simulation (mold filling, and solidification); finite element stress analysis and fracture mechanics and fatigue/creep analysis for life prediction. The use of rapid tooling including Rapid Prototyping (RP) and Computerized Numerical Control (CNC) machining of patterns after the design is finalized brings products faster into the market. Fig. 1 explains how CAE tools and Rapid prototyping are integrated to bring agile product developments. Essentially, the design optimization through Finite Element Analysis (FEA) and Casting Process modeling results into a final design which then is transformed into the physical product through the use of rapid prototyping and tooling, casting, product testing and validation. Casting Process modeling is a part of the CAE tool kit and this paper demonstrates it's usefulness to new cast product development and product conversions from fabrication/forging/non-metals to castings.

Extensive research and development all over the world over the last 15 years or so to understand the science and physics behind metal casting along with faster computers have resulted into the development of many commercially available software products which simulate various casting processes. Casting process modeling software essentially provides the numerical computation for solving physics behind mold flow, solidification and microstructure evolution. Casting process modeling in a concurrent engineering environment helps the product engineer design a sound castable geometry before any tooling is constructed by validating casting digitally on computer. The paper explains typical inputs, outputs, the applications and future directions in the area of casting process simulation. A brief discussion about the usefulness of the web based collaboration tools for communication in the concurrent engineering environment is also presented.

Designs can be improved through optimization of cycle time, thermal loads and cooling lines in case of permanent mold and die-casting processes. The casting yield can also be optimized by on-screen testing of the rigging.

Potential casting defects related to mold filling and solidification shrinkage could be identified through the use of the numerical casting process model. Defects such as primary and secondary shrinkage, porosity, hot-tear, gas-entrapment, re-oxidation and dross formation, and mold/core superheating can be visualized on the computer monitor. This validates the cast component's design, rigging and process parameters. These steps ensure the cast components are right the first time without the delay and expense of traditional trial-and-error methods. The relevant inputs required to carry out casting process simulation and typical out put from such commercially available tools are discussed. Most of the casting process modeling tools provide the information such as cooling rate, gradient, velocity and temperature of the flow front during filling, local solidification time, micro structure, predicted mechanical properties, residual stress, deformation etc. A brief presentation about the state of the art Internet based communication tools available to achieve a true collaborative concurrent engineering environment is presented.

Science Behind Metal Casting

Research over the years has enabled metal casters to understand the liquid alloy flow behavior using as simple a model as Bernoulli's principle to as sophisticated and accurate a model as Navier Stokes equations. These equations which simulate the physics behind mold flow, momentum and heat transfer are solved numerically using either finite element method or finite difference method.

Some software uses the strictly empirical equations or a combination of empirical with numerical methods. Using either enthalpy or entropy models in conjunction with energy equation for conduction, convection, and radiation heat transfer modes, solidification of the casting alloys up to room temperature is modeled. Solidification kinetics, nucleation and grain growth models are simulated numerically which help predict the microstructure of various cast alloys. Using empirical relationship between microstructure and mechanical properties, mechanical properties in the different areas of the cast geometry under a given set of process parameters are simulated. Selection of the computer simulation software largely depends on the casting process to be modeled, the type of casting geometry – thin wall Vs thick wall; small Vs large overall size; computation time available; analyst's skill and experience available; and the main objective behind the simulation.

Typical Inputs to Casting Process Simulation

The first and foremost input to the process simulation is the geometry. Cast geometry with machine stocks, rigging (risers, chills, feeding systems such as exothermic and insulating sleeves, filters, chills, gates, vents etc.), mold box and core geometry are either created or imported from another CAD software program. The geometry of the complete casting process is then enmeshed either into the fine elements in case of finite element based software or control volumes/cuboids in case of finite difference method. Fig. 2 shows the complete casting system for a steel cast pump body. Each color represents different cast components: white/ yellow the casting area, green/blue the risers, etc. This pump body was reverse engineered from a failed pump for a captive power generation plant. Thermo-physical properties such as specific heat, density, thermal conductivity, viscosity, latent heat of fusion, etc. are applied for each components: casting, rigging, mold an core materials, filters, riser sleeves, chills etc. These properties are input for the entire temperature range from pour temperature to the room temperature. Another important input required is inter-facial heat transfer co-efficient, in other words, contact conductance. This input essentially simulates the resistance to heat flow between different interfaces such as sand to metal; metal to metal, and metal to air. It has been found experimentally that the output of simulation results is very sensitive to inter-facial heat transfer co-efficient, especially in permanent mold and die casting applications. Process parameters such as pouring temperature, initial mold/core temperatures, pouring rate or time or velocity or pressure, die cycle time, cooling and heating channels initial temperature and flow rates in case of permanent mold and die casting processes are some of the important inputs which are considered for casting process simulation.

Typical Output Results

After hours of computation, which depends on the type of the software, type of solver and computer hardware configuration, a massive database is created for each simulation. Some simulation results are viewed as a snap shot while some software animates the results to enhance the visualization. Moldfilling simulations give out information about the velocity vectors, and partial filled mold cavity with temperature profile. The results are useful to visualize the flow pattern; to look for any vortex and turbulence in the flow, and to look for any mis-runs and cold shuts. Typical solidification simulation results comprise of cooling rate, thermal gradient, local solidification time, hot spots, temperature profile at different fraction solids, and criterion functions such as Niyama and feeding to predict primary and secondary shrinkage. In case of permanent mold and die casting processes, multiple die cycles can be modeled. Temperature profile in the mold and core also provide useful information to foundry design engineers. Porosity predictions from casting process modeling are superimposed with finite element stress analysis results and using fracture mechanic study critical flaws and casting specifications are derived. In case of iron castings, microstructure in different areas can be predicted which then predict the casting mechanical properties in as-cast condition.

Applications and Versatility of Casting Process Modeling

Casting process modeling is an integral part of the casting product design process. The technology is very useful for any new product development, product re-designs, problem-solving for reducing the scrap as a problem solving tool, for improving the quality, and for reverse engineering. Sand, plaster molding, vertically parted molding, micro-gravity and counter gravity, permanent mold, die (low and high-pressure) casting, investment casting, centrifugal casting and other conventional casting processes can be modeled using current technology. Simulation technology is being used for newer processes such as lost-foam and semi-solid molding (thixo-forming and thixo-molding). Also the thermo-physical database enable design engineers to model any alloys; from plain carbon to alloyed steel to irons to non-ferrous to super-alloys for single crystal directionally solidified turbine blades. The similar database exists for most commonly used mold, core and die materials, and riser sleeves.

Advantages Using Casting Process Modeling

Following are some of the benefits casting users, designers and manufacturers achieve using casting process modeling technology:

- Right at the first time - no trial and error method involved, reduction or virtual elimination of the sampling time, and associated cost.
- Rigging and process parameters optimization.
- Reduction or elimination of the tooling rework, very important for the permanent mold and die casting process.
- Improved productivity by fine tuning the process before any tooling and castings are made.
- Design for castability, manufacturability.
- Development of achievable casting specification.
- Virtual casting on computer before any hard tooling is made.

Future Trends in Casting Process Modeling

The research is on going in optimizing the code to reduce the run time such that simulation is practical in the real world situation. Efforts are underway to enrich the accurate thermo-physical and inter-facial heat transfer co-efficient data. Software developers are working on predicting residual stresses and distortion for dimensionally critical to help design near net shaped castings and working on predicting the segregation tendency for large castings. Also, the developments are underway to reduce the reliance on analyst's knowledge about the rigging design principles using artificial intelligence so that the near-optimum solutions are derived using the simulation software. The simulation is also being extended for simulating the emission of the by-products of the binders and for simulating the core blower sand to help design the core-boxes for large intricate shaped automotive castings.

Engineering Collaboration Over the Internet

In the current global economy, a product development team can easily be composed of a design engineer, a foundry engineer, a tool maker and a machinist located in different buildings, different cities, or even different countries. These team members need to work concurrently. Tools such as AC Notebook allow the concurrent engineering team members to collaborate, interact, exchange ideas and documents over the internet in real time which further brings agility to the product development.

SUMMARY

The need for agility in bringing new products to market is being forced upon manufacturers around the world. Companies that want to prosper must become low-cost producers of rapidly made high-quality products. Computer Simulation is very effective tool helping design engineers to validate their part geometry and to predict the casting quality before any tooling and castings are made;

helps foundry engineer to design and optimize the rigging and process parameters. Most of the automotive and aircraft components are currently being developed using this technology. More work is underway in the areas of generating accurate thermo-physical properties for more alloys and molding mediums. As with any analysis, the accuracy off the data determines the result accuracy and correlation between the simulation results and actual results; and the interpretation of the results largely depends on the experience of the analyst. Casting process modeling is a tool to validate the foundry and design engineer's designs, but doesn't automatically create designs!

ACKNOWLEDGMENTS

Author acknowledges that AC Notebook software discussed in the paper is a result of the research efforts by Agile Casting Consortium to which K+P Agile is a member. The contract was funded by DARPA under contract number N00014-96-3-001 through the Office of Naval Research.

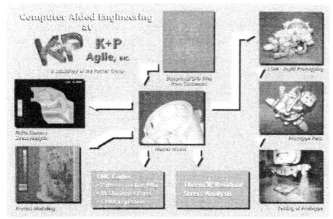

Figure 1 - Computer Aided Engineering at K+P Agile

CONTACT

For more information either visit the web site of K+P Agile at www.kpagile.com where there are more case studies on the application of casting process modeling or contact author by telephone at 630-505-4334; by fax at 630-577-1988 or by e-mail at jvs@kpagile.com.

REFERENCES

Applications of CIM Metal casting by Jiten Shah, AFS Transactions, Vol 101, 1993.

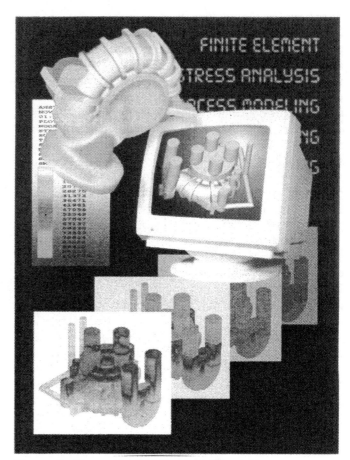

Figure 2 - Pump Casting Process Simulation

2000-01-0755

Flow Modeling of Casting Processes

Ken A. Williams
Flow Simulation Services, Inc.

Copyright © 2000 Society of Automotive Engineers, Inc.

ABSTRACT

Intended for the designer of automotive components, this paper emphasizes the importance, and feasibility today, of using casting modeling early in the design process. Usage of computer modeling for metal casting has expanded greatly in just the past few years. This is due to both advances in computer power, and to the economical benefits from modeling. Benefits include optimization of the process parameters to ensure sound parts, reduction of scrap, and minimization of defects. Given the complexity of automotive castings and the expanded range of materials being cast, computer simulation has gained an important role with designers as well as foundrymen. However, most computer simulations to date have focused on solidification and shrinkage modeling. Only recently has modeling begun to include the metal flow behavior with its inherent complexity. Recent advances in casting-specific flow modeling are showing great opportunity to provide additional improvements to automotive castings, especially for powertrain components. Specifically, this includes the processes of lost foam, high-pressure die-casting, and even with sand-core blowing. This paper covers the recent developments with casting modeling in all three casting process areas.

INTRODUCTION

Designers of automotive components today routinely make usage of computer modeling for stress analysis to ensure performance of a (critical) part. However, they often do not consider how this part will be manufactured. Any process, including casting, can lead to un-sound mechanical properties, or an undesirable surface finish. To help ensure that a component can indeed be cast as a sound part, designers should similarly employ computer-modeling software for casting flow and solidification. The following section discusses necessary conditions for such flow software, and how its usage can become an integral part of the initial design process.

CASTING MODELING REQUIREMENTS

For computer modeling to be feasible within the early design process there are two primary requirements. First, the modeling process must be conducted in a timely manner, including any "parametric" studies.

Second, the accuracy must be sufficient to ensure confidence in the conclusions. The goal of the casting modeling is to identify (and change) any features of the component that would make it "defect prone." Such modeling, in conjunction with foundrymen and casting suppliers, can help identify the most promising casting option to be employed for a given part. Since production costs can vary dramatically with the process, modeling may indeed suggest design modifications that could enable a more cost-effective process; or one that would be less prone to "typical" defects. Even if plans are to subcontract the part, this could head off future production problems.

TURNAROUND-TIME FOR FLOW MODELING

The primary steps required for modeling are: preprocessing setup, flow solver, and graphics. Tremendous progress has been made within the last few years on the "user friendliness" of flow modeling software. For example, some software packages allow direct importing of solid model(s) with semi-automatic meshing. Modelers supplied with a computer-aided-design (CAD) stereo-lithography (stl) model of the part can often have the geometry meshed within a few hours, or less. An illustration of three-dimensional meshing of a (stl) CAD model is shown in Figure 1. This mesh was generated within minutes, and a higher density meshing can be obtained with a simple input change. Specification of boundary and initials conditions, plus metal thermophysical properties is likewise straightforward. At this stage of the problem "setup" it will be necessary to work with foundrymen to specify the metal gating or feedsystem for the particular process. For casting simulation engineers who routinely work with foundry process this is a normal step.

The flow-solver stage accomplishes simulation of the metal filling and solidification processes. Accuracy discussions are presented below, however the computer run-time for the flow solver stage with today's personal computers (PCs) has dropped enormously. A sufficiently accurate solution should be obtainable within less than 24 hours, perhaps with parametric studies also necessary. Finally, understanding of the computed (three-dimensional) results has likewise progressed enormously with graphical post-processors. They readily facilitate identification of defects and problems

71

with metal flow. Working with the designer, the modeler can suggest potential changes to the part that facilitates its "castability."

MODELING ACCURACY

Having the ability for a "fast turnaround" is helpful only if the modeling conclusions are reliable. This means the software must have physically-based models for the underlying fluid mechanics and thermal phenomena. That is, they must be truly predictive, and not simply empirical. Again, today's computing power makes this feasible.

Application of computer modeling to casting has until recently focused on solidification. While this has paid considerable dividends after a part's design is given, flow modeling is required to evaluate which process is "best" for any particular part. This is because the flow of molten metal from the pour, through the feedsystem and within the cavity can have a major effect on its quality, or "soundness." For example, trapped air can induce porosity; or cold shuts can easily occur within thin sections. To quantify these effects the metal free-surface must be accurately represented during its entire flow path. Examples of such flow behavior in three different processes are now discussed.

High-Pressure Die Casting (HPDC)

The metal's free-surface behavior during cavity filling can be seen in Figure 2 from a simulation of a high-pressure die casing process. Filling of the cavity is strongly influenced by the flow patterns and momentum-induced jetting. Accurate determination of where trapped air may occur is important for (porosity) defect reduction. Figure 3 presents the computed last-to-fill region in this HPDC part. Examination of the final part (Walkington) reveals flow-induced defects (from trapped air) that can be mitigated by process modifications. Flow modeling is even being used to enable routine HPDC with "new" materials, such as copper (Daugherty and Williams).

Lost Foam

Lost foam casting has numerous benefits including casting thin-wall, near-net-shape parts. However, maturation of the process has been slowed in large part due to the complications of metal flow as pattern displacement occurs. Evaporation of the foam pattern generates gases that influence the metal motion, and foam decomposition products often introduce "fold defects." However, good progress has been made on mechanistically modeling lost foam casting with the FLOW-3D® code. Metal flow against a lost foam pattern is shown at various times in Figure 4. As metal fronts converge liquid expandable polystyrene (leps) on the fronts may become trapped causing a gas bubble or "fold." Furthermore, the feedsystem (and part region) for lost foam often contains internal pockets called lighteners, or hollows. These have the singular purpose

of controlling metal flow to achieve a dominant effect on the part's soundness. Flow simulation of this phenomenon can be well computed. While modeling all details of the lost foam process has not yet been done, today's software is sufficiently accurate to support initial manufacturing process decisions for a component.

Sand Coreblowing

Finally, an area that has eluded modeling is with one of the oldest foundry techniques, coreblowing. Air blowing of sand cores is a very complex fluid dynamics process. Foundrymen are greatly challenged to locate vents and blowtubes. Recently a new software has been developed that enables flow modeling and thus, internal visualization for coreblowing (Snider). The ARENA Eulerian-Lagrangian multi-fluid software was used to simulate experimental coreblowing at Auburn University (Overfelt). Figure 5 shows frames from high-speed movies, while Figure 6 gives the ARENA predictions. Very good agreement exists with details of filling patterns and times. This software has been used for (proprietary) simulation of a production engine core having dozens of vents and blowtubes.

Other

Numerous other casting flow modeling papers have been published under the auspices of the American Foundrymen's Society (AFS) and other organizations. For example, an excellent paper on casting improvements resulting directly from modeling metal flow in a green-sand feedsystem was given by Goettsch of General Motors (1998), while Barkhudarov and Hirt (1996) report on modeling semi-solid casting processes.

CONCLUSION

The consensus is that flow modeling software has made tremendous strides just within the past few years. This includes both the user friendliness and the accuracy. Combined with today's computers, flow software is playing a key role within manufacturing analysis organizations and foundries. As with stress analysis, flow modeling can today help automotive designers ensure that when a part is cast it will be sound and provide proper mechanical strength. An additional benefit is helping ensure it can be cast using the most cost-effective process.

CONTACT

For further information please contact Ken A Williams at Flow Simulation Services, Inc. (www.flowsim.com). The telephone number is (505) 828-1284 and email address is ken@flowsim.com

REFERENCES

Flow Science, Inc., Los Alamos. NM, FLOW-3D®, www.flow3d.com

Personal communication with Bill Walkington, Walkington Engineering, www.walkengr.com

Daugherty, J. and K. A. Williams, *"Thermal modeling of mold material candidates for copper pressure die casting of the induction motor rotor structure,"* Int'l Workshop on Permanent Mold Casting of Copper-Based Alloys, Ottawa, Canada, October 1998.

Snider, D. M., Goettsch, D., Stahl, K., Couture, D. J., 1999, *"An experimental and numerical study of dense particle flow in sand core castings,"* FEDSM99-7900, Proceedings 3rd ASME/JSME Joint Fluids Engineering conference, July 18-23, San Francisco, CA.

Bakhtiyarov, S. I. & Overfelt, R. A., 1996, "A study of apparent viscosity of fluidized sand", *Proceedings, ASME International Mechanical Engineering Congress and Exposition*, vol. 4, D. A. Siginer, et. al., ed., United Engineering Center, NY.

Goettsch, D. *"Baseline Casting Analysis Of a Grey Iron Engine Block"*, CASTEXPO '99, St. Louis, MO, March 13-16, 1999

Barkhudarov, M. R. and Hirt, C. W., *"Thixotropic Flow Effects under Conditions of Strong Shear"*, Proc. ASM-TMS, 1996 Material Week, Cincinnati, OH 7-10 Oct.

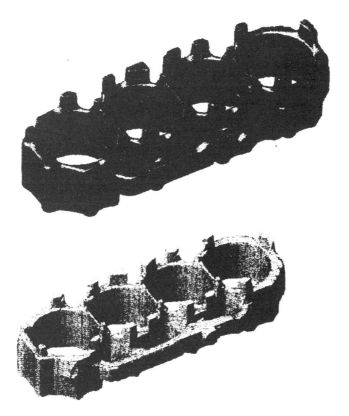

Figure 1 CAD file in stereolithography (stl) format (top) and meshed for flow simulation

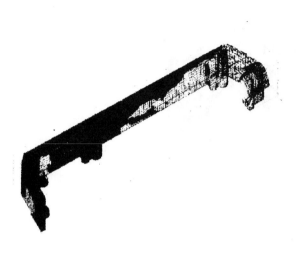

Figure 2   Metal "jetting" during cavity filling of HPDC process

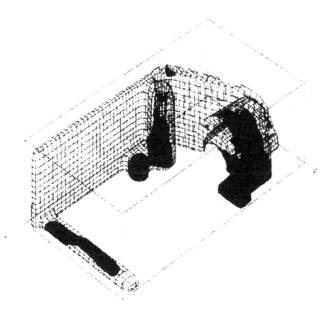

Figure 3   Last-to-fill region in HPDC casting can cause air entrapment and porosity

Figure 4 Lost Foam simulation showing pattern evaporation and metal temperature profiles

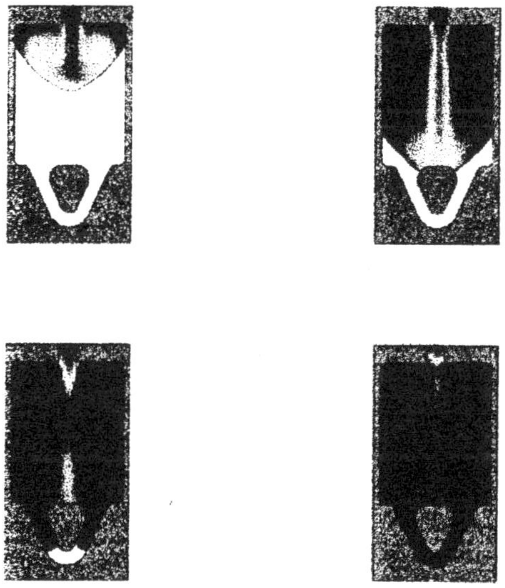

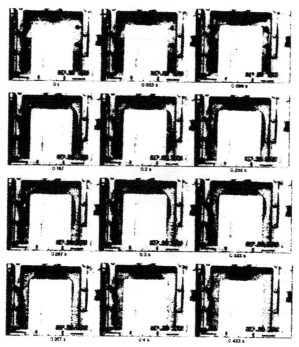

Figure 5 University of Auburn sand blowing experiment (Bakhtiyarov & Overfelt)

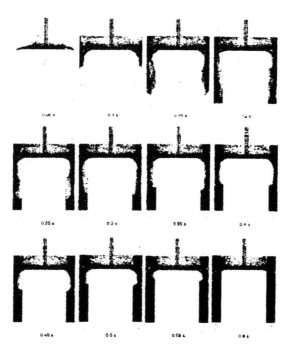

Figure 6   Calculation of the University of Auburn experiment
Interphase drag multiplier = 50.

2000-01-0756

Ensuring Castable Designs with Casting Process Simulation

Christopher Rosbrook and Ralf Kind
MAGMA Foundry Technologies, Inc.

Copyright © 2000 Society of Automotive Engineers, Inc.

ABSTRACT

Today's leading casting manufacturers employ many new technologies to produce high quality engineered castings. Foremost among these technologies is casting process simulation. With casting process simulation, casting designers and process engineers use sophisticated physical models to optimize casting filling and solidification patterns, microstructure and mechanical properties distributions, and residual stresses and distortion. Using casting process simulation early in the development cycle leads not only to higher quality castings, but also to shorter product development times, more castable designs, higher productivity, and castings that go well beyond what were once considered to be the limits of the casting process. This paper illustrates through case studies how both designers and producers of castings are using simulation to meet the increasing demands being placed on castings by the automotive and transportation industries.

INTRODUCTION

For a wide range of automotive components, castings and casting processes offer design engineers significant advantages over competitive products and manufacturing processes. Castings offer increased design flexibility where complex shapes are required; lighter weight, a key requirement of many automotive applications; and a near net-shape alternative that may not otherwise be available. Additionally, casting processes often provide lower manufacturing costs and reduced lead times.

Making high quality engineered castings, however, is more than pouring molten metal into a mold. Casting is a complex process that requires expertise in metal melting and handling, competence in metallurgy, and an understanding of the fluid flow, heat transfer and solidification phenomena that occur when the metal is cast.

Many new technologies help foundries to produce defect-free castings with tighter dimensional tolerances and superior mechanical properties. One such technology, casting process simulation, provides a window inside the mold that allows casting designers and process engineers to evaluate and optimize both the casting and the casting process – filling and solidification patterns, microstructure and mechanical properties distributions, and residual stresses and distortion – before any metal is poured.

Using casting process simulation early in the development cycle leads to higher quality castings, shorter product development times, more castable designs, and higher productivity. These benefits are highlighted in the following case studies.

APPLICATION CASE STUDIES

Over the past decade, designers and process engineers have applied casting process simulation to hundreds, if not thousands, of automotive components. The following three case studies – conversion of a seat frame fabrication to a magnesium die casting, improving quality and productivity for a gray iron brake drum, and conversion of a cast iron engine block to aluminum – typify the application of casting process simulation to automotive components.

CONVERSION OF A FABRICATION TO DIE CASTING – MAGNESIUM SEAT FRAME

Converting fabrications, stampings, and aluminum castings to magnesium can provide important weight savings for many automotive components. Working together, design and process engineers used casting process simulation to assist conversion of the automobile seat frame, Figure 1, from a fabrication of many sheet metal components to a single magnesium die casting. The proposed casting geometry was transferred from the CAD system to the simulation software as an STL file, Figure 2. The computational grid used for the simulation is shown in Figure 3.

Because of the combination of thin walls and large overall casting dimensions, early engineering efforts focused on determination of a gating system to achieve and adequate filling pattern. Two very different gating concepts – one in which the casting was gated from the inside and one in which the casting was gated from the outside – were evaluated. Results of the initial simulations indicated the superiority of the "inside"

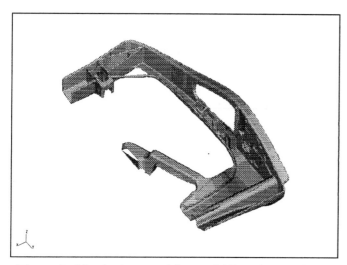

Figure 1. Magnesium seat frame CAD geometry (one-half of symmetric model)

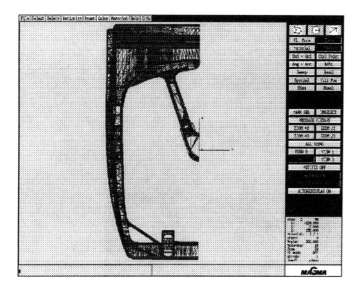

Figure 2. STL file imported from CAD system into simulation software

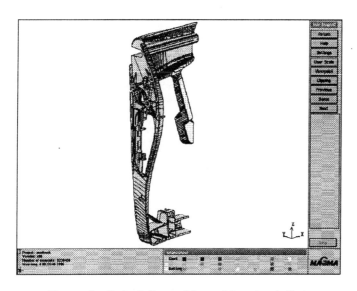

Figure 3. Calculation grid used for simulation

gating, and the inside-gating concept was chosen for further refinement using simulation.

Simulation of cavity filling provided detailed information on the flow pattern, air entrapment, knit lines, and metal velocities and pressures, as well as the melt heat losses that occur during filling. Because simulation was employed before the final casting design was fixed, it was possible to make changes to the casting itself to improve the filling of the cavity. A total of three simulations were conducted to design the runner and gate geometry and to properly locate the vacuum runners. These simulations ensured that the casting would fill without any critical entrapped air, without any critical knit lines, and without any misruns. Figures 4 and 5 show results of the filling simulation for the final gate and runner design.

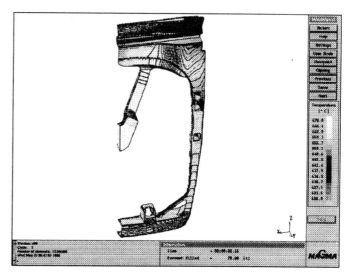

Figure 4. Fill pattern and temperature distribution in casting (70% filled)

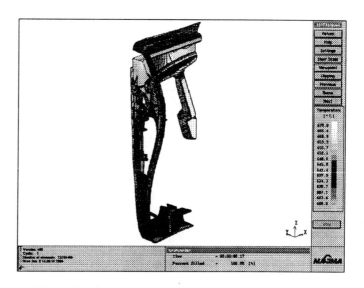

Figure 5. Temperature distribution at end of filling

Once the gating system had been designed, additional simulations were used to establish the locations of water and oil channels and to determine the cycle time. And finally, after all simulations had been completed, the die was constructed. The benefits of the simulations were

seen when the casting went into production without any problems.

HIGHER QUALITY AND HIGHER PRODUCTIVITY – GRAY IRON BRAKE DRUMS

Figure 6 shows the calculation grid used for simulation of the casting of gray iron brake drums. Foundry process engineers had two reasons to simulate these castings: eliminating an intermittent porosity defect and finding a way to increase productivity in light of increased pressure for lower costs. The first simulation of the existing process was conducted to determine the cause of the intermittent porosity defect. The computer prediction of the defect is shown in Figure 7.

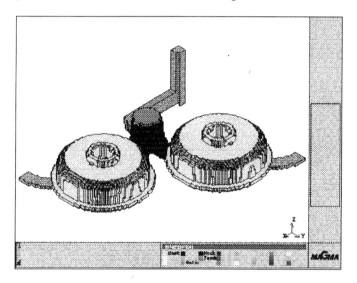

Figure 6. Horizontal mold layout for brake drum castings (one quarter of symmetric model – eight castings per mold)

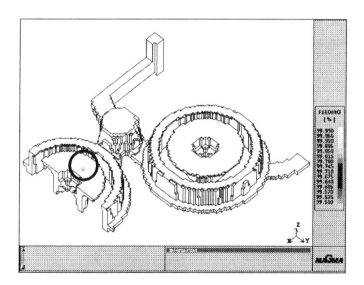

Figure 7. Simulation predicts intermittent porosity defect in current production

The results of the initial simulation indicated that the riser was not effectively feeding the casting and could be removed without any negative consequences, and that the intermittent porosity could be removed with a

better inoculation practice. (By modeling solidification kinetics, casting process simulation takes into account the effects of the specific iron chemistry as well as the foundry's inoculation practice. This level of detail is necessary for accurate shrinkage prediction in iron castings.) These observations were confirmed in a second simulation. Figure 8 shows defect-free castings made without the riser. Elimination of the riser improved the yield (the ratio of casting weight to the overall weight of metal poured) by eight percent, thereby reducing costs.

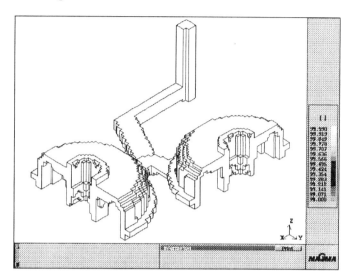

Figure 8. Modified design eliminates porosity defect

To increase productivity, several more simulations were performed to determine how best to increase the number of castings per mold. Figure 9 shows the final successful configuration with 16 castings per mold where there had previously been only eight.

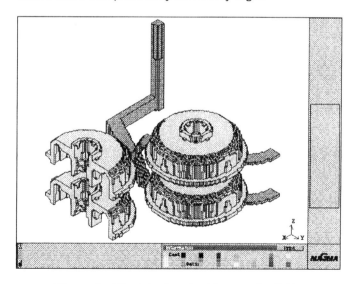

Figure 9. Final design doubles productivity

Having evaluated their process extensively with simulation, the foundry process engineers moved confidently toward the new mold design, even though it had the added complication of requiring a core to be placed between upper and lower castings. This new production process doubled productivity, improved casting quality through the elimination of the intermittent porosity defect, and further reduced costs by improving casting yield from 75% to 90% – an increase of 20%.

CONVERTING AN IRON CASTING TO AN ALUMINUM DIE CASTING – ENGINE BLOCK

In the continuing quest for lighter weight, castings traditionally made from gray iron are being converted to aluminum. This conversion has been made simpler in many cases through the application of casting process simulation. Simulation allows design engineers and process engineers to evaluate simultaneously and interactively the effects of engineering changes on castability and the effects of changes required for castability on the engineering design.

The four cylinder engine block shown in Figure 10 was converted from an iron sand casting to a high pressure aluminum die casting with the help of casting process simulation. As engineers worked through design changes, mold filling simulations were used to define the gating system, determine filling process parameters, and to properly locate the overflows, Figure 11.

Figure 10. Original gray iron engine block (left) and aluminum replacement

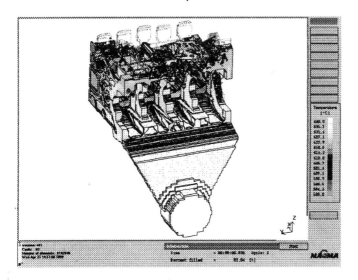

Figure 11. With a proper filling pattern, the overflows (top) are the last to fill

Simulation of the casting solidification pattern highlighted the regions that would likely exhibit shrinkage porosity, Figure 12, and the mold cooling system was designed to control the level of shrinkage in these regions. It was also determined that the heavy casting sections in the bearing section would require local squeeze pins; the position and timing of the squeeze pins was determined with simulation.

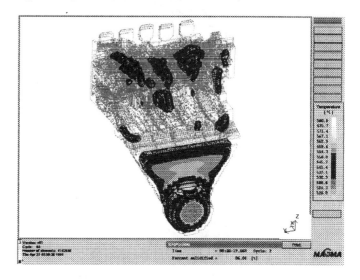

Figure 12. Solidification pattern highlights regions where shrinkage porosity was addressed through mold cooling and squeeze pins

The cast-in iron liners required by the aluminum design were evaluated for their effects on filling, solidification, casting distortion, and residual stresses. Distortion and stresses were of particular concern because of the different thermal expansion coefficients between iron and aluminum. The initial liner design was modified – the liners were made thinner – when simulation indicated that the residual stresses in the casting near the liners exceeded the yield stress of the cast aluminum alloy. Figures 13 and 14 show the casting distortion and residual stresses, respectively.

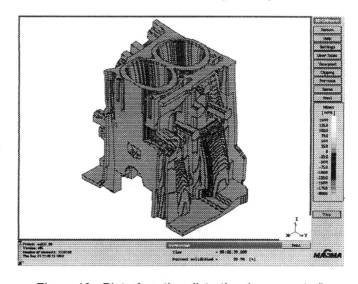

Figure 13. Plot of casting distortion (exaggerated)

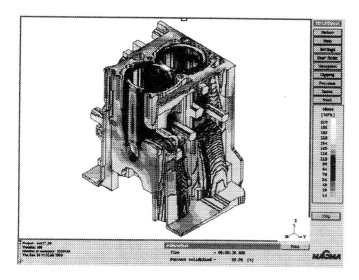

Figure 14. Mises residual stresses in the aluminum casting

All together, ten simulations were conducted to design the die and to assess the behavior of the cast-in liners. Finally, the engine block was launched successfully into production just eighteen months after the initial simulation efforts began.

SUMMARY

These three examples illustrate how design and process engineers are successfully applying casting process simulation to meet the continuously increasing demands being placed automotive components and automotive suppliers. As simulation tools continue to improve and as their application gains greater acceptance, these tools will continue to shape the way castings are designed and produced in the future.

ABOUT AUTHORS

Christopher Rosbrook and Ralf Kind are Vice President and Manager Die Casting Applications, respectively, at MAGMA Foundry Technologies in Arlington Heights, Illinois (www.magmasoft.com). Mr. Rosbrook joined MAGMA in 1992 upon graduating from The Ohio State University. His master's thesis on simulation of heat checking in die casting dies was conducted at the university's Center for Die Casting. Mr. Kind joined MAGMA in 1998 after 11 years at Ford Motor Company's casting plant in Cologne, Germany.

Both authors have been active in casting process simulation for more than ten years. They can be reached by phone at 847-427-1001.

Automotive Casting Defect Reduction by Process Simulation

Yun Xia
K + P Agile, Inc.

TingXu Hou
Citation Corporation

Copyright © 2000 Society of Automotive Engineers, Inc.

ABSTRACT

The automotive foundry industry is still facing greater challenge to make casting component lighter, stronger, tougher and cheaper. As computer process simulation technology has become a very helpful tool, more and more companies are popularly applying this tool in their optimizing casting structure and casting process designs. Fighting against casting defects is usually one of the major subjects in optimizing both casting structure design and casting process design. Computer simulation can reasonably predict "casting results" based on the structure/process data designed for a casting component previously or even conceptually. This prediction can provide us with some information about castability of a casting structure and then allow us to recommend for further improvement in its "original structure design" or to make a better casting process design to minimize the risk, i.e., those potential casting defects. For such purpose, a very important step is that computer process simulation must be performed before, not after, a casting is poured on the floor. This is an efficient way and also a successful way in improving casting quality, and reducing casting scrap and production costs.

In this paper, some experiences as well as several examples in applications of computer simulation for automotive castings are presented. By combining the casting experience with computer simulation technique, both casting structure and casting process designs such as casting orientation in mold, gating/risering designs, and many metallurgical factors in foundry operations can be optimized.

INTRODUCTION

Process simulation not only helps foundrymen in optimizing casting gating/risering design, but also helps to achieve an ideal cast microstructure through process parameter control.

Automotive castings have unique requirement regarding mechanical/metallurgical properties, mass production, and low cost. Computer process simulation assists in meeting these goals.

Computer simulation technology applied in optimizing process design for automotive casting components has proved to be successful. A good simulation can assist many parameters in a casting process design, which include gating/risering size, position, pouring time, pouring temperature and filling rate.

Mold filling simulation can help to achieve an uniform, even, and non-turbulent metal flow pattern. Defects caused by jetting, oxide entrapment, dross inclusions, and misruns can be reduced significantly. Solidification simulation can predict cooling rates, metal shrinkage, and riser pipe, as well as potential hot tearing and warpage related to thermal stress/strain distributions at elevated temperature during solidification. The latest progress in simulation software enhances micromodeling ability and can enable users to predict some features related to casting microstructure including matrix structure, ratio of pearlite/ferrite, hardness, nodularity, nodule counts, carbide formation, etc.

Specific database and parameters must be defined for simulating a particular casting process. These data and parameters should be as accurate as possible to achieve the realistic solutions for a particular process. Such parameters include the orientation and location of the casting component in the mold, gating/risering system layout (horizontal/vertical), and physical conditions and thermal data. Sometimes, factors relating to melting method (Cupola/Induction), metal treatment method, microstructure (pearlite/ferrite), inoculation operation (ladle/in-mold) should also be considered before setting up a simulation. Other available data helpful during process simulation include variable cooling curves, shrinkage factors, riser pipe and feeding efficiency.

Simulation trials are more cost effective than production trials. Making modifications to the gating/risering system is an effective way to optimize processes. This is the most efficient way to improve confidence in process design resulting in better casting, less scrap, lower cost, and higher profit.

CHARACTERISTICS OF AUTOMOTIVE CASTINGS

Mass production - ferrous casting production for auto part components typically uses automatic molding lines such as DISA, Osborne, or Hunter machines, as does the core making process. In North America, commonly cast ferrous automotive components include suspensions, chassises, knuckles, beams, brake calipers, control arms, crankshafts, camshafts, engine blocks, and cylinder heads. All of these parts are usually produced in high volumes with tight quality requirements.

Expensive tooling - normally the automotive industry uses permanent tooling such as metallic pattern boards, as opposed to the wood, plastic, and urethane rubber commonly used by short run casting industries. Alterations to permanent tooling require cost, time and labor.

Why not make it right the first time - most of the automotive castings listed above are made of ductile iron, gray iron. Unlike steel casting, these ferrous and aluminum parts are very hard to salvage with welding processes if a defect occurs.

High quality requirement - Automotive castings require both mechanical properties and specific microstructures since they need to work in wide temperature ranges, cyclic loading, vibration, and corrosive conditions.

COST FROM CASTING DEFECTS

As mentioned above, the automotive casting components usually require a high volume of production. The cost from the scraps is not only related to direct expenses such as those on operations, power, labor, alloy treatments, and machine usage, but also influences the customer's cost. For example, in the DISA 2070 model, 300-350 molds can be made within one hour. Each mold may have multiple cavities. There may be thousands of castings produced in an hour. If scraps happen, thousands of castings will be thrown away. This is the so-called "in-house" scrap. As to some castings with sub-surface problems, such as gas holes, pinholes, inclusions and internal carbides, these defects are usually difficult to find out using ordinary in-house inspection. If the castings are supposedly shipped to a machine shop, these defects are finally discovered with machining operations. Unfortunately, it is at times too late since costs have already been paid by now. No matter with who will be the payee to pay the cost, a bundle of money has already lost. On the other hand, cost for the process design corrections on the tooling and riggings is also money consuming. As such, controlling the casting quality and reducing the scrap can be the largest saving in the auto casting industries.

ONE TIME SUCCESSFUL

To prevent the situations mentioned above, it is better make automotive castings successfully the first time. Otherwise, there will be a headache thing to pay the expenses on the corrections of tooling and process parameters to meet the customer's specifications. To achieve good quality in a casting project, especially for a new casting project, the most important is to thoroughly understand any potential problems with the casting and how to prevent or minimize the problems with an optimized process design prior to placing it into production.

One time successful can be as a piece of foundry rule: never pour a single ladle of casting before having performed computer process simulation.

EXAMPLES

MOLD FILLING BALANCE

Unbalanced mold filling usually comes as a result of an incorrect calculation of the gating system. Figure. 1 shows the gating which does not evenly fill the cavities. This may result in turbulent flow, misruns, and an ill-sequenced solidification order. This kind of mistake usually happens at both horizontal and vertical gating systems. To have an even filling system, the tooling engineer should calculate the gating ratio, pressure, flow rate at different layers, and should consider using tapered or step runner and ingate, etc. Of course, the calculation is time consuming and relies on people's experience. Computer simulation can usually give reasonably accurate results as well as a time savings. Adjusting the runner, ingate size and shape on the computer model by trial and error, you will get a much better filling pattern. Figure. 2 shows the balanced mold filling results by changing the ingate areas and runner shapes.

Uneven filling can usually be found from the gating system design in foundry shops, which may result in lots of casting defects. The reason may be that the designer did not accurately calculate parameters, or did not reasonably use tapered/step sprue, runner and gates, especially for multiple layer vertical gating. Fortunately, computer process simulation can be applied to evaluate the designs. An improved filling system can then be achieved with some corrections on the gating after reviewing the information from the simulation results.

In production of automotive castings, the filtration system is frequently used to eliminate impurities such as inclusions and dross that come from liquid metal treatment stage such as inoculation and pouring operations. To some extent, the filter can also help in liquid metal movement through a gating or casting system with a stable and smooth manner. However, it may reduce the kinetic pressure and velocity in some areas. A gating system with wrong filter settings may cost produce some defects such as cold shot, misrun, and even short pour. Again, computer process modeling will help evaluate the filter settings with the information about mold filling such as those distributions of pressure, velocity, and temperature. This will optimize the filter setting and achieve better casting quality.

SOLIDIFICATION, POROSITY, AND RISER PIPING PREDICTION

In steel, ductile iron, and aluminum castings, shrinkage porosity is usually one of the biggest problems. Successful prediction of the shrinkage positions, as well as its levels is the most important issue. In many cases, although it is difficult to eliminate all of the shrinkage porosity out of castings, it is still possible to reduce them by applying appropriate risers, chills, and other features. With these features, solidification sequences of castings can be under controllable. As a result, those hot spots that are the sources of porosity can be moved into an incorporated riser or a non-critical area. Therefore, the computer predictions on those potential porosity sites, their locations and sizes, are the critical objective to the computer simulation professionals

Figure. 3 shows the shrinkage in the part. Figure. 4 shows the shrinkage level is reduced by changing the feeding speed and hot riser position. The results match the x-ray inspection.

Several criteria being used for evaluations of casting defects such as porosity formed during casting solidification are also available in some commercial solidification simulation packages. These criteria are mostly derived from some solidification features such as solidification time, thermal gradient, cooling rate, solidification rate, variation of fraction of solid with time, variation of density with time, and so on. Niyama criterion is one of the popularly used for evaluating the piping shrinkage porosity formed in steel castings. On the foundry floor, after checking the appearance of a solidified riser such as its piped levels, an experienced professional can usually give his judgment on the casting quality. Figure. 5 illustrates a piped riser pattern. The riser piping situation can be simulated by some computer software packages. This provides users with a clear direction with viewable results on the computer screen to adjust those factors relating to a feeding riser, if necessary, such as the sizes of a riser, types of an insulating sleeve, and the details of riser contacts. The feeding volume is defined as a certain amount or percentage of liquid metal in a riser can be enable to play its feeding function to its neighboring casting region. Figure. 6 shows an example of a well-piped riser after modified the riser size and the neck shape. How to apply the casting parameters in an appropriate way? This is depending on the individual experiences of the professionals. Computer simulation is a useful tool for this purpose. However, the optimal accomplishment for it will usually be achieved by an excellent combination of computer technology and casting process experience.

MICRO-PROCESS MODELING

Most of the automotive castings are made of cast iron including gray, ductile, and compact irons. Casting quality also depends on the microstructure conditions. In the current commercial software world, some simulation packages incorporate a micro-modeling module and can be used to predict the metal matrix, strength at variable temperature values, carbide quantity and nodularity/nodule count, etc. Figures 7 and 8 are examples of the computed metal matrix and nodule counts.

The microstructure modeling can help process people to control the chemistries in metal castings as well as those metallurgical factors related to the formation of microstructures. To use the computer module, people can input the alloy composition and process parameters in adjustable levels to reflect a particular application. For example of ductile iron casting process, the names and concentrations of chemical elements in iron castings such as C, Si, Mn, S, P, Ni, Mg, Cu and other trace elements like Sn, Ti, Zn, Al can be as input data for a microstructure simulation. In addition, those process parameters such as the inoculation methods as well as its amount can also be input into the preset data to describe a particular treatment.

In ductile iron, graphite expansion also plays an important role in shrinkage porosity levels. Stronger mold can usually keep the casting expansion less and make the growing graphite inward to fill those porosity and shrinkage. Shakeout time often affects the microstructures of a casting such as percentage of matrix compounds and the shape and numbers of graphite nodules. In general, micro-modeling can help adjust these process parameters in meeting the needs of achieving particular casting microstructures. However, at the current stage, this technique is still under development and will be improved to reach realistic application in the near future.

PROCESS SIMULATION VALIDITY

Both successful and unsuccessful simulation results can be seen in simulation engineering houses. It often depends on how much the user can combine simulation technique with his own casting experience. Normally, every simulation software provides databases for the user's use. They usually cover thermal properties such as density, thermal conductivity, specific heat, latent heat of fusion, liquidus and solidus temperatures, viscosity for variable alloys and mold sands, and some physical conditions such as interfacial heat transfer coefficients, etc. They can all be constant or temperature dependent. However, the built-in data does not mean that they can always match your own company's specific case. Most of the software packages also provide the capabilities for the user to modify an existing database or establish a new material database. Users need to do some basic investigation for some specific metal alloys to obtain a more reliable database. Users might also need to do some experiments to measure the heat transfer coefficients for their specific casting and mold system. In some large foundries, there are various casting processes such as green sand, no-bake sand, shell mold, permanent mold and even die casting. It is a smart idea to create their own special databases for particular processes. More investigation works have been done, and more confidences in using the simulation software to reduce the casting defects will be achieved. If one always uses the same database provided by the software company without modification or update, they will not be taking full advantage of the simulation.

Another very important point is how to explain the simulation results to colleagues or clients. It is better to use those color scales in software to quantitatively illustrate those shrinkage porosity levels, temperature distributions across castings and molds, turbulent flow patterns, and etc. The recognition of a defect nature such as a shrinkage porosity, a gas problem, or a sand inclusion is also a plus to successfully perform an explanation on the simulation results.

QUALIFICATION OF SIMULATION SOFTWARE USERS

The person to use the simulation software should have adequate process experiences. It is not a good idea to employ computer background professionals to run the simulation software, as some companies do. Although It looks like they can save some on labor cost, they might not really take advantage of the usage of the simulation. In addition, the users should also have basic knowledge of fluid flow and heat transfer. If the simulation tool user has a strong background in metallurgy, process control, melting, treatment, tooling, sand and core system, casting parting surface design, gating and risering system design, the user will be beneficial to the company.

Furthermore, cooperation between the process simulation team, structure/design team, and tooling makers can bring about more advantages in optimization of casting structure, process design, and tooling making. Immediate improvements in casting quality, production cost, and customer service can also be achieved. These improvements may include better castability of casting design, optimized gating/risering system design for preventing casting defects, less pour weight and higher metal yields, easily trimmable gates, ease of engineering modifications, and less overall production costs. A good simulation user should perform multiple tasks. For example, some technical recommendations should follow up your simulation reports for future casting production, and some information related to production, such as optimal mold sand weight, casting/sand ratio, and shakeout time may also be useful for operation staff to consider.

SUMMARY

Casting production for auto components is facing more serious competition than ever before. Its special characteristics require that fighting against casting defects be one of the most important tasks for a foundry. It is usually true that improvement in casting quality can result in lower reject rate and lower overall cost. Computer process modeling is successfully used to simulate the casting process, including the gating design. This is an effective tool to improve casting quality, increase yield and reduce cost.

The mold filling module is used to assist gating design both for vertical and horizontal systems, especially for gating systems with multiple layers. Uneven mold filling patterns, turbulent flow manners, short pours, and misruns can be optimized by adjusting the gate ratio, runner/gate size, venting, etc.

A solidification module is used to predict hot spots, shrinkage porosity, etc. Locations and sizes of risers, shapes and sizes of contact neck, and locations and sizes of chills can be optimized.

The micro-modeling module is used to check casting microstructure, which is helpful to decide the casting thickness, process parameters, and molding conditions.

REFERENCES

1. R. C. Cresse, , Yu Xia, "The Tapered Riser Design Optimization", AFS Transaction, 1991.
2. Yun Xia, "Automotive Casting Gating Design", Magma User Annual Conference, 1995.
3. David C. Schmidt, "Combo Modeling Method Provides Extra Solidification Insight, Modern Casting, October 1997.
4. Anthony C. Midea, "Accurate Thermal Data for Exothermic/Insulating Feeding Systems", Foundry Management and Technology, August, 1999.

Figure 1. Uneven Mold Filling. Metal Comes into the Mold in Different Velocity

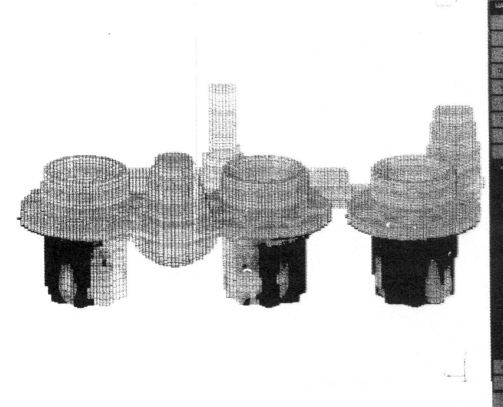

Figure 2. Balanced Mold Filling. Metal Temperature and Velocity Distribute Evenly

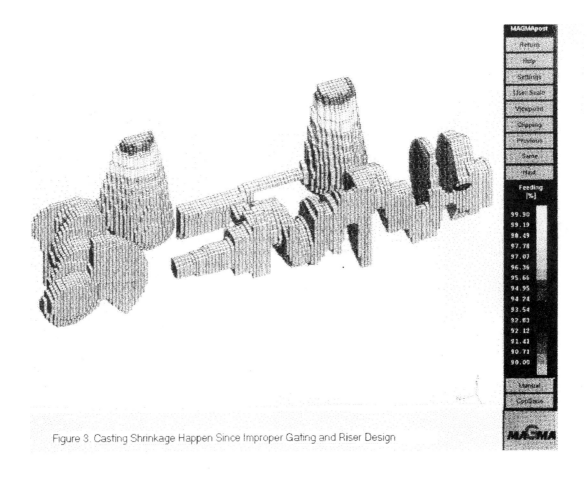

Figure 3. Casting Shrinkage Happen Since Improper Gating and Riser Design

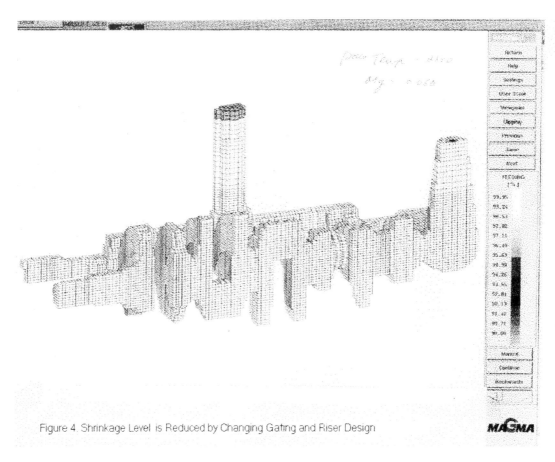

Figure 4. Shrinkage Level is Reduced by Changing Gating and Riser Design

Figure 5. Riser Piping to Feed the Casting

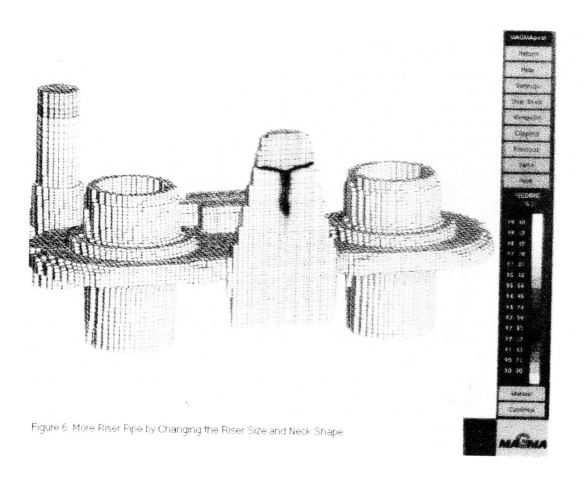

Figure 6. More Riser Pipe by Changing the Riser Size and Neck Shape

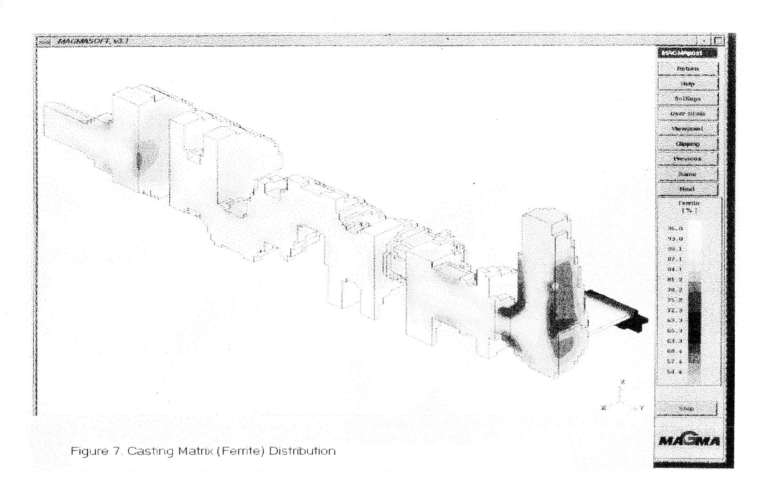

Figure 7. Casting Matrix (Ferrite) Distribution

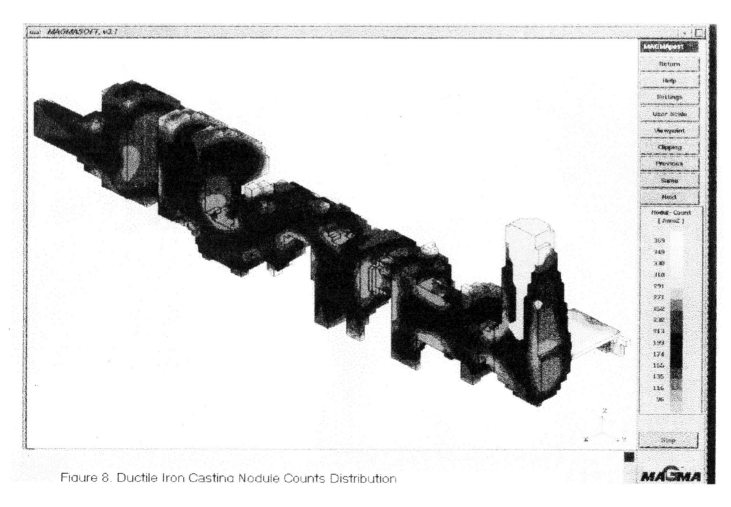

Figure 8. Ductile Iron Casting Nodule Counts Distribution

INVESTIGATIONS OF
MATERIAL PROPERTY DATA

2000-01-0758

Monotonic and Cyclic Property Design Data for Ductile Iron Castings

John M. Tartaglia, Paige E. Ritter and Richard B. Gundlach
Climax Research Services

Lyle Jenkins
Ductile Iron Society

Copyright © 2000 Society of Automotive Engineers, Inc.

ABSTRACT

Data on the low and high cycle fatigue response as well as monotonic (non-cyclic) and cyclic flow properties are required by design engineers for the proper design of many components. Currently, there are no readily available sources for such information on ductile/nodular cast iron. The purpose of this study was to determine property design data similar to those in SAE standard J1099 for SAE Grade D5506 ductile iron. In this study, the monotonic and cyclic strin hardening properties, and the variation of elastic modulus after repetitive cyclic testing were determined for eight ductile iron castings selected to represent the range of properties possible in Grade D5506 ductile iron. Strain-life testing was conducted on four of the eight materials to calculate the strain and stress versus fatigue life (reversal) constants.

INTRODUCTION

Low and high cycle fatigue data, as well as monotonic (non-cyclic) and cyclic flow properties are required before ductile/nodular iron can be used in many design applications. Although these data are available in SAE standard J1099, June 1998, "Technical Report on Fatigue Properties" for many competing materials, no readily available source exists for such information on ductile cast iron. Typical tensile and compression properties of ductile iron are well known, but the (1) monotonic and cyclic strength coefficients, (2) strain and stress versus fatigue life (reversal) constants, and (3) the variation in elastic modulus after repetitive cycling have not been published in the open literature.

The objective of this investigation was to determine many of the important constants used by engineers in the design of structural components , i.e., items (1) and (3) above, for eight ductile iron samples representative of the hardness range, nodularity, and nodule sizes typical for ferrite-pearlite SAE grade D5506 ductile iron. Four of the eight samples were selected for strain-life

fatigue testing with fully-reversed axial loading, i.e., item (2) above. Three of the selected materials represent the full range expected for this grade of ductile iron using hardness as the principle determinant. A fourth material was selected to compare the strain-life fatigue properties between ductile iron castings with similar hardness values and microstructures, but different cast cross-sectional areas. All data were analyzed with respect to the hardness and microstructure for each material.

PROCEDURES

DUCTILE IRON CASTINGS

Eight grade D5506 ductile iron heats were supplied by Ductile Iron Society (DIS) member foundries. The objective was to obtain castings that cover the full hardness range for D5506 (187-255 HB) in a range of cast section sizes. The categories were established as follows: three material conditions with nominally 187 HB, two material conditions with nominally 223 HB, and three material conditions with nominally 255 HB hardness. Monotonic and cyclic property tests were conducted on all eight material conditions in an initial survey. Based on the results, four ductile iron heats representative of the overall range of material characteristics for Grade D5506 ductile iron were selected for a subsequent comprehensive survey. The eight sets of castings ranged in cast section size from 2.54 cm (1 inch) diameter rounds to 7.62 cm (3 inch) Y-blocks.

CHEMISTRY

A comprehensive chemical analysis was performed on the eight materials. Two samples were removed from the end of a bar for each material. On one sample from each material condition, all outer edges of the casting were either cut or ground off to remove the cast surface before analyzing the carbon content. The other sample was used to determine the other elemental concentrations. Concentrations of fourteen elements were determined by the following methods: carbon and sulfur contents by combustometric methods; copper and magnesium by atomic absorption spectrophotometry; and silicon, manganese, chromium, nickel, molybdenum, aluminum, titanium, cerium, and tin by optical emission spectrometry on a remelted and chill-cast sample. The remainder of the bar was used for hardness testing, tensile testing, and microstructural analysis.

TENSILE TESTS

Three standard round tensile specimens were machined from separate bars for each of the eight ductile iron materials in accordance with ASTM standard E 8-99. The specimens had gauge sections 5.08 cm (2 inches) long and 1.27 cm (0.5 inch) in diameter. Both resistance strain gauges and an extensometer were mounted on the specimens. The specimens were tested to fracture in a screw-driven tensile machine.

The ultimate tensile strength, 0.2% offset yield strength, fracture elongation, and percent reduction of area were determined in accordance with ASTM standard E 8-99. The fracture elongations of the specimens were determined by reassembling the specimen halves subsequent to fracture and measuring the final gauge length.

The elastic modulus was determined by linear regression of the stress-strain (gauge) data in the elastic region in accordance with ASTM standard E 111-97. The monotonic strength coefficient (K) and the strain hardening exponent (n) were determined by log true stress-log true strain regression of the extensometer data in the plastic region in accordance with ASTM standard E 646-98. The K and n constants characterize the stress-strain response in a (monotonic) tensile test in the plastic region.

The following parameters based on SAE standard J1099, June 1998, "Technical Report on Fatigue Properties" were determined from the tensile tests:

S_{ys} = 0.2% Offset Yield Strength (engineering)
σ_{ys} = 0.2% Offset Yield Strength (true)
S_u = Ultimate Tensile Strength (engineering)
σ_f = Ultimate Tensile Strength (true)
%RA = Percent Reduction of Area
%El = Percent Elongation
E = Modulus of Elasticity
ε_f = True (monotonic) Fracture Ductility
K = (monotonic) Strength Coefficient
n = (monotonic) Strain Hardening Exponent

BRINELL HARDNESS

Samples were removed from the grip ends of each tensile specimen after the tensile testing for Brinell hardness measurement. The Brinell measurements were performed in accordance with ASTM standard E10-98 using a 3000 kg load, a 10 mm steel ball, and a 15 second dwell time. The average of three hardness tests

was used to provide the baseline for all subsequent comparisons.

METALLOGRAPHY

Metallographic samples were taken from the gauge region of one fractured tensile specimen half and mounted with a transverse polish plane. The samples were polished using conventional methods for ductile cast iron, and etched in 2% nital. The samples were examined optically and the nodularity, nodule count, and ferrite content were measured using computerized automated image analysis techniques.

INCREMENTAL STEP TESTING – INITIAL SURVEY OF CYCLIC PROPERTIES

Three specimens conforming to the requirements of ASTM standard E 606-98 were machined with gauge length and diameter of 3.81 cm (1.5 inches) and 0.95 cm (0.375 inch), respectively, for each of the eight material conditions. Incremental step tests (IST) were performed on an MTS closed-loop servohydraulic machine by cycling the specimens at a series of strain levels until the stress-strain hysteresis loops were stabilized at each strain. Data from these hysteresis curves were used to calculate an average cyclic strength coefficient (K') and the cyclic strain hardening coefficient (n').

The tests were performed in fully reversed strain control using a constant ramp time of 10 seconds. The specimens were cycled at ±0.1% increments from ±1.5, ±1.4, ±1.3... ±0.2%, and ±0.1% total strain for each "unloading" IST block. The specimens were then reloaded starting with ±0.1% total strain and continuing in a similar progression to ±1.5% total strain. The entire process was repeated until the cyclic stress-strain curve was stabilized upon unloading, i.e., no change in the load-strain values between the last two unloading IST blocks was observed. The seventh IST pass (where one pass unloads from ±1.5% to ±0.1%, and then reloads from ±0.1% back to ±1.5% total strain) was compared to the sixth pass and analyzed for the cyclic stress-strain curve at saturation.

The following parameters based on SAE standard J1099, June 1998, "Technical Report on Fatigue Properties" were determined from the incremental step tests:

n' = Cyclic Strain Hardening Exponent
K' = Cyclic Strength Coefficient
S'_{ys} = 0.2% Offset Cyclic Yield Strength (engineering)
σ'_{ys} = 0.2% Offset Cyclic Yield Strength (true)

TENSILE TESTING AFTER INCREMENTAL STEP TESTING

After performing incremental step testing, the IST samples were tested for tensile properties in the same manner (including modulus determination with strain gauges) as described earlier for the monotonic properties. The post-cyclic tensile properties were recorded and the elastic modulus, sometimes called the "service" modulus, was calculated for comparison to the monotonic properties.

DETERMINATION OF CYCLIC PROPERTIES – FINAL SURVEY

Four of the eight materials with widely differing properties were selected for axial strain-control low-cycle fatigue tests. (Due to the costs involved with testing, it was not possible to perform these tests on all eight material conditions.) Conditions #2, 4, and 8 were chosen to represent the low, medium, and high hardness regime of SAE Grade D5506 ductile iron, respectively. Condition #7 was very similar to Condition #8 in hardness and microstructure, but behaved somewhat differently throughut the study. This was attributed to the significantly larger coss section of the casting; therefore, it was included in the study to observe the differences caused by the cast cross-sectional areas.

Sixteen axial fatigue test specimens were machined for each material using low stress machining procedures in accordance with ASTM standards E 606-98 and E 466-96, with the exception of the Condition #7 which had sufficient material for only fifteen specimens. The gauge diameter and length of the test specimens were 8 mm and 16 mm, respectively.

Axial strain-controlled low-cycle fatigue tests were performed under the guidelines of ASTM E 606-98 to develop a strain-life curve over the range from approximately 100 cycles to approximately 5,000,000 cycles. Each specimen was cycled using fully reversed triangular waveform loading at a frequency of 1 Hz. The tests were conducted at the following total strain amplitudes: one at 0.15%, one at 0.18%, three at 0.20%, two at 0.25%, two at 0.30%, three at 0.50%, two at 0.80%, and two at 1.00%. Those tests with anticipated lives exceeding 1 million cycles were changed to load-control mode at 50 Hz after 100,000 cycles (i.e., load saturation) to conserve machine time and cost. Strain-life curves (ε-N_f) were developed from the results.

The total strain-reversals (2 times life) equation is as follows: $\Delta\varepsilon/2 = \sigma_f'/E(2N_f)^b + \varepsilon_f'(2N_f)^c$. This equation models the strain-life behavior of materials being loaded in the plastic region. The following parameters were determined based upon SAE J1099, June 1998, "Technical Report on Fatigue Properties" from the strain-life fatigue tests in accordance with the procedures stated in ASTM standard E 739-98.

σ_f' = Fatigue Strength Coefficient
b = Fatigue Strength Exponent
ε_f' = Fatigue Ductility Coefficient
c = Fatigue Ductility Exponent

Note - for each specimen, the plastic strain range at half-life was calculated as follows:

- The elastic strain amplitude at half-life was calculated by dividing the stress amplitude by the elastic modulus. For specimens with total strain amplitudes of 0.25% or less, where there was no significant plastic strain, the elastic modulus from the tensile tests conducted prior to incremental step testing was used for this calculation. For specimens with total strain amplitudes of 0.30% or more, where there was significant plastic strain, the elastic modulus measured after the incremental step tests was used.

- The calculated elastic strain amplitude was then subtracted from the total strain range at half-life to determine the plastic strain amplitude.

- The total strain amplitude curve was calculated by adding the predicted elastic and plastic strain amplitudes. The calculation for the total strain-reversals curve was performed using the elastic modulus from the tensile tests conducted prior to incremental step testing.

The calculation for the total strain-reversals regression curve was performed using the elastic modulus from the tensile tests conducted prior to incremental step testing.

RESULTS AND DISCUSSION

MATERIAL CHARACTERIZATION

Eight ductile iron materials ranging in hardness from 186 to 270 HB were evaluated in this investigation. The test bars represented a wide range in cast section size varying from 2.54 cm (1 inch) rounds to 7.62 cm (3 inch) Y-blocks. All the castings were produced with the intent to cover the full range of properties (see SAE standard J434 Jun86), especially the Brinell hardness range, for SAE grad D5506. Table 1 contains the descriptions, microstructural analyses, and chemical compositions of all the materials employed in this study. All samples met the typical minimum tensile strength of 550 MPa. Two samples at the low end of the hardness range were somewhat below the typical minimum yield strength of 380 MPa. One material at the high end of the hardness range did not quite meet the typical minimum elongation (6%). Pearlite content ranged from a low of 49% to greater than 99%. Optical micrographs for the eight ductile iron samples are presented in Appendix A.

Overall, the eight materials were an appropriate group of alloys representing the full range of properties attainable in Grade D5506, with a wide range in hardness, microstructure and section size. There was sufficient variation in hardness and strength to determine their influence on high-cycle fatigue properties, and there was sufficient variation in microstructure and ductility to study their effects on low-cycle strain-life properties.

From the onset of the study, it was discovered that most properties varied with hardness. Therefore, the following

Table 1: Metallographic Characteristics and Chemical Compositions of Eight Grade D5506 Ductile Irons.

Condition (Rank Based On Hardness)	Symbol	Units	1	2	3	4	5	6	7	8
Casting Type			1" diameter circular bars	1" Y-Blocks	2" Y-Blocks	2" Y-Blocks	7/8" Round Keel Bars	2" Y-Blocks	3" Y-Blocks	1" diameter circular bars
Material Properties										
Brinell Hardness		HBS 3000	186	189	205	228	236	244	250	270
Pearlite Content		%	63.0	49.3	65.2	74.7	84.2	86.3	99.4	99.7
Ferrite Content		%	37.0	50.7	34.8	25.3	15.8	13.7	0.7	0.3
Nodule Count		per mm²	176	187	210	356	196	300	68	147
Nodularity		%	94	95	85	91	96	94	89	93
Chemistry Data										
Carbon	C	wt%	3.70	3.68	3.75	3.70	3.65	3.75	3.56	3.60
Sulfur	S	wt%	0.009	0.013	0.01	0.01	0.016	0.011	0.012	0.009
Phosporus	P	wt%	0.022	0.012	0.016	0.017	0.019	0.017	0.017	0.021
Silicon	Si	wt%	2.38	2.39	2.72	2.85	2.18	2.61	2.41	2.10
Manganese	Mn	wt%	0.29	0.26	0.23	0.25	0.23	0.25	0.31	0.35
Chromium	Cr	wt%	0.04	0.04	0.02	0.02	0.09	0.02	0.05	0.09
Nickel	Ni	wt%	0.02	0.03	0.02	0.02	0.05	0.02	0.03	0.04
Molybdenum	Mo	wt%	<0.01	0.01	<0.01	<0.01	0.01	<0.01	0.01	0.01
Aluminum	Al	wt%	0.026	0.022	0.037	0.04	0.034	0.042	0.019	0.029
Copper	Cu	wt%	0.13	0.44	0.53	0.54	0.40	0.66	0.36	0.62
Magnesium	Mg	wt%	0.031	0.039	0.026	0.038	0.044	0.036	0.057	0.049
Titanium	Ti	wt%	0.006	< 0.005	<0.005	<0.005	0.007	<0.005	<0.005	<0.005
Cerium	Ce	wt%	0.0048	0.0028	0.0069	0.0081	0.0056	0.0069	0.0047	0.0063
Tin	Sn	wt%	<0.005	0.006	0.005	0.006	< 0.005	0.008	0.037	<0.005
Carbon Equivalent	CE*		4.50	4.48	4.66	4.66	4.38	4.63	4.37	4.41

*CE = wt% C + 1/3 (wt% Si + wt% P)

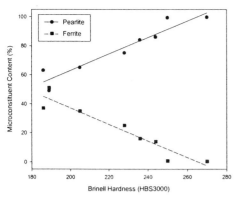

Figure 1: Pearlite and ferrite percentage as a function of hardness.

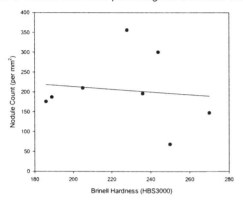

Figure 2: Nodule count as a function of hardness.

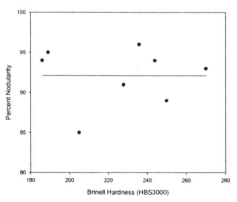

Figure 3: Nodularity as a function of hardness.

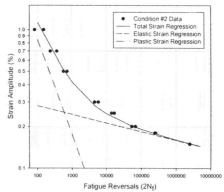

Figure 4: Strain-life fatigue data and predictions for Low-Hardness, Condition #2.

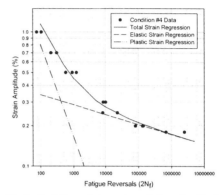

Figure 5: Strain-life fatigue data and predictions for Medium-Hardness, Condition #4.

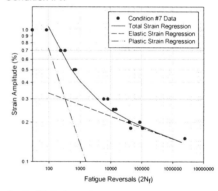

Figure 6: Strain-life fatigue data and predictions for High-Hardness, Thick Section, Condition #8.

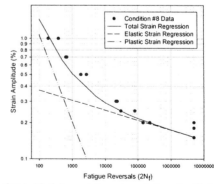

Figure 7: Strain-life fatigue data and predictions for High-Hardness, Condition #8.

discussions each significant monotonic and dynamic property is evaluated and correlated with hardness.

The hardness was directly proportional to the amount of pearlite in the microstructure. As shown in Figure 1, hardness increased linearly with increasing pearlite content. Linear regression of the nodule count and percent nodularity with respect to hardness showed no significant correlation, see Figures 2 and 3. Therefore, correlations of hardness with other mechanical properties are independent of graphite structure.

MECHANICAL PROPERTIES

All of the monotonic mechanical properties data and the incremental step testing data are given in Table 2. The strain-life fatigue constants for each condition are shown in Table 3. Linear regression constants and predicted values of many characteristic properties at 186 HBS and 270 HBS, based upon the data presented in Table 2, are tabulated in Table 4. The corresponding linear

Table 2: Monotonic Tensile and Cyclic Property Results.

Condition (Rank Based On Hardness)	Symbol	Units	1	2	3	4	5	6	7	8
Brinell Hardness		HBS 3000	186	189	205	228	236	244	250	270
Tensile Properties										
Ultimate Tensile Strength (Engineering)	S_u	MPa	604	612	631	725	759	754	775	863
0.2% Offset Yield Strength (Engineering)	S_{ys}	MPa	356	368	389	439	419	447	437	474
Percent Elongation	%El	%	11.9	13.7	9.7	10.4	8.1	7.7	4.4	6.3
Percent Reduction Area	%RA	%	11.2	12.1	8.9	8.2	7.7	6.8	3.9	5.7
Modulus of Elasticity	E	GPa	177	170	168	168	169	165	174	176
Monotonic Strength Coefficient	K	MPa	910	887	924	1100	1300	1250	1590	1760
Monotonic Strain Hardening Exponent	N		0.17	0.17	0.16	0.18	0.21	0.20	0.25	0.25
Incremental Step Test (IST) Results										
0.2% Offset Yield Strength (Engineering-Tension)	S_{ys}'	MPa	427	434	447	486	470	505	488	500
0.2% Offset Yield Strength (Engineering-Compression)	S_{ys}'	MPa	428	444	449	488	462	510	487	505
Cyclic Strength Coefficient (Tension)	K'	MPa	793	754	816	922	1020	986	1120	1230
Cyclic Strength Coefficient (Compression)	K'	MPa	1140	1140	1230	1450	1510	1610	1640	1820
Cyclic Strain Hardening Exponent (Tension)	n'		0.10	0.09	0.10	0.10	0.12	0.11	0.13	0.15
Cyclic Strain Hardening Exponent (Compression)	n'		0.16	0.15	0.16	0.18	0.19	0.19	0.20	0.21
Testing Properties After Incremental Step Testing										
Ultimate Tensile Strength	S_u''	MPa	592	591	634	690	a	788	705	823
0.2% Offset Yield Strength (Engineering)	S_{ys}''	MPa	425	433	449	490	a	510	490	503
Percent Elongation	%El	%	9.3	11.7	8.0	5.5	a	6.9	2.5	4.1
Percent Reduction Area	%RA	%	7.7	10.9	7.5	5.8	a	6.3	2.4	4.0
Monotonic Strain Hardening Exponent	n''		0.13	0.11	0.14	0.16	a	0.19	0.21	0.24
Monotonic Strength Coefficient	K''	MPa	862	804	938	1140	a	1400	1480	1770
Modulus of Elasticity	E''	GPa	160	155	158	158	a	160	160	162

a. samples fractured during incremental step testing.

Table 3: Strain-Life Fatigue Test Data Results

Condition	Symbol	Units	#2	#4	#7	#8	Combined
Brinell Hardness		HBS 3000	189	228	250	270	221
Fatigue Strength Coefficient	σ'_f	MPa	723	895	983	1030	971
Fatigue Strength Exponent	b		-0.062	-0.074	-0.087	-0.083	-0.084
Fatigue Ductility Coefficient	ε'_f		0.506	0.494	0.573	0.813	0.599
Fatigue Ductility Exponent	c		-0.683	-0.686	-0.728	-0.722	-0.707
Modulus of Elasticity	E	GPa	177	168	174	170	170

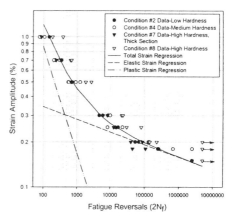

Figure 8: Strain-life fatigue data for all four conditions with predictions for the combined data set.

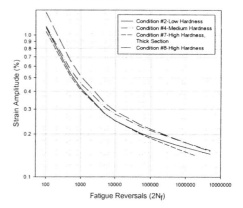

Figure 9: Predicted total strain-life curves for each individual condition.

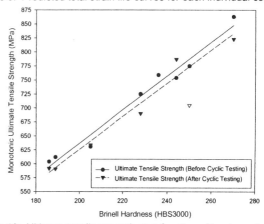

Figure 10: Ultimate tensile strength as a function of hardness before and after cyclic tests.

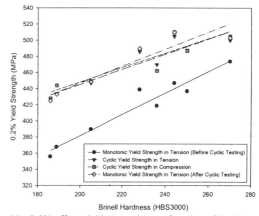

Figure 11: 0.2% offset yield strength as a function of hardness before and after cyclic testing.

regression lines are superimposed on all the figures. The coefficients of determination (r^2) varied from 0 to 1, indicating increasing correlation from none to perfect correlation between the particular property and hardness. Note the strain-life constants and the plot intercepts are based on reversals-to-failure ($2N_f$).

The strain-life (reversals) data are plotted in Figures 4 through 7 for material conditions #2, 4, 7, and 8, respectively. Each plot also shows the linear logarithmic regression lines predicted for the elastic and plastic strain amplitude components, calculated from the strain-life data, as well the logarithmic total curve obtained by adding these two components.

Figure 8 shows that when all the raw data for the four conditions are plotted simultaneously, the data scatter was minimal (approximately ½ a logarithmic decade), and no clear distinction in fatigue life data was obtained as a function of hardness. A few data points revealed the expected trend of high hardness exhibiting lower and higher lives at higher and lower applied strains, respectively.

Figure 9 shows a summary plot of all the total strain-life predictions. No clear-cut trend was revealed, but there was some slight separation in the predicted fatigue life for the high hardness materials as compared to that of the low and medium hardness materials. The high hardness conditions #7 and 8 exhibited higher lives in the high cycle (low strain) regime, but only the thin section condition #8 showed higher life in the low cycle (high strain) regime. Predicted strain values at various lives for the low hardness, medium hardness, high hardness/thick cross-section, and high hardness samples (conditions #2, 4, 7, and 8, respectively) are summarized in Table 5.

CORRELATION OF MECHANICAL PROPERTIES WITH HARDNESS

A correlation of ultimate tensile strength with Brinell hardness is shown in Figure 10. The monotonic ultimate tensile strength increased with hardness, and showed a very slight reduction in strength between the monotonic

101

Table 4: Linear Regression Constants and Predicted Values as a Function of Brinell Hardness

Property	Symbol	Units	Intercept at Ordinate	Slope	Coefficient of Determination, r^2	Predicted Value at 186 HBS	Predicted Value at 270 HBS
Monotonic Ultimate Tensile Strength (Before Cyclic Testing)	S_u	Mpa	34.7	0.44	0.98	595	848
Monotonic Ultimate Tensile Strength (After Cyclic Testing)	S_u''	MPa	32.1	0.43	0.97	584	834
Monotonic 0.2% Yield Strength in Tension (Before Cyclic Testing)	S_{ys}	MPa	115	0.19	0.94	363	475
Monotonic 0.2% Yield Strength in Tension (After Cyclic Testing)	S_{ys}''	MPa	258	0.14	0.87	432	511
Cyclic 0.2% Yield Strength in Tension	S_{ys-t}'	MPa	269	0.13	0.81	436	511
Cyclic 0.2% Yield Strength in Compression	S_{ys-c}'	MPa	244	0.15	0.87	432	517
Monotonic Percent Elongation (Before Cyclic Testing)	%El	%	29.0	-0.09	0.78	12.6	5.1
Monotonic Percent Elongation (After Cyclic Testing)	%El'	%	26.0	-0.08	0.76	10.1	3.0
Monotonic Modulus of Elasticity in Tension (Before Cyclic Testing)	E	GPa	169	0.00	0.00	171	171
Monotonic Modulus of Elasticity in Tension (After Cyclic Testing)	E''	GPa	148	0.01	0.49	157	161
Monotonic Strength Coefficient in Tension (Before Cyclic Testing)	K	MPa	-1075	1.47	0.89	810	1660
Monotonic Strength Coefficient in Tension (After Cyclic Testing)	K''	MPa	-1280	1.60	0.97	775	1700
Cyclic Strength Coefficient in Tension	K_t'	MPa	-268	0.79	0.93	740	1190
Cyclic Strength Coefficient in Compression	K_c'	MPa	-433	1.20	0.99	1110	1810
Monotonic Strain Hardening Exponent in Tension (Before Cyclic Testing)	n		-0.04	0.001	0.77	0.16	0.24
Monotonic Strain Hardening Exponent in Tension (After Cyclic Testing)	n'		-0.15	0.001	0.95	0.11	0.23
Cyclic Strain Hardening Exponent in Tension	n_t'		-0.02	0.001	0.77	0.09	0.14
Cyclic Strain Hardening Exponent in Compression	n_c'		0.02	0.001	0.96	0.15	0.21
Pearlite Content	%P	%	-51	0.57	0.90	55	103
Ferrite Content	%F	%	151	-0.57	0.90	45.1	-2.6
Nodule Count	Nod Ct.	per mm²	283	-0.35	0.01	219	190
Nodularity	Nod	%	92	0.000	0.00	92	92

Table 5: Predicted Cyclic Strain at Selected Fatigue Lives.

Reversal	Low Hardness (Condition #2), Δε/2 (%)	Medium Hardness (Condition # 4), Δε/2 (%)	High Hardness-Thick Cross-Section (Condition #7), Δε/2 (%)	High Hardness (Condition #8), Δε/2 (%)
	186 HB	228 HB	250 HB	270 HB
500	0.72	0.75	0.68	0.90
1,000	0.54	0.57	0.51	0.66
5,000	0.33	0.36	0.32	0.39
10,000	0.28	0.31	0.28	0.33
50,000	0.22	0.25	0.22	0.25
100,000	0.20	0.23	0.20	0.23
500,000	0.18	0.20	0.17	0.20
1,000,000	0.17	0.18	0.16	0.19
5,000,000	0.15	0.16	0.14	0.16

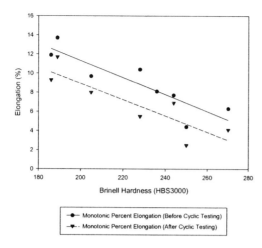

Figure 12: Percent elongation as a function of hardness before and after cyclic testing.

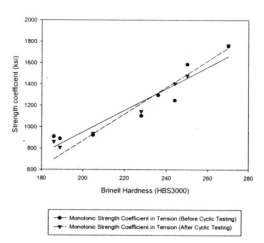

Figure 14: Strength coefficient as a function of hardness before and after cyclic testing.

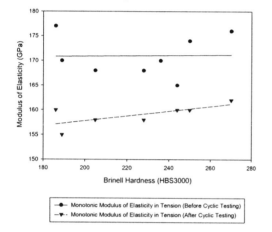

Figure 13: Modulus of elasticity as a function of hardness before and after cyclic testing.

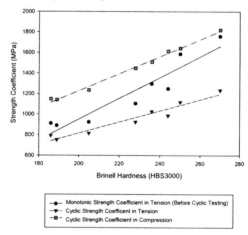

Figure 15: Monotonic and cyclic strength coefficients as a function of hardness.

tensile test results before and after cyclic testing. Note that one outlying point (condition #7 with high hardness/thick cross section, represented by an open symbol) was not used in the regression.

A correlation of 0.2% offset yield strength with hardness is shown in Figure 11. The monotonic yield strength prior to cyclic testing displayed more dependence on hardness than after cyclic testing. There was very little difference between the cyclic yield strength in tension, in compression, and the yield strength after cyclic testing.

Tensile elongation was strongly affected by hardness, see Figure 12. The elongation dropped uniformly after cyclic testing. This indicates that the materials harden with cyclic testing but the rate of change in elongation as a function of hardness remained the same.

The monotonic modulus of elasticity (Young's modulus) was nearly independent of hardness with wide-spread scatter in the data, see Figure 13. After cyclic testing there was an overall decrease in the modulus values, as is consistent with the observed behavior historically. There was a significant reduction of scatter in the data,

and the development of a slight modulus dependence upon hardness as well. At 186 HBS, the elastic modulus after cyclic testing decreased by approximately 13.8 GPa. At 270 HBS, the elastic modulus decreased by only 10.3 GPa after cyclic testing.

The strength coefficient in monotonic tension is correlated with hardness in Figure 14. The strength coefficient was a strong function of hardness. As observed with the ultimate tensile strength, there were no significant changes in the strength coefficients before and after cyclic testing.

Figure 15 shows the strength coefficient in cyclic testing as a function of hardness. The strength coefficients in cyclic tension and cyclic compression were less dependent on hardness than the monotonic values, and the cyclic tension values changed less with increasing hardness than the cyclic compression values. The cyclic tension strength coefficient was similar in value to the monotonic coefficient at low hardness values, but the cyclic value diverged rapidly with increasing hardness. Since monotonic compression tests were not performed and a tension cycle preceded the first compression cycle

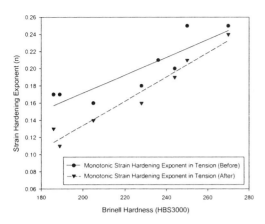

Figure 16: Monotonic strain hardening exponent as a function of hardness before and after cyclic testing.

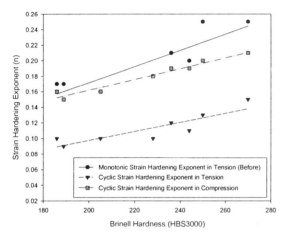

Figure 17: Monotonic strain hardening exponent before cyclic testing and cyclic strain hardening exponents as a function of hardness.

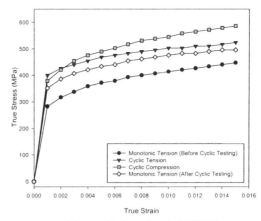

a) Lowest Hardness Sample (186 HBS)

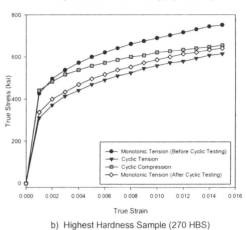

b) Highest Hardness Sample (270 HBS)

Figure 18: Predicted stress-strain curves for a) low hardness (Condition #2), and b) high hardness materials (Condition #8).

in the cyclic tests, monotonic values were unavailable for comparison to the cyclic compression strength coefficients.

A correlation of the monotonic tension strain hardening exponent obtained in monotonic tension testing with hardness is shown in Figure 16. The strain hardening exponent increased with increasing hardness. It was lower for all hardness values after cyclic testing, but the strain hardening exponent after cyclic testing exhibited a stronger correlation with hardness. At low hardness values the monotonic and cyclic values were different, but at high hardness the regression lines converged.

In Figure 17, the cyclic strain hardening exponents in tension and compression are shown to be slightly less a function of hardness when compared to the monotonic tension strain hardening exponents. The cyclic tension exponents were similar in value to the monotonic tension exponents at low hardness, but the monotonic and cyclic values diverged as hardness increased. The rate of change as a function of hardness was equal in both cyclic tension and cyclic compression. Note that the monotonic strain hardening exponent was not included because it is equal to the cyclic strain hardening

exponent in tension once the cyclic test specimen has reached strain saturation. The act of conducting a tensile test on the cyclically tested sample is essentially the same as continuing the cyclic test an additional quarter cycle.

Stress-strain curves were predicted for the lowest and highest hardness samples using the equation:

$$\sigma = K\varepsilon^n,$$

using the strength coefficients (K) and strain hardening exponent (n) values calculated from the incremental step test results and the monotonic tensile results before and after cyclic testing. The predicted curves are shown in Figure 18. The low and high hardness materials cyclically strain-hardened in tension within the strain range used while conducting these tests. (A comparison can not be made between cyclic and monotonic compression because the monotonic compression data are unavailable.)

At very low cyclic strains, a greater level of cyclic strain hardening occurred in tension than in compression (as shown by the higher stress values obtained at, for

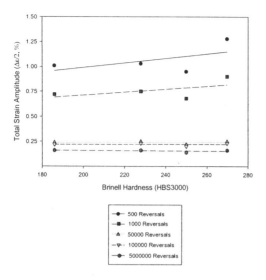

Figure 19: Predicted cyclic strain at selected fatigue lives as a function of hardness.

example, 0.001 strain). The trend quickly reversed itself with increasing strain values, and the strain value for this trend reversal decreased with increasing hardness. The cyclic compression curves behaved similarly to the monotonic tension curve before cyclic testing in that each curve predicted the same proportional increase in true stress at a given true strain. However, the cyclic tension curve is neither parallel to the monotonic tension curve nor the cyclic compression curve; the predicted curves indicate that the materials would transform from cyclic strain hardening to strain softening at levels of strain higher than what was used in testing (That is, materials strained in excess of 1.5% would conceivably strain soften as indicated by the cyclic tension curve intersecting with, and falling below the monotonic curve.)

The predicted cyclic strains at selected fatigue lives are presented in Figure 19 and Table 5. The calculated constants from the fatigue life tests were used to predict the cyclic strains at various fatigue life expectancies. The strain limits for high cycle life predictions were independent of hardness. Conversely, the strain limits for low cycle life expectancies increased with increasing hardness. (Only the predicted cyclic strains at 500 and 1000 cycles showed a modest increase with hardness.) As a result, Figure 8 and the last column of Table 3 can be treated as a valid combined data set to describe the general cyclic behavior of Grade D5506 ductile iron over its full hardness range.

CONCLUSIONS

1. This study compared the chemistries, microstructures, tensile properties, and fatigue properties of several ductile iron materials covering the entire range in hardness (187-255 HBS3000) for SAE grade D5506.

2. All the constants contained in SAE standard J1099, June 1998, were determined for four materials. The tensile properties and monotonic and cyclic strain hardening coefficients and exponents were determined for all eight materials. The cyclic strain-life coefficients and exponents were determined for four of the materials, covering the full range of hardness.

3. Although the monotonic properties varied with hardness before and after fatigue testing, cyclic stress-strain properties and fatigue lives remained primarily independent of hardness. One set of constants may be used to describe the general cyclic properties of the Grade D5506, regardless of the differing hardness, microstructure, and tensile properties.

ACKNOWLEDGMENTS

The authors gratefully acknowledge the help of Mr. Richard V. Wagner for the extensive mechanical testing performed, and the financial support of this work by the Ductile Iron Society (DIS), North Olmsted, OH.

CONTACT

John M. Tartaglia, Ph. D.
Climax Research Services
51229 Century Court
Wixom, MI 48393
Tel: (248) 489-0720
Fax: (248) 489-8997
E-mail: tartagliaj@climaxresearch.com

REFERENCES

1. Rice, Richard C., editor, "SAE Fatigue Design Handbook", 3rd edition; Society of Automotive Engineers, Inc., Warrendale, PA; pgs. 22-25

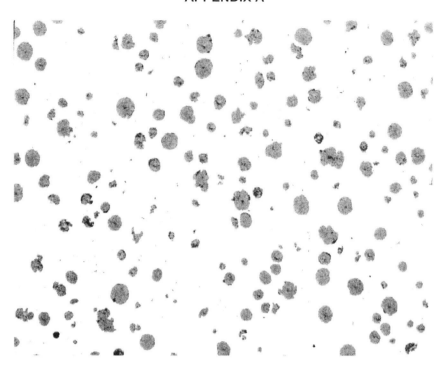

As-Polished, 100x

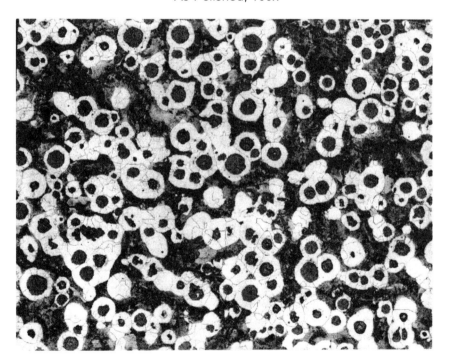

2% Nital, 100x

Condition	Hardness (HBS3000)	Material Type	Yield Strength (MPa)	% Nodularity	% Ferrite
1	186	1" round	356	94	37

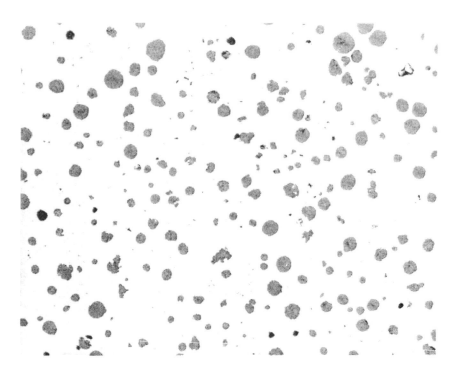

As-Polished, 100x

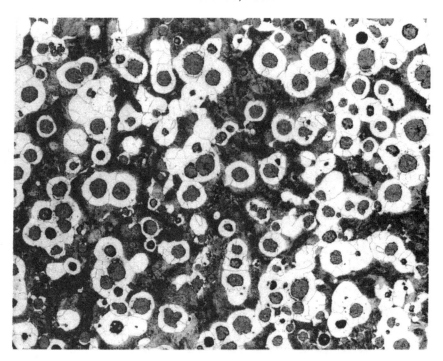

2% Nital, 100x

Condition	Hardness (HBS3000)	Material Type	Yield Strength (MPa)	% Nodularity	% Ferrite
2	189	1" Y-block	368	95	51

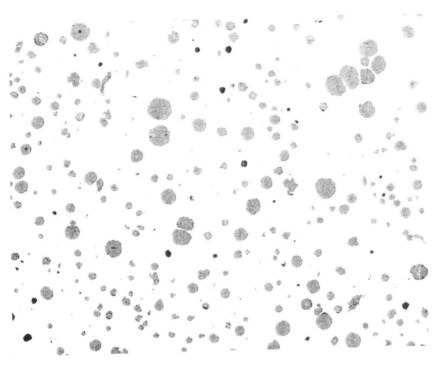

As-Polished, 100x

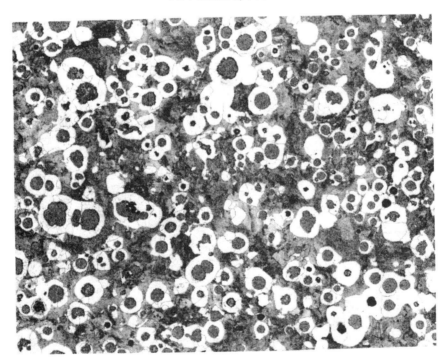

2% Nital, 100x

Condition	Hardness (HBS3000)	Material Type	Yield Strength (MPa)	% Nodularity	% Ferrite
3	205	2" Y-block	389	85	35

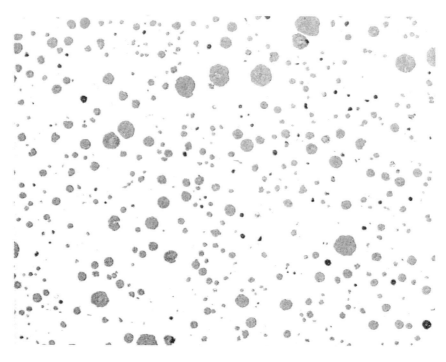

As-Polished, 100x

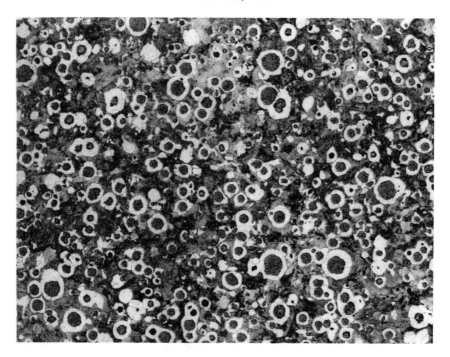

2% Nital, 100x

Condition	Hardness (HBS3000)	Material Type	Yield Strength (MPa)	% Nodularity	% Ferrite
4	228	2" Y-Block	439	91	25

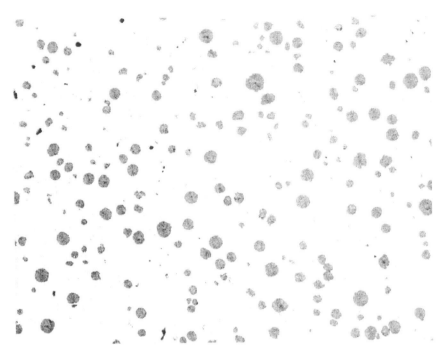

As-Polished, 100x

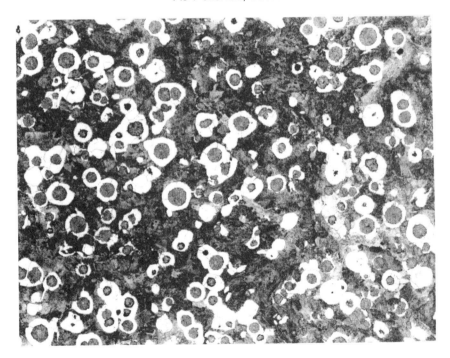

2% Nital, 100x

Condition	Hardness (HBS3000)	Material Type	Yield Strength (MPa)	% Nodularity	% Ferrite
5	236	7/8" Keel bars	519	96	16

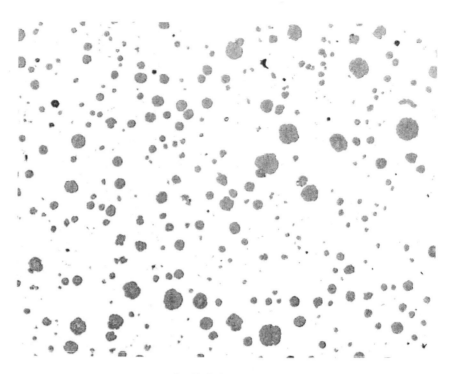

As-Polished, 100x

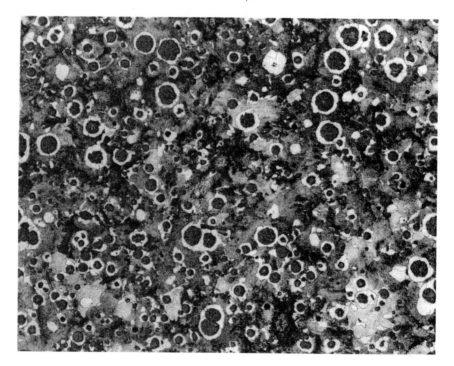

2% Nital, 100x

Condition	Hardness (HBS3000)	Material Type	Yield Strength (MPa)	% Nodularity	% Ferrite
6	244	2" Y-block	447	94	14

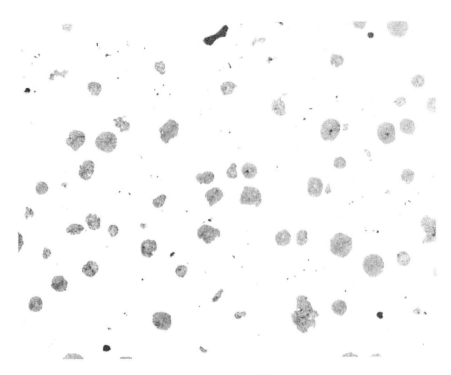

As-Polished, 100x

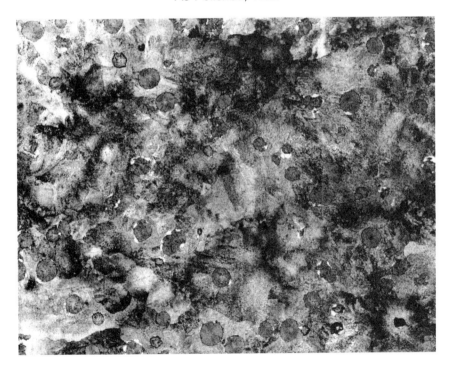

2% Nital, 100x

Condition	Hardness (HBS3000)	Material Type	Yield Strength (MPa)	% Nodularity	% Ferrite
7	250	3" Y-Block	437	89	<1%

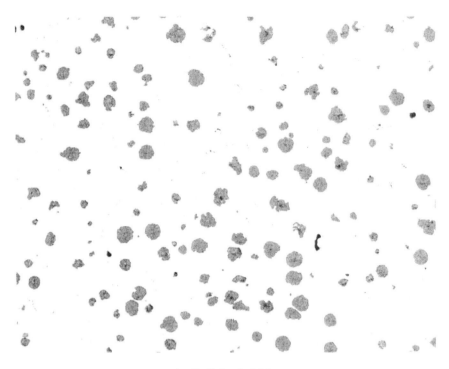

As-Polished, 100x

2% Nital, 100x

Condition	Hardness (HBS3000)	Material Type	Yield Strength (MPa)	% Nodularity	% Ferrite
8	270	1" round	474	93	<1%

2000-01-0759

The Effect of Copper Level and Solidification Rate on the Aging Behavior of a 319-Type Cast Aluminum Alloy

Carla A. Cloutier and J. Wayne Jones
University of Michigan, Department of Materials Science & Engineering

John E. Allison
Ford Motor Company, Ford Research Laboratories

Copyright © 2000 Society of Automotive Engineers, Inc.

ABSTRACT

Compositional and microstructural variations in a casting can often result in rather significant variations in the response to a given aging treatment, leading to location dependent mechanical properties. The objective of this study is to determine the effect of copper content and solidification rate on the aging behavior of a type 319 cast aluminum alloy. The nominal composition of the alloy is Al-7% Si-3.5% Cu-0.25% Mg, however, typical secondary 319 aluminum specifications allow copper levels to vary from 3-4%. Solidification rates throughout a casting can vary greatly due to, among other factors, differences in section size. To determine the effect of copper level and solidification rate on the aging response, aging curves were experimentally developed for this alloy. Three different copper levels (3, 3.5, 4%) and two solidification rates were used for this study. Aging temperatures ranged from 150-290°C with nine aging times at each temperature. The results show that both copper level and solidification rate have an effect on the aging response at certain aging temperatures

INTRODUCTION

The purpose of age hardening is to produce a uniform dispersion of hard precipitates in a softer and more ductile matrix. The presence of the precipitates creates local barriers to dislocation movement in the matrix and consequently increases strength and hardness. There are three steps in the age hardening heat treatment: solution treatment, quench, and age.

The main objective of the *solution treatment* is to place into solid solution the maximum practical amount of soluble hardening elements. The process consists of heating the alloy at a temperature sufficiently high, but below the liquidus temperature, for a time long enough to achieve a nearly homogeneous solid solution [1]. The coarser microstructures associated with slower solidification rates require a longer solution heat treatment [2, 3]. The *quench* immediately follows solution treatment and consists of cooling rapidly from the solution temperature in order to obtain a supersaturated solid solution. *Aging* is accomplished by holding the supersaturated solid solution at temperatures below the solvus temperature to allow nucleation and growth of strengthening precipitates.

Jahn, et al, [4] have extensively studied precipitation hardening in cast 319 aluminum. They found that age hardening in 319 is primarily due to the precipitation of plate-shaped θ' (Al_2Cu). This is consistent with the high copper content of this alloy. Magnesium containing precipitates are also observed in samples aged from 150-305°C. At peak aged conditions in an alloy with a fast solidification rate, the microstructure contains binary θ'-Al_2Cu platelets and needles which are either ternary S'-Al_4CuMg or Q-$Al_4Cu_2Mg_8Si_7$. In this complex alloy, small variations in the chemical composition can affect the amount and type of precipitate present. Differences in the volume fraction of precipitate can have significant effects on the mechanical properties. According to Silcock [6] and Hardy [7] who studied binary Al-Cu alloys, the time to peak hardness at low aging temperatures was essentially independent of copper concentration. However, there was a strong influence of copper content on hardness levels. Higher aging temperatures and higher copper contents led to higher hardness and the shorter the time to peak hardness [6].

The microstructure of a cast component is strongly influenced by the rate of solidification. The secondary dendrite arm spacing (SDAS) is governed by the solidification rate and thus provides a direct measurement of the solidification rate in a local area of a casting. Faster solidification rates result in lower SDAS and general improvements in strength [8-11]. Ultimate tensile strength, fracture strength, and ductility decrease with decreasing solidification rate. The effect of solidification rate on yield strength is not as straightforward. Kattamis [9] claims that yield strength increases with solidification rate in an Al-7% Cu alloy. He found that the increased solidification rate results in a finer SDAS, which also corresponds to finer intermetallics, lower porosity levels, and higher copper concentration in the matrix due to an decrease in interdendritic phases. On the other hand, Frederick [10], in 356, and Samuel [12], in a 319-type alloy, report that yield strength remains essentially constant, meaning that variation in the solidification rate does not effect the stress required to initiate plastic flow. Boileau, et al [13] have reported that solidification rate has no effect on the yield strength for 356 but a strong effect on yield strength in a 319-type alloy.

The purpose of this study was to characterize the effect of copper content and solidification time on the aging response of a specific 319-type aluminum alloy, W319, to allow optimization of the heat treatment of this alloy.

EXPERIMENTAL PROCEDURE

The alloy used for this study is a variant of the Aluminum Association 319 alloy and is referred to as W319 in this paper. To study the effect of copper level on the aging response of W319, the copper level was varied while the rest of the alloying elements remained constant. The three different copper levels examined are designated as W319L, W319M, and W319H. The compositions of the three W319 variants and the composition for AA319 are listed in Table I. Chemical compositions were determined by optical emission spectrometry. W319 has higher silicon and magnesium levels but lower iron compared to the standard Aluminum Association 319 alloy. Strontium is added to modify the morphology of the silicon phase.

For the present study, a wedge was cast which produces a variety of solidification rates. To determine the effect of solidification rate on the aging response of W319, samples with two different solidification rates were examined. The majority of the investigation focused on samples with a fast solidification time (approximately 17 seconds), which corresponds to a dendrite arm spacing of about 20 μm (+/- 4 μm). This data is compared with work done by Reeber, et. al., [14] on W319 with a longer solidification time (320 seconds) and corresponding dendrite arm spacing of about 40 μm (+/- 8 μm). Dendrite arm spacing was determined using a Kontron IBAS Image Analysis System. Figures 1a and 1b are representative micrographs of the alloy examined in this study. Important features include the aluminum dendrites, the Al-Si eutectic, and intermetallics such as $Al_{15}(Mn, Fe)_3Si_2$ and Al_2Cu.

Table I: Compositions of W319 Alloys in Weight Percent

	W319-L	W319-M	W319-H	AA319
Cu	2.92	3.46	4.02	3.0-4.0
Si	7.58	7.48	7.38	5.5-6.5
Fe	0.42	0.32	0.32	1.0 max
Mn	0.24	0.25	0.25	0.5 max
Mg	0.24	0.26	0.24	0.10
Sr	0.010	0.010	0.010	-

Rough-cut bars were removed from their respective areas of the wedge and were given a simulated thermal sand removal (TSR) treatment that consists of 1h at 495°C followed by an air cool. The samples were then solution heat treated for 8h at 495°C and quenched in boiling water. Between solution treatment and artificial aging, the samples were held at 0°C to prevent natural aging. The samples with the faster solidification rate were artificially aged for 9 different times at 5 temperatures (150, 190, 230, 260, 290°C). These were compared with samples at a slower solidification rate [14] that were aged for 10 different times at 190, 230, 260°C. Three samples were heat treated at each time-temperature combination. The samples aged at 150°C were aged in air in a tube furnace while all other samples were aged in a Partherm 190™ molten salt bath. All samples were quenched in ice water after aging.

Following aging, the rough-cut bars were machined into cylindrical tensile specimens with a gauge length of 31.75mm and diameter of 6.4mm. Six samples at each copper level were also tested in the "as-solution treated" condition. These samples were machined prior to solution treatment. Between solution treatment and testing, these samples were stored at 0°C. They were equilibrated at room temperature for 7 minutes and then tested. All tensile specimens were tested using a hydraulic MTS 810 load frame in stroke control. The stress-strain data was acquired digitally and 0.2% offset yield strength and ultimate tensile strength were calculated in accordance with ASTM E8. All tests were performed at room temperature in laboratory air and the initial strain rate was 8×10^{-4}/sec. An axial extensometer with a 12.7 mm (0.5 inch) gauge length was used to measure elongation. All reported values for elongation are plastic elongation at fracture.

RESULTS

Figure 2 is a plot of the yield strength versus aging time for W319-M. The peak yield strength ranges from 415 MPa (100 hours at 150°C) to 265 MPa (1 minute at 290°C). At all copper levels, these alloys exhibit conventional precipitation hardening behavior. The time required to reach peak strength decreases with increasing aging temperature and the peak strength also decreases with increasing aging temperature. In the 3.0% Cu alloy, the peak strength ranges from 395 MPa (100 hours at 150°C) to 235 MPa (1 minute at 290°C). In the 4.0% Cu alloy, the range is from 417 MPa (100 hours at 150°C) to 265 MPa (1 minute at 290°C).

For over 90 percent of the samples tested the ultimate tensile strength was equivalent to the fracture strength, that is, the maximum strength exhibited was that at which the sample fractured. Ultimate tensile strength, as shown in Figure 3, follows the same general trends as yield strength: peak ultimate tensile strength decreases with increasing aging temperature and the time to peak ultimate tensile strength also decreases with increasing aging time. The peak ultimate tensile strength for the 3.5% Cu alloy ranges from 445 MPa (100 hours at 150°C) to 355 MPa (1 minute at 290°C). This is a much smaller range in strength compared to the range in yield strength (90 MPa vs. 150 MPa). Thus, the effect of aging time and temperature is not as significant on ultimate tensile strength as it is on yield strength. There is significantly more scatter in the ultimate tensile strength data than in the yield strength data. The range in ultimate tensile strength of the as-solution treated samples is approximately 90 MPa while the range in yield strength of the as-solution treated sample is approximately 30 MPa.

Figure 4 is a plot of plastic elongation to fracture versus aging time for W319-M for three aging temperatures. There is a substantial amount of variability in this data, especially at the shorter aging times. Even in the as-solution treated condition the scatter is large, with values ranging from 1 to 7 percent elongation. The effect of age hardening on elongation is better seen in Figure 5, which is a plot of plastic elongation to fracture versus yield strength. As yield strength increases to approximately 325 MPa, the ductility decreases. At yield strengths above 325 MPa, the percent elongation plateaus between 1-3%. In general, ductility levels below one percent are only observed at strengths greater than 350 MPa. Elastic modulus is not affected by aging conditions, composition, or solidification rate. The modulus is 74 +/- 2 GPa, regardless of composition or solidification rate.

EFFECT OF COPPER LEVEL

Copper content has a substantial effect on the peak yield strength, as shown in Figure 6. With increasing copper, the peak yield strength for a given aging temperature increases; however, this effect is non-linear and tends toward an asymptotic value at higher copper levels. For instance, the average peak yield strength for the alloy containing only 3.0% Cu subjected to an aging temperature of 230°C is 330 MPa. While the 4.0% Cu alloy subjected to the same aging temperature has an average peak yield strength of 370 MPa. Additionally, with increasing aging temperature the scatter in the peak yield strength increases. As shown in Figure 6, the relationship between copper content and the peak yield strength is similar at all aging temperatures, that is, the curves are parallel.

The copper level of the alloy also influences the time to peak yield strength. Figure 7 shows the time to peak yield strength versus copper content. At temperatures higher than 150°C, the time to peak yield strength decreases with increasing copper content. Furthermore, with increasing aging temperature, the decrease in time to peak yield strength with increasing copper content becomes more substantial. For instance, at 190°C, increasing the copper level of the alloy from 3% to 4% reduces the time to peak yield strength from 5 hours to 3 hours. This is a 40% reduction in aging time. However, at 260°C, increasing the copper level from 3.0% to 4.0% reduces the time to peak yield strength from 25 minutes to 5 minutes, which translates to an 80% reduction in aging time.

Figure 8 describes the effect of copper content on the yield strength of W319 at 230°C. The increase in yield strength with increasing copper content and the decrease in time to peak yield strength with increasing copper content can be seen clearly in this figure.

The effect of copper content on the ductility of W319 (Figure 9) is not as straightforward due to the variability in the elongation data. However, with increasing copper content, the likelihood that the ductility is at or below the one percent level increases.

EFFECT OF SOLIDIFICATION RATE

Figure 10 shows the variation of yield strength with aging time at 230°C for two different solidification rates. It is clear from the plot that the material with the faster solidification rate has higher yield strengths (365 MPa vs. 320 MPa) and a shorter time to peak yield strength (approximately 45 minutes vs. 90 minutes) than the material with the slower solidification rate. It is especially interesting to note that in the as-solution treated condition all yield strengths fall into the range of 210-250 MPa, regardless of solidification rate. Thus, in the as-solution treated condition, solidification rate has no noticeable effect on the yield strength of the alloy. However, with as little as 5 minutes of aging at 230°C, there is a significant difference (approximately 60 MPa) in yield strength between the two solidification rates.

For the three aging temperatures considered, peak yield strength decreases with decreasing solidification rate (Figure 11) and the time to peak strength increases with decreasing solidification rate (Figure 12). The slopes of the lines in both Figure 11 and in Figure 12 are essentially parallel, indicating that the differences in peak yield strength and time to peak yield strength due to different aging temperatures is the same regardless of solidification rate. Therefore, both the decrease in peak yield strength and the increase in time to peak yield strength with decreasing solidification rate appear to be temperature independent.

The effect of solidification rate on the ultimate tensile strength of W319-M, as shown in Figure 13, is very similar to that of the effect on the yield strength. The samples with the faster solidification rate have higher ultimate tensile strengths (407 MPa vs. 346 MPa) and reach peak strength at shorter times (approximately 0.5 h vs. 2 h) than those with a slower solidification rate. Unlike yield strength, the ultimate tensile strength of W319 aluminum in the as-solution treated condition depends on the solidification rate, i.e., decreasing in the coarser microstructure condition.

Solidification rate also has an effect on ductility. Though there is substantial scatter in the elongation data (Figure 14), the material with the faster solidification rate generally has higher ductility. The majority of the samples with the slower solidification rate have ductilities of less than one percent while very few of the faster solidification rate samples have less than one percent elongation.

DISCUSSION

The aging response of W319 is typical of conventional age hardening alloys. As the aging temperature is raised, diffusion of solute atoms through the matrix increases which results in an increased aging response. Faster aging rates are associated with lower peak hardness because larger and fewer precipitates quickly form at higher temperatures. In addition, as the aging temperature increases, the degree of solute supersaturation decreases, thus, lowering the driving force for precipitation. This results in a lower volume fraction of precipitates and lower strength levels. Thus for a given composition, as aging temperature is increased, the precipitates will be more widely spaced and, therefore, less effective in inhibiting slip [15].

EFFECT OF COPPER CONTENT

The increase in strength with increased copper was expected because strength should increase with increasing volume fraction of precipitates and the volume fraction of Al_2Cu precipitates is directly proportional to the copper level above the solubility limit. Yield strength is the sum of the contributions from the intrinsic strength of the matrix (σ_i), the strengthening due to solid solution ($\Delta\sigma_{ss}$), and the strengthening due to precipitates ($\Delta\sigma_{ppt}$):

$$\sigma_{net}(t) = \sigma_i + \Delta\sigma_{ss} + \Delta\sigma_{ppt} \qquad [1]$$

The precipitate strength can be described as a competition between precipitate shearing and precipitate bypassing, given the following relationships:

$$\Delta\sigma_{ppt} = \left[\left(\frac{1}{\Delta\sigma_{sh}}\right) + \left(\frac{1}{\Delta\sigma_{bp}}\right)\right]^{-1} \qquad [2]$$

Here σ_{sh} and σ_{bp} are the shearing and bypassing components of precipitation strengthening, which can be expressed in terms of volume fraction and precipitate size.

$$\Delta\sigma_{sh} = c_1 f^{1/2} r^{1/2} \qquad [2a]$$

$$\Delta\sigma_{bp} = \frac{c_2 Gb}{l} = \frac{c_3 f^{1/2}}{r} \qquad [2b]$$

f is the volume fraction of precipitate, r is the precipitate radius, b is the Burgers vector, G is the shear modulus, and l is the spacing between precipitates. c_1, c_2, and c_3 are constants. For both σ_{sh} and σ_{bp}, an increase in the volume fraction of precipitate leads to an increase in strength. The strength increases up to a point of saturation, which is consistent with both equations 2a and 2b in which the volume fraction of precipitate is a function of $f^{1/2}$.

The aging behavior is controlled by coarsening kinetics [7, 15-17]. This relationship is well established and can be written as the following:

$$r^3(t) - r_o^3 = \frac{c_4 t}{T} \exp\frac{-Q_A}{RT} \qquad [3]$$

Where r is the particle radius, c_4 is a kinetic factor which depends on the matrix composition, t is time, T is temperature, R is the universal gas constant, and Q_A is the activation energy for volume diffusion. An increase in solute concentration increases the coarsening kinetics and, therefore, reduces the time to peak strength for a given aging temperature, as shown in Figure 7. The density of precipitates present at a given aging time and temperature increases with increasing solute concentration, thus, the shorter the diffusion distance required for precipitate coarsening.

EFFECT OF SOLIDIFICATION RATE

At the three aging temperatures studied, the material with the faster solidification rate has higher yield and ultimate tensile strengths than the material with the slower solidification rate. The increased strength with faster solidification rates is in agreement with the literature. Coarser microstructures associated with slower solidification rates require a longer solution heat treatment for an equivalent amount of copper to be placed in solution compared to that required for a finer microstructure material [3]. Thus, for a given solution heat treatment time and temperature and given composition, more copper would be present in solution in the aluminum dendrites in a finer microstructure than in a coarser microstructure. Finer microstructures have a shorter diffusion path, thus for a given time more solute diffuses into the dendrites during the solution.

As with increased copper content, increasing solidification rates result in shorter times to peak strength. As previously discussed, precipitation kinetics is based, in part, on the coarsening rate which is a function of the matrix composition. As discussed above, the finer microstructure would thus result in shorter times to peak strength.

Elongation decreases with decreasing solidification rates. The decreasing solidification rates result in coarser microstructures. Larger pores and coarser intermetallics or brittle particles, which are often associated with coarser microstructures, thus have a detrimental effect on the ductility.

CONCLUSIONS

Both copper level and solidification rate have a significant effect on the aging response of W319 aluminum. Increasing the copper level increases the strength of the material and also decreases the time to reach the peak strength. Increasing the solidification rate has the same effect on the aging behavior. Samples with a faster solidification rate have higher strengths and shorter times to peak strength than do samples with a slower solidification rate but subjected to identical heat treatments. The effects of increased copper level and increased solidification rate are due to the same phenomenon: an increase in the volume fraction of Al_2Cu precipitates. There is a high degree of variability in the elongation data. Elongation decreases with increasing strength levels and with increasing copper levels and slower solidification rates. The influence of strength level on ductility is substantial while the influence of copper content and solidification time are less dramatic.

ACKNOWLEDGMENTS

The authors would like to thank P. M. Reeber-Schmanski for her work on the slower solidification rate material. They would also like to thank J. W. Zindel and L. A. Godlewski for providing the alloys used for this study. C. A. Cloutier and J. W. Jones acknowledge the financial support of Ford Motor Company.

REFERENCES

1. N. F. Budgen, The Heat-Treatment and Annealing of Aluminium and its Alloys. London: Chapman & Hall, 1932.
2. ASM. "Foundry Products." *Aluminum & Aluminum Alloys - ASM Specialty Handbook*, ASM International, Materials Park, OH, 1993.
3. Hangas, J., W. T. Donlon, J. E. Allison, unpublished results, 1999.
4. Jahn, R., W. T. Donlon, J. E. Allison, submitted to *Automotive Alloys III*, TMS conference proceedings, San Diego, 1999.
5. J. M. Silcock, T. J. Heal, and H. K. Hardy, "Structural Aging Characteristics of Binary Aluminum-Copper Alloys," *J. I. M*, vol. 82, pp. 239-248, 1953.
6. H. K. Hardy and T. J. Heal, "Report on Precipitation," in *Progress in Materials Science*, vol. 5, B. Chalmers and R. King, Eds. New York: Interscience Publishers, 1954, pp. 143-278.
7. Kashyap, K. T., Murali, S., Raman, K. S., and Murthy, K. S. S. "Casting and Heat Treatment Variables of Al-7Si-Mg Alloy." *Materials Science & Tech.*, 189-203, 1993.
8. T. Z. Kattamis, "Solidification Microstructure of Aluminium Alloys and its Effects on Mechanical and Corrosion Behaviors," *Aluminium*, pp. 225-229, 1982.
9. S. F. Frederick and W. A. Bailey, "The Relation of Ductility to Dendrite Cell Size in a Cast Al-Si-Mg-Alloy," *Trans. AIME*, vol. 242, pp. 2063-2067, 1968.
10. M. C. Flemings, S. Z. Uram, and H. D. Taylor, "Solidification of Aluminum Castings," *AFS Trans*, vol. 68, 1960.
11. A. M. Samuel and F. H. Samuel, "Effect of Melt Treatment, Solidification Conditions and Porosity Level on the Tensile Properties of 319.2 Endchill Aluminium Castings," *Journal of Materials Science*, vol. 30, pp. 4823-4833, 1995.
12. Reeber-Schmanski, P., Jones, J. W., Allison, J. E. Unpublished work, 1998.
13. J. M. Boileau, P. C. Collins, and J. E. Allison, "The Effect of Solidification Time and Heat Treatment on the Tensile and Fatigue Properties of a Cast 319 Aluminum Alloy," presented at The Fifth International Conference on Molten Metal Processing, Des Plaines, IL, 1998.
14. A. H. Geisler, "Chapter 15: Precipitation from Solid Solutions of Metals," in *Phase Transformations in Solids*, R. Smoluchowski, J. E. Mayer, and W. A. Weyl, Eds. New York: John Wiley & Sons, 1951, pp. 387-535.
15. H. R. Shercliff and M. F. Ashby, "A Process Model for Age Hardening of Aluminium Alloys - I. The Model," *Acta Metallurgica et Materiala*, vol. 38, pp. 1789-1802, 1990.
16. Martin, J. W., and Doherty, R. D. *Stability of Microstructure in Metallic Systems*, Cambridge University Press, London, 1996.

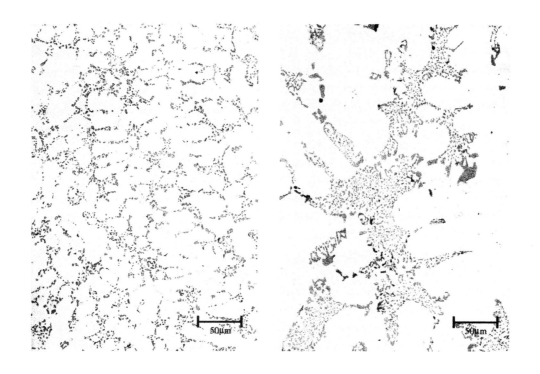

Figure 1: Micrographs of W319-M: (a) solidification time of 17 seconds, (b) solidification time of 320 seconds.

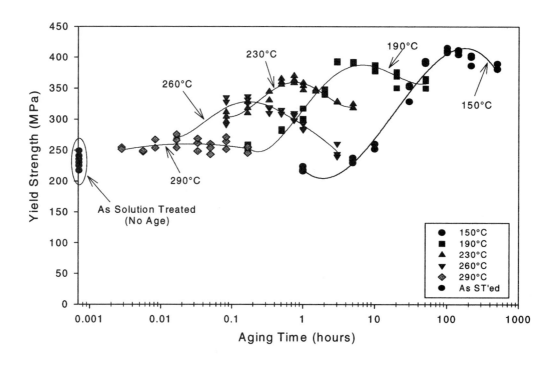

Figure 2: Yield Strength vs. Aging Time in 3.5% Cu Alloy

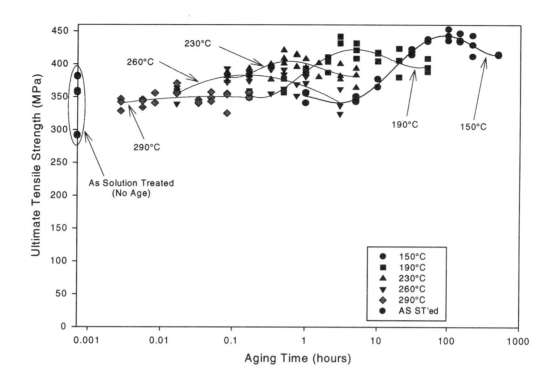

Figure 3: Ultimate Tensile Strength vs. Aging Time in 3.5%Cu Alloy

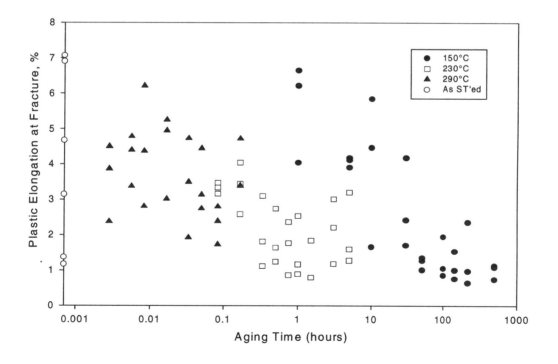

Figure 4: Elongation at Fracture vs. Aging Time in 3.5% Cu Alloy.

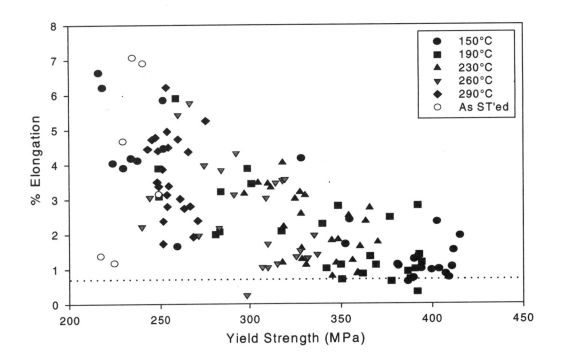

Figure 5: Elongation at Fracture vs. Yield Strength in 3.5% Cu Alloy

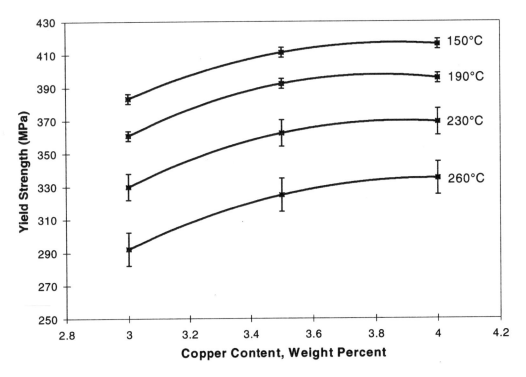

Figure 6: Peak Yield Strength vs. Copper Content

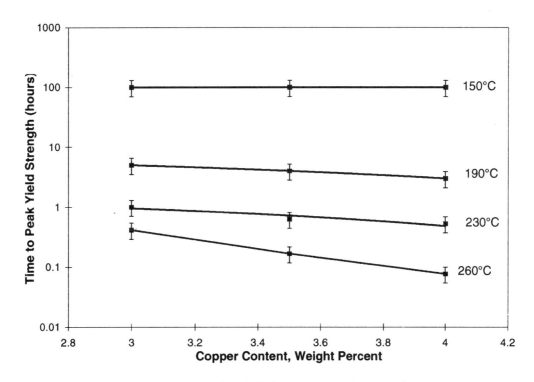

Figure 7: Time to Peak Yield Strength vs. Copper Content

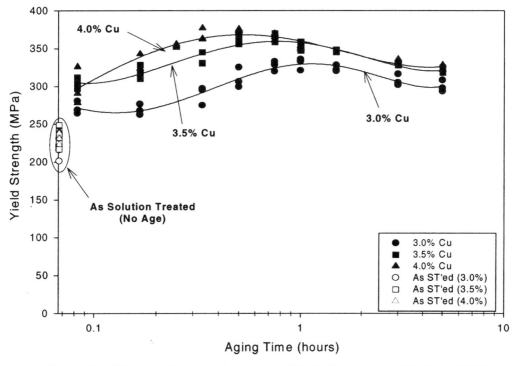

Figure 8: Effect of Copper Content on Yield Strength in W319 at 230°C

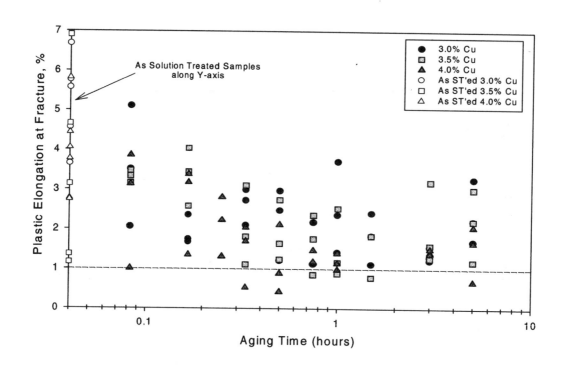

Figure 9: Effect of Copper Content on Ductility in W319 at 230°C

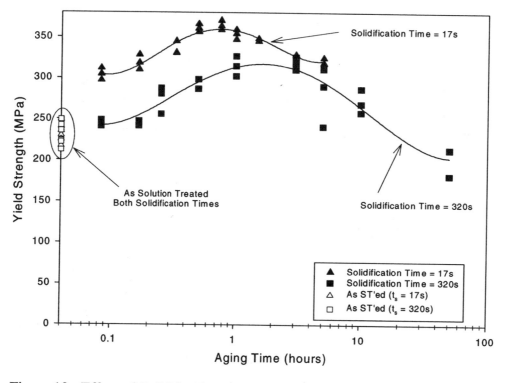

Figure 10: Effect of Solidification Time on the Yield Strength of W319 at 230°C

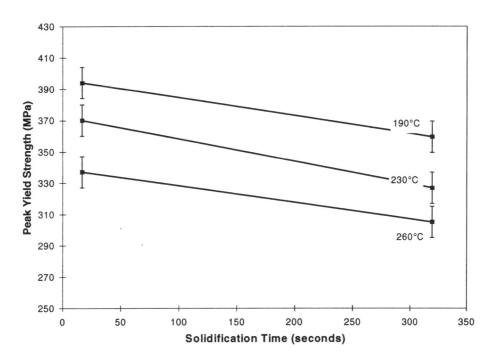

Figure 11: Peak Yield Strength vs. Solidification Time in W319

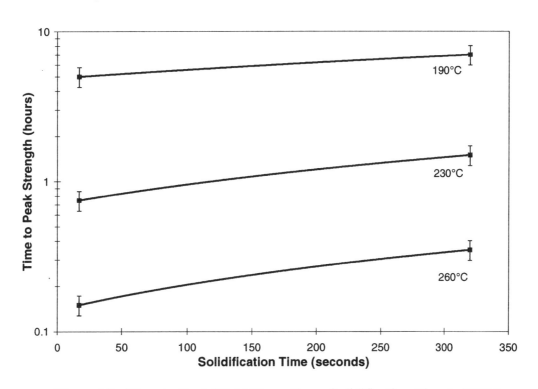

Figure 12: Time to Peak Yield Strength vs. Solidification Time in W319

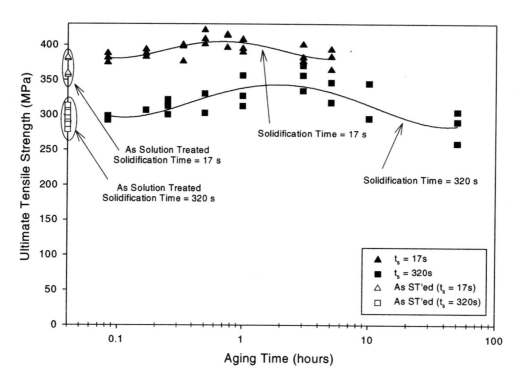

Figure 13: Effect of Solidification Time on Ultimate Tensile Strength in W319 at 230°C

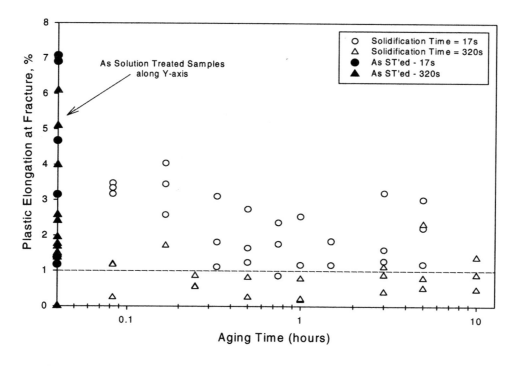

Figure 14: Effect of Solidification Time on Ductility in W319 at 230°C

UNDERHOOD APPLICATIONS FOR CAST COMPONENTS

2000-01-0760

High Integrity Structural Aluminum Casting Process Selection

Robert Wolfe and Rob Bailey
Madison-Kipp Corporation

Copyright © 2000 Society of Automotive Engineers, Inc.

ABSTRACT

Proper alloy and process selection is critical to the commercial production and application of any high-integrity casting. These activities must be focused directly on critical part performance criteria. This paper presents examples of how a casting supplier, with a sound foundation in a broad range of the high-integrity casting techniques, can select and optimize critical criteria in the areas of product design, alloy design, casting process design and heat treatment to achieve a commercial manufacturing success which satisfies the casting customers' functional needs. Three case studies are described which show how proper process selection aided the casting customer in choosing the correct casting process.

Case Study 1 -- Optimization of a 357 semi-solid metal casting (SSMC) alloy with T-5 heat treatment for a swaging application.

Case Study 2 -- Optimization of a 365 alloy and T-5 heat treatment for Johnson Apparent Elastic Limit (JAEL).

Case Study 3 -- Optimization of a 365 alloy heat-treated die casting for impact resistance.

INTRODUCTION

Automotive casting producers and end-users are faced with ever increasing challenges regarding component design and cost. Consideration to how the part is to be produced, assembled and used are all part of the manufacturing process selection. This paper will show three case studies that demonstrate how a high integrity, structural aluminum casting processes, were developed to meet the end users product requirements.

CASE STUDY #1

AUTOMOTIVE IDLER HOUSINGS

Automotive idler housings require both yield strength for part function and ductility for assembly manufacturing.

This application has been historically satisfied with a machined iron casting. During the assembly manufacturing process the idler arm assembly is retained within the idler housing by swaging. This forming process bends a lip around the idler arm assembly and, therefore, requires good ductility. Figure 1 shows a completed assembly. Aluminum afforded an opportunity for a great weight savings versus iron if adequate yield strength and ductility could be assured.

Idler Housing

The Idler Housing part and process design had been validated in aluminum by the customer in single cavity development. The process selected was semi-solid metal casting (SSMC) of aluminum alloy 357.0 (AlSi7Mg) with a T6 heat treatment. The part design reflected the maximum weight savings possible. This part design encountered quality problems–inconsistency in the swaging properties when the program was scaled up to a multi-cavity production die. The customer allowed the part to be redesigned to improve castability but did not allow consideration of alternative heat treatments versus T6 (solutionizing, followed by precipitation hardening).

Pre-production and product launch was done using the T6 heat treating process but quality issues were apparent considering the part's surface appearance. At this time the process development to investigate a T5 heat treatment was initiated. The development question was asked: could a precipitation hardening T5 process satisfy the semi-solid metal casting (SSMC) idler housing's functional requirements, yield strength for part function and ductility for assembly manufacturing?

To attempt to answer this question, an understanding of which physical properties had the most significant impact on the part's function was necessary. Yield strength and ductility (% elongation) were determined to be more significant than ultimate strength and hardness. These were the four properties specified in the customer's material specification. These target values were a UTS of 310 MPa, a YTS of 240 MPa, a hardness range between 83.5-93.5 on the Rockwell Hardness "E" scale (HRE) and a minimum elongation of 7%. Yield strength was selected over ultimate strength since, once the material had exceeded its relative yield strength, it had effectively, permanently, changed its dimensions. It was assumed this condition would be considered severe enough to affect the performance of the assembly. Ductility was considered more significant than hardness since it was more applicable to the requirements of the assembly manufacturing process. Hardness provides a good process monitoring criteria but could not be correlated to how well the casting would perform during the swaging operation.

Initial research was performed on castings using sub-standard flat tensile specimens machined from the round tube wall of the casting. This was the technique used to develop the initial physical property specifications during the single cavity prototype stage. A heat treatment study was performed on 357.0 SSMC castings to attempt to frame the capabilities of the T5 process. The aim of this development was to match the T6 capabilities. The initial time and temperature levels evaluated were $350^{\circ}F$, $450^{\circ}F$ and $550^{\circ}F$ at 3, 5, 7 and 10 hours, respectively. The results of this benchmarking study are shown in Figure 2.

As shown by this graph, the $350^{\circ}F$ for 7 to 10 hours resulted in the best yield strength performance. These results suggest that precipitation hardening was occurring within the $350^{\circ}F$ range and overaging was occurring at the $450^{\circ}F$ and $550^{\circ}F$ temperature levels. Another result of this study was that the technique for preparing the sub-standard samples was not very reproducible.

Two follow-up studies were initiated from these results. First, raw material was sent from the North American supplier to Europe where full size tensile rods could be made in a production SSMC cell. Second, while the full size specimens were being produced, an additional casting heat treatment study was initiated to optimize the $350^{\circ}F$ recipe. Samples were heat treated at $310^{\circ}F$ and $350^{\circ}F$ for 3 to 7 hours. Results of this study are shown on Figure 3. The lack of correlation between the two tests, Figures 2 and 3, caused the disqualification of the flat sub-standard technique as an analytical method. The same conclusion was confirmed with the flat sub-standard specimen performance in T6 heat treatment development.

Using the yield strength performance as a guide, when the round, full size tensile rods were available, the T5 ($350^{\circ}F$ for 7 hour precipitation hardening recipe) was used for comparison with the T6 process. The results of this comparison are shown in Figure 4. Based on this comparison, sample castings were submitted to the customer for functional and durability testing. The functional test for the assembly is a push-out test that attempts to push the idler assembly out of the housing by breaking the spin lip. Six assemblies were built up and tested. In two out of the six, a different part failed at 4368 and 4685 pounds, respectively (with 2500 pounds being the minimum specification). The spin lips on these two idler housings did not fail. On the four other assemblies the spin lip failed between 3902 and 4421 pounds. For durability testing, a minimum of 2.5 schedules is specified. The housing and assembly were in good condition when the testing was suspended after 46 schedules. Two additional assemblies were submitted to fatigue testing. In both cases a part in the assembly other than the idler housing failed well above the minimum peak load.

Based on this development, the standard manufacturing process was changed from a T6 heat treatment requirement to a T5 heat treatment requirement. To date, several hundred thousand castings have been machined, assembled and put into the field in this aluminum idler housing application without any spin lip failure occurrences.

To summarize:

- The conversion from iron to aluminum reduced part weight by 50%.

- The conversion to 357 alloy, SSMC, T-6 was successful.

- The conversion to the T-5 heat treatment eliminated the high temperature defects and warpage.

- The T-5 heat treatment provided the ductility needed for the swaging operation.

- The T-5 heat treatment met all assembly test requirements for the iron casting including ultimate, dynamic and fatigue.

- Several hundred thousands of parts have been produced and used in the T5 condition without any assembly failures.

CASE STUDY #2

AUTOMOTIVE GEAR SHIFT ACTUATOR SHAFTS

Automotive gear shift actuator shafts require a unique combination of strength and part geometry. The application within the assembly places a torque load on the casting that requires high yield strength and must be machined to close tolerances to control noise and vibration. In the past, this application has been satisfied with ferrous investment castings and, more recently, with aluminum 357.0-T6 semi-solid metal castings. The SSMC aluminum solution delivered a significant weight and cost reduction over the ferrous casting. However, it was felt that, with proper part and process development, a liquid metal casting process and a T5 heat treat process would satisfy the functional requirements at a lower cost.

Actuator Shafts

The first step in evaluating the actuator shaft was to reconcile the part design with the design's impact on casting process feasibility. This part's general shape is a very heavy shaft connected to a relatively thin wall box on one end. (See Figure 5) During sub-assembly of the steering column, the gearshift is attached to the shift actuator by this shaft. A new process and a new die was needed. As part of the new die design, metal flow into the cavity and the solidification of the metal was modeled to optimize metal soundness. The process impact on the porosity which is due to turbulence as the metal fills the cavity and the potential lack of intensification (squeeze) during solidification was also optimized by the modeling. Within the multi-cavity die required for this product, there was a concern for cavity-to-cavity variation in dimensions and mechanical properties. The part and process was redesigned to minimize variation. This decision was the foundation for the casting process to succeed in meeting the project goal.

An integral part of the revised part design was the gate and runner system and cavity-filling scheme. The challenge presented by this part's design and function required a casting process which needed the soundness of a squeeze casting in the shaft and the net-shape, thin wall dimensional repeatability of a die casting process within the broach box. This drove the runner design towards a thick runner so that the metal could fill the cavity in a slow, planar manner while maintaining high pressure and metal feed during intensification. Control of the thermal environment (and, therefore, solidification direction) is maintained with proper design of die cooling lines.

Casting process feasibility also played a large part in alloy and heat treatment design. The SSMC process used the aluminum alloy 357.0 (AlSi7Mg) combined with a T6 process. This process produces a high quality material with excellent yield strength, ultimate strength and elongation. The liquid metal casting process would have to perform equal with this process on the critical physical properties. From discussion with the customer, it was known that the most important physical property for this application is the Johnson's Apparent Elastic Limit (JAEL). This property is another method of defining Offset Yield Strength in that it describes the transition of a sample (or in this case an assembly) from the elastic range to the plastic range. The JAEL is the point at which permanent deformation has occurred. JAEL is calculated by plotting the stress strain curve for the part. The slope of the curve is determined for the elastic range. A new line is then established at an angle of 1.5 times the elastic slope. The JAEL is determined by the target point of the new 1.5x line and the stress strain curve. The JAEL is the stress (load) determined by this method (Figure 6). This test was done on finished machined castings built into a test apparatus that simulates actual part loading in the steering column. This provided a direct one to one comparison of the 357.0-T6 SSMC to the M365-T5 liquid metal parts.

The initial alloy chosen to die cast was 365.0 (AlSi10Mg). This alloy approaches the strength and elongation properties of A356 or 357 alloy without the aggressive die soldering associated with those alloys.

A single cavity prototype die was produced with the revised part design. Over 1000 sample castings were produced in an automatic, continuous 16 hour production trial to confirm casting feasibility. Magnesium content was varied during this run from 0.2% up to 1%. The intention of this level of variation was to determine if the yield strength (and, therefore, the JAEL) could be optimized to the SSMC performance.

Sub-standard round tensile specimens were produced from the actual runner and casting over these various Mg levels to optimize the heat treatment. These were subjected to various heat treatment temperatures and times of 300°F, 350°F and 400°F, with time frames at 1, 3 and 5 hours. Figures 6 and 7 display the averaged data for these various levels. For clarification, averaging means that all 11 Mg levels were taken into account for the temperature and time data point and for the Mg data point, all 9 heat treatment group results were used for that point. As can be seen from these graphs, the optimum Mg levels were from 0.9 to 1% and the optimum heat treat recipes were 350 °F for 5 hours and 400 °F for 3 hours.

A confirmation heat treat study using actual castings was done comparing the two optimum recipes indicated by the tensile specimen yield strength performance. These castings again varied over the full range of Mg levels. The results of this study showed that the higher temperature actually decreased the peak load, regardless of Mg level. Peak load, which corresponds to UTS, was used at this time to determine an optimum heat treat recipe. A second generation of heat treat studies was performed using mid-level Mg (0.6 to 0.7%)

castings, again using peak load as the metric. The temperatures chosen were 325 °F and 375 °F, with time frames of 3, 5 and 7 hours. Figure 8 shows the results of this development. Based on peak load, the 325 °F at 7 hours was chosen as the heat treatment process for the JAEL comparison with the 357.0-T6 SSMC machined castings.

Samples of the 357.0-T6 SSMC castings were obtained from the customer for evaluation. Using the same assembly components and testing fixture, the high density modified 365-T5 machined castings were compared with the SSMC parts. Figure 9 shows these results. The JAEL of the M365-T5 parts equaled the performance of the 357.0-T6 parts (212 pounds versus 213 pounds) with a tighter six sigma range (88 pounds versus 59 pounds). This satisfied the development goal.

The automotive customer evaluated a large quantity of the actuator shafts from the optimized alloy and heat treatment. The pieces passed all assembly, ultimate and durability requirements. Implementation of this process development into a multi-cavity production process has also been completed with slight modification to the target heat treatment temperature. Production castings from this multi-cavity process have matched the success of the single-cavity prototypes regarding the JAEL performance and the assembly, functional and durability tests.

It was possible to convert a gear shift linkage shaft from a SSMC to a high integrity liquid casting.

In summary:

- The SSMC aluminum substituted for an investment cast steel part providing both weight and cost reductions.

- The SSMC 357 alloy, T-6 performed well in this application.

- A hybrid squeeze casting/die casting process was developed as a single cavity prototype.

- The liquid cast, 365 alloy T-5 parts equaled the JAEL yield strength of the SSMC parts. This is the primary performance criteria.

- Multi-cavity capability was demonstrated to be equal to the single cavity prototype.

- The 365, T-5 parts were validated through ultimate and dynamic assembly testing.

- A significant cost-savings was generated.

Case Study #3

COMMERCIAL PAINT GUNS

The integrity of paint guns is highly dependent on design and material of construction. Aluminum is used because of its lightweight and chemical resistance to a broad range of solvents. The low cost guns are produced from standard die castings. These parts are vulnerable to brittle failures when dropped or mishandled. The best guns are from aluminum forgings, which are very expensive. The challenge is to produce a line of guns with forging performance in a die casting format.

Paint Gun

The initial marketing opportunity was to produce a high-end commercial paint gun (Figure 1) as a semi-solid metal casting. Historically this gun would have been produced as a forging because of the mechanical properties required to meet the function of the part. Their primary concern was for high ductility while at the same time providing near net shape to minimize finishing operations and machining capital.

Process engineering evaluated the semi-solid request. SSMC would certainly provide all of the product needs but the part design was too restricted to yield a robust production process in this fabrication. A counter proposal was offered. This counter-proposal was that the part could be produced in a high ductility liquid alloy and meet all product performance criteria. This set into action a series of activities.

First, it was necessary to demonstrate the capability of the alloy system to provide the necessary ductility. We started with a 365 (AlSi10Mg) alloy and modified the magnesium content and heat treatment to optimize mechanical properties. Three levels of magnesium were chosen; namely, 0.2%, 0.35% and 0.75%. ASTM tensile bars were produced at each composition. These bars were than tested at four heat-treat conditions: 1) as cast; 2) 350°F for six hours; 3) 500°F for six hours; and 4) 650°F for six hours. Results are presented graphically in Figures 11a, 11b and 11c. The mechanical properties for this alloy were very good under all conditions. Of particular interest is the high elongations that were attained. Several conclusions were obvious: 1) as cast properties were quite good; 2) UTS and yield strengths could be optimized by a T-5 heat-treatment at 350°F with some decrease in elongation; 3) over-aging at 500°F and 650°F increased elongation but decreased UTS and yield; and 4) increasing magnesium content increased UTS and yield particularly in the T-5 heat treatment but it also decreases ductility.

Secondly, it was necessary to demonstrate that the ductility attained in tensile bars could be attained in the parts. A prototype die was made to produce part of the casting as a test coupon. See Figure 12. These parts had to be made in an actual die casting die. This could not be simulated from another casting process or cut from solid bar stock. Parts were cast at the 0.2% magnesium level and tested in the as-cast and heat-treat conditions.

The test consisted of a one kilogram weight dropped one meter on to the relatively thin hook detail of the casting. Acceptance criteria was that the hook could deform (bend) but could not crack or separate. A minimum of ten drops per sample was established as the minimum acceptance criteria. Standard die cast parts (380 alloy) failed on the first drop. The 365 alloy die cast parts passed this impact test with 10 to 20 drops per part depending upon heat treatment. The best results were attained with a 500°F treatment for six hours.

The final phase was to build the production tool and certify that the same impact performance could be attained in the production parts. A production die was completed. Parts were cast and heat-treated to the optimized coupon schedule. The impact test was conducted in the same manner and the results were the same as demonstrated on the coupon. This process has produced more than 100,000 parts.

What was significant in this effort:

- We were able to substitute a high ductility die casting for a forging and provide additional benefits.

- Near net shape internal and external features – four deep intersecting holes were cored.

- Accurate surface detail so that all machining locators and all logo and safety operating instructions were cast into the part.

- A smooth surface with minimum die parting lines which could be easily buffed and polished.

- All design and performance criteria specified for the forging were attained.

- Provided a significant cost-savings in both direct cost and machine line capital.

SUMMARY

The ability to work with the casting end user to select the appropriate casting process requires a sound understanding of not only the high integrity structural aluminum materials and casting processes, but also a sound understanding in the metallurgical requirements of the casting and end product. Reconciling the feasibility of how to make the casting with the overall programs' economic and functional goals is paramount to succeeding in the launch of any casting process. This paper has described the steps taken to positively meet the end users requirements in three separate functions:

- Assembly via swaging which requires ductility.

- Yield strength as defined by the Johnson's Apparent Elastic Limit.

- Impact resistance.

While each of these functions were unique to the casting, the method used (initial process selection, prototype validation and production validation) is relatively the same. By committing to development and validation, a casting supplier can reliably satisfy the customer's component requirements.

ACKNOWLEDGMENTS

The following individuals contributed with background development work:

Justin Heimsch, Undergraduate Intern, University of Wisconsin-Madison

Scott Brown, Undergraduate Intern, University of Wisconsin-Madison

AUTHORS

Rob Bailey, Senior Process Engineer, Madison-Kipp Corporation, 201 Waubesa Street, Madison, WI, USA

Robert Wolfe, Vice President of Technology, Madison-Kipp Corporation, 201 Waubesa Street, Madison, WI, USA

Phone   (608) 242-5312
Fax   (608) 244-4674

Figure 1
Idler Housing Assembly

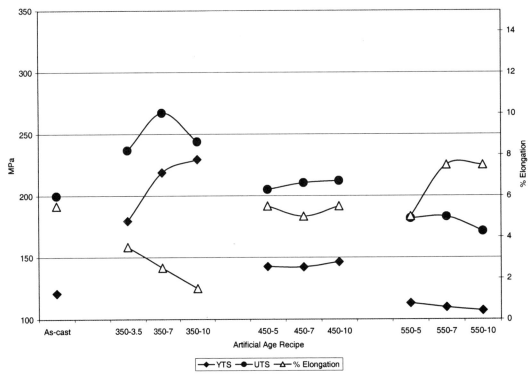

Figure 2
SSMC 357.0-T5 Tensile Study

Using Flat, Sub-standard Tensile Bars

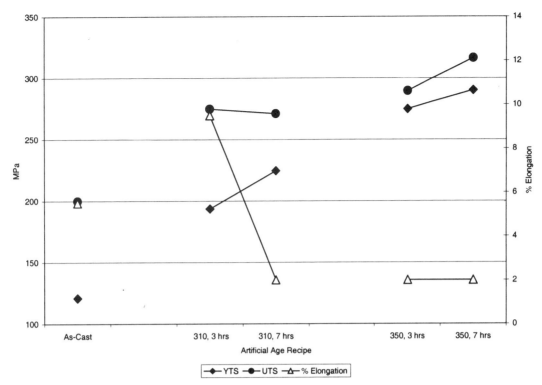

Figure 3
Yield Strength And Elongation
Over A Tighter T-5 Aging Range

(Using Flat, Sub-Standard Tensile Bars

	T6	T5
0.2% YTS (MPa)	198.4	216.3
UTS (MPa)	301.1	300.4
% Elongation	13%	8%

Figure 4
Comparison Of The T-5 Vs. T-6 Heat Treat
Properties For Ssm-357 Alloy

(Using SSMC 357.0 Full-Size Round Tensile Bars)

Figure 5
Shift Actuator

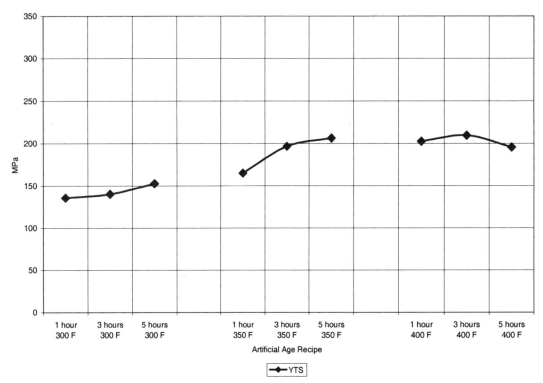

Figure 6
Jael Yield Strength Vs. T-5 Aging Cycle

(Yield Strength Vs. T5 Aging Recipe)

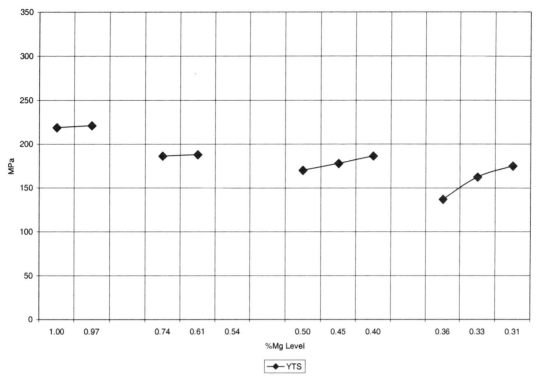

Figure 7
Jael Yield Strength Vs. Magnesium Content

(Yield Strength Vs. %Mg Content)

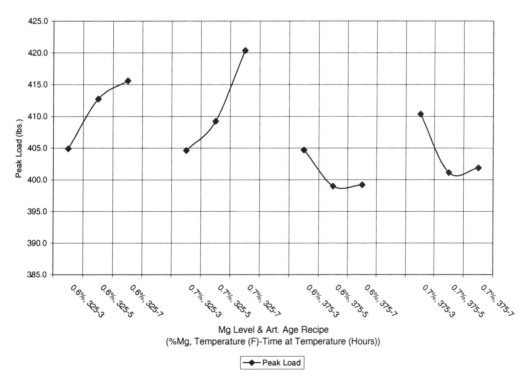

Figure 8
Jael Yield Strength Vs.
Aging Time And Temperatures

(Part Ultimate Strength Vs. Mg Level And T5 Recipe)

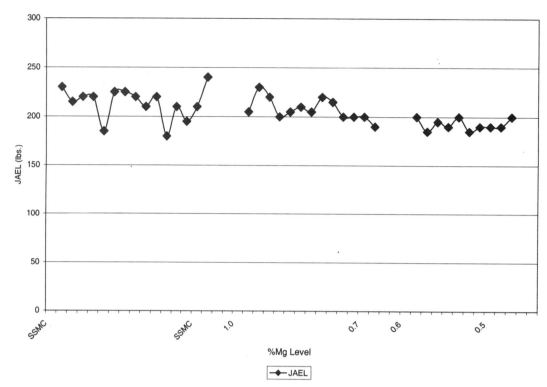

Figure 9
Jael Yield Strength -- SSM-T6 Vs. 365-T5 Alloy

Part Jael Vs. %Mg Level & SSMC

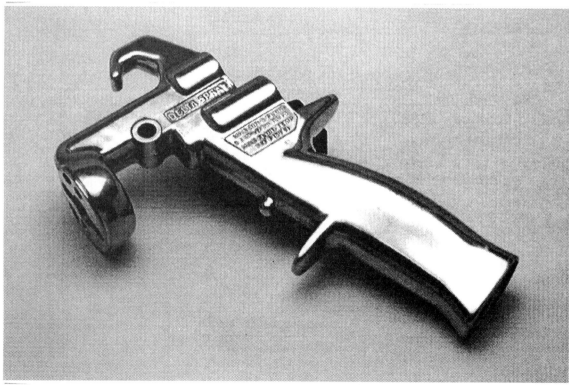

Figure 10
Paint Gun

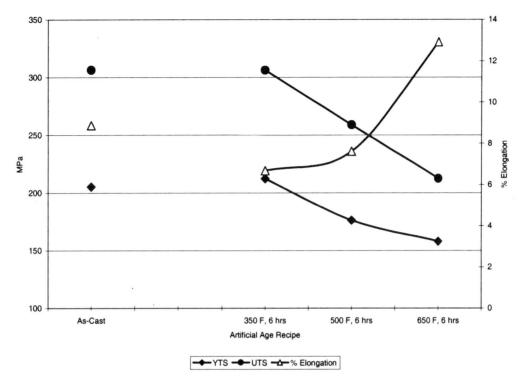

Figure 11a
Mechanical Properties Of 365 Alloy (0.2mg)
At Various T5 Aging Conditions

(0.20% Mg Content)

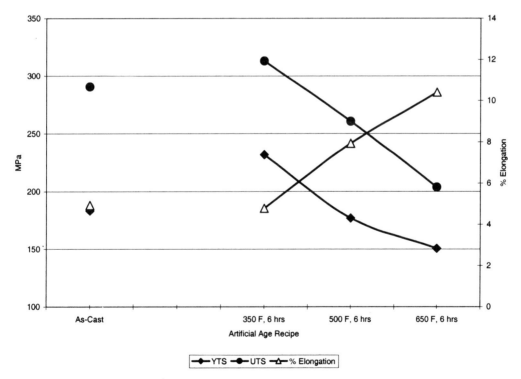

Figure 11B
Mechanical Properties Of 365 Alloy (0.35mg)
At Various T5 Aging Conditions

0.35% Mg Content

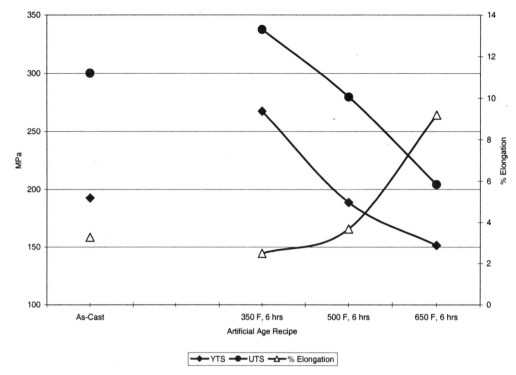

Figure 11C
Mechanical Properties of 365 Alloy (0.75 %Mg)
At Various T5 Aging Conditions

0.75% Mg Content

Figure 12
Impact Test Coupon

2000-01-0761

Design Review of Cast Aluminum Scroll Compressor Components

David T. Gerken
Casting Technology Company

John Calhoun
Sanden International (U.S.A.), Inc.

Copyright © 2000 Society of Automotive Engineers, Inc.

ABSTRACT

Automotive air conditioning compressors utilizing aluminum scrolls offer improvements in engine performance and fuel economy by lowering energy consumption, reducing weight, and allowing smaller packaging. This alternative compressor design was first commercially produced in 1981. Since this time, scroll compressors have continually increased their share of the original equipment compressor market for Japanese, European, and US automotive manufacturers. Two essential components in the compressor assembly are the aluminum scroll castings (fixed and orbiting).

The first production aluminum scrolls were machined from sand castings. This process was then replaced by squeeze casting, which has now been in use for over 12 years. Forging has recently emerged as an alternative process. The design and structural requirements of the aluminum scroll component challenge both squeeze casting and forging processes. Scrolls are a unique combination of thin and thick sections with deep low draft walls requiring minimum machining stock for optimum machinability. Over 90% of the scroll surfaces are machined. In some areas, the remaining stock is less than 2 millimeters wide and over 30 millimeters tall. Operating conditions for the scroll compressor require the aluminum scroll component to withstand the very high temperatures and pressures of the discharge gases. These requirements have established new standards for dimensional capability, internal integrity, and material properties (selection and control) in the high volume automotive aluminum casting market.

This paper will first describe the basic design and operational benefits of scroll compressors over traditional piston types. The discussion will include operational differences between the compressors and the effect on manufacturing/assembly tolerances. Secondly, the paper will identify the key design, material,

and quality requirements of the aluminum scroll. The discussion will focus on how machining and operational requirements drive design requirements such as machining stock, draft, dimensional control, and internal integrity. Finally, a comparative summary will explain the difference in processes and materials used in the manufacture of aluminum scrolls. Benefits and potential issues for squeeze castings and forgings will be discussed relative to manufacturing, processing, and compressor performance/reliability testing.

INTRODUCTION

Aluminum scroll compressors have established themselves as a reliable option for air conditioning compressor systems in the automotive market. Scroll compressors consume less engine power to operate thereby improving engine operating performance. The compressors are lighter in weight contributing to increasingly stringent CAFÉ requirements. The smaller packaging of the unit allows for more efficient engine compartment usage. Finally, the operating characteristics and mechanical layout of the compressor design significantly reduces engine compartment noise.

These benefits have increased market share of the automotive aluminum scroll compressor as demonstrated by increasing worldwide usage as original equipment. Market share is approximately 10% and continues to grow steadily.

COMPRESSOR OPERATION

Traditional piston compressors pull gas into the compression chamber as the piston withdraws and compress during the return stroke. It is a proven system being utilized in the majority of automotive air conditioning systems today.

The scroll compressor consists of two separate aluminum castings. The fixed half is permanently mounted to the housing assembly. The orbiting half orbits eccentrically about the center. This motion pulls in gas between the fixed and orbiting walls and continuously compresses them towards the center. A reed valve allows the compressed gas to escape through the base of the fixed scroll. The action is shown graphically in Figure 1 below. Note that 2 compression zones are created during each cycle.

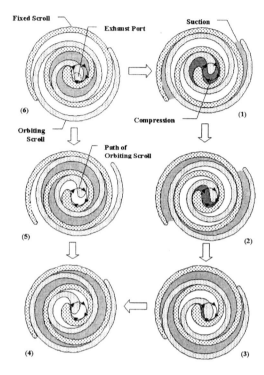

Figure 1 Operation of a Scroll Compressor

Comparatively, the operating efficiency of a scroll compressor exceeds the traditional piston compressor. The volumetric efficiency of a typical piston compressor is 65%. The scroll counterpart can typically achieve 85% efficiency. The engineering basis for this improvement is beyond the scope of this paper; however, a brief listing is provided below for reference.

1. Harmonic vibration reduced
2. Several compression pockets moving simultaneously
3. Near perfect dynamic balancing
4. Nearly unnoticeable torque variations
5. Compression seal by involute wall/refrigerant oil wedge effect vs. line contact of piston/cylinder
6. Low moment of inertia by small radial eccentric movement of orbiting scroll
7. No top dead clearance or blow-by

A typical cycle comparison between scroll and piston type compressors is shown in Figure 2. The chart graphically demonstrates the differences due to the operational efficiencies listed above. Previous papers written on scroll compressors are noted in the reference section and provide substantial discussion on the operation of scroll compressors.

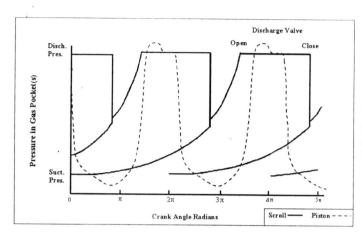

Figure 2 Typical Compressor Cycle

The driving mechanism allows the scroll walls to separate under certain conditions. Therefore, "slugs" of liquefied refrigerant that can develop in air conditioning compressors are able to pass through with minimal impact. Piston compressors can be severely damaged by attempting to compress liquids.

Additional material on scroll compressor operation can be found in references 1 and 2 noted at the end of this paper. These articles cover design and operation in detail.

DESIGN REQUIREMENTS

Geometrically, the scroll shape presents many challenges for casting and machining operations. A typical scroll is shown in Figure 3.

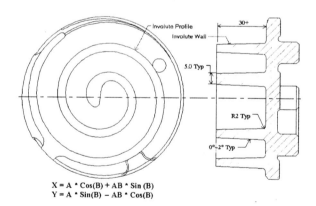

$$X = A * Cos(B) + AB * Sin(B)$$
$$Y = A * Sin(B) - AB * Cos(B)$$

Figure 3 Typical Scroll Casting

As shown above, the profile of the involute is not a primitive arc or line. The involute is a continuously unwrapping curve increasing in distance from the center as it uncurls. Each point on the curve is a mathematical function of the base circle radius and the angle (0 to ∞) of unwrap. An involute profile was therefore difficult to program until the development of computerized numerical control (CNC). Effective machining of the involute walls for both die manufacturing and final part machining was made possible only after the development of CNC. Precision CNC with high-speed controllers are required to handle the amount of data required to machine the profile without creating a faceted appearance.

The efficiency of the compressor is dependent on the ability of the fixed and orbiting halves to seal along the interior walls of the involute profiles as well as the between the base plate and involute top. Sealing surfaces are shown in Figure 4 below. As stated above, precision CNC allows for effective machining of these surfaces.

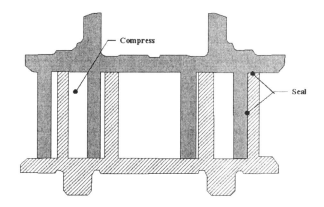

Figure 4 Scroll Seal Surfaces

A second challenge to machining relates to the depth of the involute wall, amounts of casting stock, and amount of draft present. To maintain constant finish, the walls must be milled with a single continuous pass at full depth. Minimal stock (~0.3 mm Typical) is allowed for reduced tool loads at this depth. Draft angles on the casting run from 0° to 2° maximum.

Control of each of these 3 factors is important for machining feeds, speeds, tool loads, tool wear, and tool breakage. The overall effect directly relates to machining cycle rate and surface finish. The general relationships between these factors are graphically expressed in Figure 5.

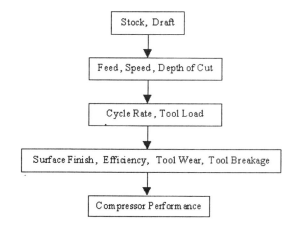

Figure 5 Performance vs. Machining Stock

During operation, the highest load applied by the compression of gas occurs at the center of the involute. This is graphically demonstrated in Figure 6. Structural

integrity of the casting at this location is a critical control feature for manufacturing. Process development and quality inspection for casting of the scroll component must reflect this high integrity requirement.

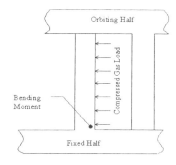

Figure 6 Involute Wall Loading

CASTING REQUIREMENTS

Both fixed and orbiting scroll castings require exceptional quality standards be applied to the casting. A mechanical property comparison between forged and cast product is shown in Table 1. Both listing of properties are shown at room temperature and 150° C. *Properties shown are from handbook references listed at the end of this paper and do not necessarily reflect properties available/required from either process.* As demonstrated, 4032 as a forged material offers properties that are higher than 354 cast material under both conditions.

	Temp.	UTS	YS	% Elong
354 Cast Material	Rt	379 MPa	283 MPa	6%
	150° C	290 MPa	241 MPa	6%
4032 Forged Material	Rt	380 MPa	315 MPa	9%
	150° C	315 MPa	285 MPa	9%

Table 1 Typical Mechanical Properties

In principle, the ideally perfect forged part could be superior to the ideally perfect cast part. However, the shape of the scroll component creates severe challenges to the forging process due to the extensive amount of material movement required. In practice, the squeeze cast scroll components offer comparable strengths to forged scroll components. The choice between a well developed forging process and a well developed squeeze casting process for scrolls elements, therefore, hinges on many other factors.

Materials differ between processes. A comparison of the alloy compositions is shown in Table 2. Casting alloys commonly used are 354 or A332. The 332 alloy is commonly used in permanent mold aluminum pistons. The most common alloy for U.S. manufactured squeeze cast scrolls is 354. This alloy offers premium strength with T6 heat treatment. The high silicon contents are favorable for wear resistance between the involute walls. However, control of the eutectic modification may be required for machinability and post machining surface treatments. Additionally, precise control of heat treat temperatures must be maintained to prevent incipient melting of intermetallics during solid solution heat treatment. These intermetallic compounds tend to concentrate in isolated areas of comparatively larger cross sections. Properly controlled heat treatment will result in no discernible difference in material properties or function of the casting. Loss of control can result in the formation of voids. Quality assurance inspections during casting and subsequent to heat treat should consider this issue.

A common forging alloy for scrolls is A4032. The primary elements are silicon, magnesium, copper and nickel. This alloy offers improved high temperature strength and low coefficient of thermal expansion. The forging technology necessary to manufacture a scroll is comparatively new. Process controls focus on forcing an aluminum blank into the shape of the scroll involute without imparting flow lines or metal folds. Should this phenomenon occur in the forging process, the mechanical strength of the involute is reduced. Any intermetallics that would exist in a forging alloy would be equally distributed throughout the blank prior to the forging operation and would therefore not be of primary consideration during subsequent heat treatment. However, proper refinement of the primary silicon particles in the blank used for forging is a key material control factor. Lack of proper refinement can be detrimental to fatigue properties.

Name	Element	Cu	Si	Mg	Fe	Ni
354	Maximum	2.0	9.4	0.60	0.20	0.05
AA	Minimum	1.6	8.6	0.40		
A332	Maximum	4.0	10.5	1.5	1.0	0.5
AA	Minimum	2.0	8.5	0.5		
A4032	Maximum	1.3	13.5	1.3	1.0	1.3
JIS	Minimum	0.5	11.5	0.8		0.5

Table 2 Common Scroll Materials

Mechanical properties are checked at the central region of the base plate as shown in Figure 7. This is the location of the highest load condition on the scroll casting in operation. Additionally, the previous discussions demonstrated that casting imperfections from either squeeze casting or forging process would tend to occur in this region of the part.

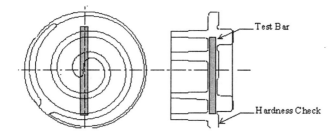

Figure 7 Mechanical Testing Location

Casting quality requirements are divided into three zones of interest. As shown in Figure 8 and Table 3, the

highest level of quality is required in zone one (highest mechanically loaded). Zone 2 requirements are less stringent mechanically, however, the seal required between mating involute walls requires a high degree of casting integrity. Zone 3 defines the base plate area of the casting.

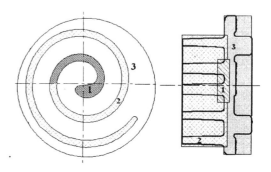

Figure 8 Casting Soundness Inspection Zones

Internal Defect	Zone 1	Zone 2	Zone 3
Sponge Shrinkage	None	None	None
Gas Hole	⇑	⌀0.3 mm	⌀0.5 mm
Gas Porosity	⇑	None	None
Shrinkage Cavity	⇑	⇑	⇑
Foreign Material Inclusion	⇑	⇑	⇑
Cracks	None	None	None
Cold Shut	⇑	⇑	⇑
Cold Lap	⇑	⇑	⇑

Table 3 Casting Soundness Requirement

Inspections for levels of defects defined by figure 10 require destructive testing of production castings. Samples are pulled from production throughout the casting run. The samples are section cut to reveal key areas of interest indicated by figure 11, polished or milled smooth, and inspected according to figure 10 requirements. Frequency of and sample quantity are dependent on process development and levels of process control established for casting.

SUMMARY

Aluminum scroll compressors offer a number of improvements over traditional piston type air conditioning compressors. The improvements include lower weight, reduced packaging, reduced engine noise, higher efficiency, and lower power consumption. Market share has increased over the last 18 years to approximately 10% and continues to rise.

The key components in a scroll compressor are the aluminum fixed and orbiting scroll castings. Design criteria for these components offer several challenges for casting, forging, and finish machining operations. Involute walls are deep with 0° to 2° maximum draft and minimal stock. Precision machining of the continuously unwrapping involute surface to a mirror finish challenges casting suppliers to meet the highest standards of dimensional consistency. The scroll is a combination of thin and thick cross sections demanding exceptional quality standards for strength and casting integrity.

The differences in materials and processes for manufacturing of scroll castings result in comparable finished products regardless of the differences in base material properties. Both processes appear to be equally capable of manufacturing aluminum scroll products.

ACKNOWLEDGMENTS

The following individuals are acknowledged for their participation in the design and development of the squeeze cast aluminum scroll program.

Glen Meyer – Product Process Engineer, Casting Technology Company

Terry Burcham – Design Engineer, Casting Technology Company

Toshiro Ogiwara – VP Technology Transfer, Izumi Industries

CONTACT

Dave Gerken is the Manager of Tooling and New Products for Casting Technology Company (CTC) located in Franklin Indiana. CTC is North America's largest supplier of Vertical Squeeze Cast aluminum front knuckles and scroll compressor castings. Over 6.5 million aluminum scroll compressor castings have been produced from this facility since 1995. Phone number (317) 738-0282, Fax Number (317) 738-0262, E-mail dave.gerken@amcast.com

REFERENCES

1. Kiyoshi Terauchi, Yasuhiro Tsukagoshi, and Masaharu Hiraga, "The Characteristics of the Spiral Compressor for Automotive Air Conditioning", 1983 SAE paper no. 830541
2. Masaharu Hiraga, "The Spiral Compressor – An Innovative Air Conditioning Compressor for the New Generation Automobiles" 1983 SAE paper no. 830504
3. ASM, "Aluminum Properties and Physical Metallurgy", 1984, Referenced for typical mechanical properties and chemistries of alloys discussed in this paper.

2000-01-0763

Dissimilar Welding of Si-Mo Ductile Iron Exhaust Manifold Welded to Stainless Steel Catalytic Converter using NI-ROD Filler Metal 44HT

Brian Baker and Samuel Kiser
Special Metals Corporation

Peter Chen
Ford Motor Company

Brian Skinn and Rick Williams
Wescast Foundries, Ltd.

Copyright © 2000 Society of Automotive Engineers, Inc.

ABSTRACT

The demands of modern society continue to drive automotive design to greater efficiency and cleaner operation at lower cost. Higher operating temperatures are now typically required to meet these demands, making the use of more robust materials and joining techniques a necessity. This paper describes how the benefits of reduced emissions and greater fuel economy along with quieter operation are achieved by using silicon-molybdenum modified ductile iron exhaust manifolds welded to close-coupled 400 series stainless steel catalyst cans. This weldment is made possible by using a newly-developed stabilized Ni-Fe-Mn-Cr-Cb welding wire called NI-ROD® Filler Metal 44HT. Durability testing of fabricated exhaust components under extreme dynamometer testing has shown that this welding material provides successful higher temperature performance by the ductile iron than that provided by previous weldments of the same iron.

INTRODUCTION

In the early days of the "Tin Lizzy", the exhaust parts were so far down on the list of priorities that most owners couldn't even identify them. In the middle ages of automobiles, most exhaust manifolds were gray cast iron and seemed to perform well enough. Within the last 10-20 years, increasing emphasis has been placed on fuel efficiency and emissions control, forcing exhaust gas temperatures upward and challenging all of the components. Today, it is not unusual for exhaust temperatures to reach 870°C when towing extra loads up long grades. With electronic fuel injection to custom blend air and fuel for each demand of automobile operation, thermal efficiency, fuel efficiency, and emissions control can be optimized instantaneously. Unfortunately, the equipment and alloys normally used are challenged by the higher temperatures generated. One of the results of these challenges is the development of the fabricated manifold. These have been in place for some time, and have been performing admirably until the most recent demands have been positioned. The replacement for the fabricated manifold with an iron casting is an old idea refurbished with a new material. The part is a Si-Mo modified ductile cast iron manifold. With this technology introduced, several benefits are obtained, but with the added necessity of moving the catalyst can closer to the engine for faster light off, the problem of dissimilar welding arises. Once the feasibility of simply welding the two together was established, the task of optimizing the joint design, welding process, and performance of the weld were tackled. Using the measuring devices of metallographic examination, dynamometer testing, and laboratory corrosion and thermal fatigue testing, the final fabrication sequence and technique was developed. As a result of the combined efforts of a foundry, an automobile company, a welding products company, and a welding supplier, a durable close-coupled part is now being fabricated. It consists of a Si-Mo ductile iron manifold welded to a 400 series stainless steel catalyst can using a Ni-Fe-Mn-Cr-Cb welding wire.

CURRENT AND FUTURE EXHAUST ENVIRONMENTS

MATERIALS REQUIREMENTS

Today's emissions requirements and vehicle package restraints often require attachment of the catalytic converter as close as possible to the exhaust manifold. The practice of welding a fabricated stainless steel exhaust manifold to a stainless steel converter shell is becoming an increasingly common practice. The use of a cast iron manifold instead of fabricated stainless steel can potentially provide cost savings, exhaust noise reduction as well as low leak rates and low tail pipe emissions. However, welding the cast iron to stainless steel to produce a reliable weld joint of acceptable quality in high volume production poses a definite challenge. Specifically, the weld joint must meet the requirements of thermal cycle testing on engine dynamometers.

Historically, ductile iron has not been considered to be a weldable material. This has changed through recent development of new welding consumables, Ni-Rod Filler Metals 44 and 44HT (for composition see Table 1). Through the development of more oxidation resistant cast iron and optimization of welding parameters it has been possible to produce a dissimilar joint having the strength, thermal stability and ductility required for extended exhaust system service.

Collaboration among the automotive company, the producer of the ductile iron castings, and the welding product producer has resulted in the development of a production fabricated stainless steel converter welded directly to a cast ductile iron manifold via a small mushroom-shaped flange at the casting.

PERFORMANCE REQUIREMENTS

The assumption is often made that fabricated manifolds offer significantly superior emissions results that those fabricated from cast iron based on the higher thermal inertia of the casting. However, recent test data obtained using a current-model vehicle having a six cylinder engine indicates that the emission results are similar for each type of manifold (Table 2). The C_XH_Y and CO emissions were slightly lower and the NO_X emissions were slightly higher for the cast manifold. Catalyst efficiencies were slightly higher for the cast manifold (Table 3). The obtained values may be essentially equivalent between the two manifold types given inherent test variation.

Table 4 shows a comparison of emissions results for a fabricated steel (2-2.5 mm wall thickness) versus a cast iron manifold on a 2001 model year vehicle. These data indicate that the fabricated steel manifold produced, on average, 15% more unburnt hydrocarbons, 6% more carbon dioxide and 12% more NO_X. Experimental data indicate that the internal temperature of the catalyst connected to the fabricated steel manifold does not exceed that of the cast iron manifold until 40-50 seconds have elapsed in the drive cycle. This is presumed to be due to the tendency of the steel manifold to extract more heat from the exhaust gas than the cast iron manifold during the warm-up phase of the driving cycle. This can be rationalized through consideration of the higher heat transfer coefficient and lower thermal mass of the fabricated steel manifold. In order to have an optimal fabricated design it would be necessary to have a very light gauge inner wall (for less heat absorption) and a heavier gauge outer wall for mechanical strength as well as an air gap between the inner and outer wall for insulation. However, this type of product is very costly and less reliable for mass production. Further consideration is beyond the scope of this paper.

MATERIALS AND FABRICATION METHODS

SILICON-MOLYBDENUM DUCTILE CAST IRON MANIFOLD

Gray cast iron as an exhaust manifold cannot perform well for extended time periods at elevated temperatures because the characteristic graphite flakes provide ingress to oxidation and other high temperature corrosion attack. The sequence begins when surface-exposed flakes oxidize into the interior and cause swelling and spalling which is then followed by further oxidation. The newer material, Si-Mo ductile iron has several noteworthy advantages. The nominal composition of this ductile iron is given in Table I along with other materials' chemical compositions described in this paper. Of particular importance is the nearly 4% Si that imparts improved oxidation resistance and increases the ferrite-to-austenite transformation temperature (the A1 temperature) to slightly above the maximum expected operating temperature. This prevents the material from experiencing phase changes from ferrite to austenite and back again during operation. If this is allowed to happen, a phenomenon called "nodule fade" occurs and the material loses its effectiveness.

THE 409 STAINLESS STEEL CATALYST CAN

The 400 series stainless steels provide good thermal fatigue resistance due to relatively low CTE (coefficient of thermal expansion) and reasonable oxidation resistance and strength up to about 870°C, due to their chromium content. Columbium additions provide additional strength and microstructural stability. Two candidate compositions are 409 and 18Cr-Cb stainless steels. These types of materials have served well as catalyst cans for a number of years. Due to the requirement of faster light off, the cans are being moved closer to the manifold for faster heat up during cold start. In fact, the current design calls for the catalyst can to be welded directly to the manifold. This requirement has been met with NI-ROD filler metal 44 (AWS ERNiFeMn-Cl) in the past.

THE WELD AND HEAT AFFECTED ZONE AND STRESS ACCELERATED OXIDATION CRACKING

Because of earlier success, the standard approach was first attempted in the current test program. That is, Si-Mo ductile iron was welded to a 409 stainless steel catalyst can using NI-ROD filler metal 44 with pulsed gas metal-arc welding (pGMAW). The current program, however, contained some differences from the earlier one that had produced success. The first test of the current program involved a change in catalyst can design, a different weld joint configuration, and a different support mechanism during dynamometer testing. As a result of one or a combination of these factors, the first dynamometer test of the current program failed by stress-accelerated-oxidation cracking along the Si-Mo ductile iron fusion line.

As a result of the unexpected failure, static oxidation exposures and testing in a cyclic oxidation rig to generate thermal stresses were performed in the laboratory at Special Metals. Static exposures were performed in a horizontal electrically heated muffle furnace having an atmosphere of air plus 5% water vapor, added by bubbling air through a flask held at a constant temperature of 33°C. This water vapor addition is made in order to provide constant testing conditions despite fluctuation of the external humidity. The cyclic oxidation test was performed by mechanically cycling samples in air into a vertical electrically heated clamshell furnace for 15 minutes followed by removal of the samples to ambient air above the furnace for 5 minutes. The fusion line failure of the ductile iron was reproduced under cyclic conditions at 870°C. Figure 1 shows a photmicrograph of a fusion line crack at the Si-Mo ductile cast iron/NI-ROD filler metal 44 interface after one oxidation cycle at 870°C. The crack progression appears to be connected with the presence of aligned secondary graphite particles. The same type of attack was not observed after exposure to static conditions. Thus the mechanism of stress-accelerated-oxidation cracking is the likely culprit of the observed crack progression. By observing samples with only one cycle, identification and characterization of the very beginning of the failure mechanism was possible.

Due to earlier failures in the field due to graphitization of welds, Special Metals had products under development which were stabilized with Cb and fortified with Cr designed to withstand higher temperatures of operation. With the cooperation of Wescast who supplied modified castings with a different joint design to facilitate welding, Michigan Arc Products who supplied test welding facilities, and OEM oversight, welding of the second generation of prototype parts proceeded using the new

Cr-Cb modified filler metal (now known as NI-ROD filler metal 44HT). All involved in the actual welding operation were favorably impressed with the user friendliness of the new wire. It was characterized as exhibiting better wetting and greatly improved bead appearance than other wires.

After welding multiple exhaust manifold assemblies, several were sectioned and metallographically analyzed and these results were compared to previous metallographic studies. Also, some of the welds were sectioned and modified by welding with earlier iterations of Ni-Fe-Mn-Cr-Cb wires in preparation for further laboratory oxidation testing. Oxidation testing was conducted as described above but for longer periods of time, both under static conditions (100 hour exposure) and cyclic conditions (300 cycles, or 100 hours) at temperatures of 815°C and 845°C. Several differences between the respective welding products were noted. Firstly, oxide scale growth was observed to be much more rapid for the NI-ROD filler metal 44 than for the NI-ROD filler metal 44HT, based upon the cross sectional thickness of the oxide layers observed in the tested samples (Figure 2, Table 5). The NI-ROD filler metal 44HT material exhibits a distinctly different surface layer which may serve to impede cation and/or oxygen transport, while the NI-ROD filler metal 44 exhibits no such second layer. Secondly, exposure conditions resulted in the precipitation of much more secondary graphite within the weld deposit and at the interface with the ductile iron for the samples welded with the NI-ROD filler metal 44. Figure 3 shows the interface of each weld deposit after 100 hours of cyclic exposure at 1500°F. Thirdly, cyclic testing again exhibited the tendency for stress-accelerated oxidation cracking along the interface between the NI-ROD filler metal 44 and the ductile iron while the Cr-Cb modified NI-ROD filler metal 44HT deposit exhibited resistance to this phenomenon (Figure 4). Again, this behavior is conjectured to be related to the amount and linear orientation of secondary graphite at ductile iron interface of the NI-ROD filler metal 44 weld. The inherently superior oxidation resistance of the NI-ROD filler metal 44HT is also thought to increase the resistance of this material to the cracking phenomenon.

Our overall results seemed to indicate that the fusion line and heat-affected-zone (HAZ) of the ductile iron contained more carbides and higher carbon martensite as a result of welding with the conventional Ni-Fe-Mn wire than when welded with the Ni-Fe-Mn-Cr-Cb wire. After extensive investigation and reflection, we postulated that one explanation for this is that the new wire contains carbide-forming elements that would accept carbon diffusion from the ductile iron HAZ during welding while the conventional wire would tend to have a much lower affinity for carbon. Thus, during the liquidus range temperature excursion created by welding, the melted but unmixed zone of the ductile iron would generate higher carbon austenite since the conventional chemistry molten weld pool would not accept carbon diffusion as easily as the molten pool that contained chromium and columbium. Hence the HAZ of the ductile iron, when welded with conventional wire, contained more carbides and higher carbon martensite that transformed to increased secondary graphite during dynamometer testing (refer again to Figure 3).

This alignment of secondary graphite extends along the fusion line of the ductile iron. The most susceptible area for attack is at the toe of the weld where it meets the ductile iron. Here is the area where the stress-accelerated-oxidation cracking begins, as seen in Figure 1. The original series of dynamometer testing produced through-wall stress-oxidation failures that followed the fusion line such that the weld became a ring of metal fastened by an interference fit to the casting.

THE INFLUENCE OF WELDING AND DYNAMOMETER TESTING ON THE DUCTILE IRON HEAT AFFECTED ZONE

As background, the dynamometer testing consists of full load-wide open throttle (WOT) for 5 minutes followed by cold motoring of the engine with cold coolant circulated through the cooling passages to simulate the most severe thermal cycling an engine could experience. The cooling cycle can be of various lengths, and the cycles are repeated for various lengths of 150 to 200 hours. Exhaust gas temperatures are monitored and adjusted by adjusting air:fuel ratio and exhaust components are also monitored. We found temperatures of 845-870°C to be common in the weld area of the manifold. To aid in understanding the microstructures in the ductile iron, a brief discussion of metallurgy and weld cycle is presented here. The Si-Mo ductile iron is welded in the as-cast condition. The microstructure is largely ferritic with between 10%-20% pearlite. The welding operation is performed at about 250-300 amps and 24v-28v at travel speeds of about 30 in/min. At these parameters, heat-up, melting, and cool-down are all quite rapid. If one were to consult a phase-diagram, he would find that the microstructure transforms from ferrite to austenite at about 870-900°C. At and above the A1 temperature, the austenite readily absorbs carbon from both pearlite and graphite nodules.

The process of forming high carbon austenite during welding is more rapid where pockets of pearlite exist near the fusion line because the carbon is more finely dispersed and diffusion and dissolution occur more rapidly than if diffusion must occur from the nodules. Nonetheless, a band of high carbon austenite is formed immediately adjacent to the fusion line in the HAZ of the ductile iron that is heated above the A1 by the heat of welding. As the arc travels away from this area, the high carbon austenite is quenched and forms principally iron carbides and martensite. These constituents are gradually dissociated into iron and graphite with progressive cycles of engine operation. It is this secondary graphite formation that allows the ductile iron HAZ to be susceptible to stress accelerated oxidation.

As we described earlier, it appears that the amount and disposition of the secondary graphite particles are more damaging when the Ni-Fe-Mn weld metal is used than when the Ni-Fe-Mn-Cr-Cb wire is used.

THE WELDING WIRES: NI-ROD FILLER METALS 44 AND 44HT

Cast iron has been arc welded with nickel and nickel alloys since the early 1940's. INCO (International Nickel Co.) affiliates discovered the beneficial effect of low solubility (.02% at room temperature) for carbon in nickel in the 40's. Since gray cast iron was the most commonly used casting then, and since it had nil plastic ductility, a weld metal was needed to help prevent cracking in the HAZ due to shrinkage stresses imposed by the weld. Pure nickel was excellent for this job since dilution from the 3.5%C cast iron would eventually be rejected from the weld pool during solidification and, as graphite, would produce a volume expansion in the weld that would lower shrinkage stress. As both castings and weld metals became more sophisticated, ductile iron was invented that had much better plastic ductility than gray, and the need for lower stress welds was reduced.

Other innovations of Ni-Fe and Ni-Fe-Mn compositions were developed to meet higher strength and ductility requirements. NI-ROD filler metal 44 was the most recent that continued to use the graphite rejection principle however, the graphite formed in some welds has proven to be detrimental. As a result of this discovery and the realization that the graphite-rejection principle was no longer needed for some grades of ductile iron, Special Metals Corporation researchers developed a new idea for a welding wire. It contained sufficient carbide-forming elements that would combine with expected amounts of carbon dilution from the ductile iron to form carbides that would be stable at the high temperatures experienced by automotive exhaust systems. The phase stability was ensured through the use of Thermo-Calc software in the design phase. It was also designed to provide greatly improved oxidation resistance through the addition of 7% Cr, as evidenced in Figure 2 and Table 5. The improved stress accelerated oxidation cracking resistance and minimization of secondary graphite formation conferred on the ductile iron is shown in Figure 3.

SUMMARY

It has been shown that durable welds of high integrity can be made automatically at fast production rates between Si-Mo ductile iron and 409 stainless steel catalyst cans using NI-ROD filler metals 44 and 44HT. We have also reported that under severe dynamometer testing NI-ROD filler metal 44HT provides protection to the ductile iron against stress accelerated oxidation of the HAZ and exhibits improved oxidation resistance in the weld. Further testing has shown the welded assembly meets exhaust gas analysis standards and provides good leak rate and fuel efficiency results. Noise suppression is superior with the cast manifold versus the fabricated manifold. It would appear that this welded assembly is capable of meeting current and foreseeable future automotive and truck requirements throughout the world.

ACKNOWLEDGEMENTS

The authors would like to acknowledge the efforts of Chad Clary of Special Metals in testing and sample evaluation.

® - NI-ROD is a trademark of the Special Metals family of companies.

Table 1: Chemical Composition of the Alloys of this Study (Nominal Unless Indicated)

Alloy	C	Cr	Fe	Mn	Cb	Ni	Ti	Si	Mo
Si-Mo Ductile Cast Iron	3.45	0.03	Bal.	0.3	---	0.1	---	4	0.6
409 Stainless Steel	0.08*	11	Bal.	1*	---	---	6XC†	1*	---
18Cr-Cb Stainless Steel	0.03*	18.5	Bal.	1*	0.6	---	0.3	1*	---
NI-ROD Filler Metal 44	0.30	---	44	11	---	44	---	---	---
NI-ROD Filler Metal 44HT	0.03	7	37	11	1	44	---	---	---

*Maximum
†Minimum

Table 2: Comparison of Emissions Data for Fabricated Versus Cast Manifold on Current Model Six Cylinder Vehicle

Manifold Type	C_XH_Y (g/km)	CO (g/km)	NO_X (g/km)
Fabricated Steel	0.052	0.375	0.037
Cast Iron	0.048	0.335	0.038

Table 3: Comparison of Catalyst Efficiency Data for Fabricated Versus Cast Manifold on Current Model Six Cylinder Vehicle

Manifold Type	C_XH_Y (%)	CO (%)	NO_X (%)
Fabricated Steel	96.50	91.48	95.24
Cast Iron	96.55	92.00	95.42

Table 4: Comparison of Emissions Data for Fabricated Versus Cast Manifold on 2001 Model Vehicle

Test	C_XH_Y (g/mi.)	CO (g/mi.)	NO_X (g/mi.)
1	0.043	0.373	0.065
2	0.050	0.433	0.065
3	0.042	0.352	0.052
Steel Average	**0.045**	**0.386**	**0.061**
4	0.039	0.382	0.052
5	0.039	0.346	0.052
Cast Iron Average	**0.039**	**0.364**	**0.054**
Percent Reduction Afforded by Ductile Iron	15%	6%	12%

Table 5: Depth of Oxidation Observed at Surface of Samples Oxidation Tested at 1500°F

Test Conditions	Oxide Depth, Inches		% Reduction with NI-ROD Filler Metal 44HT
	NI-ROD Filler Metal 44	NI-ROD Filler Metal 44HT	
Static	0.0120	0.0051	58
Cyclic	0.0106	0.0067	37

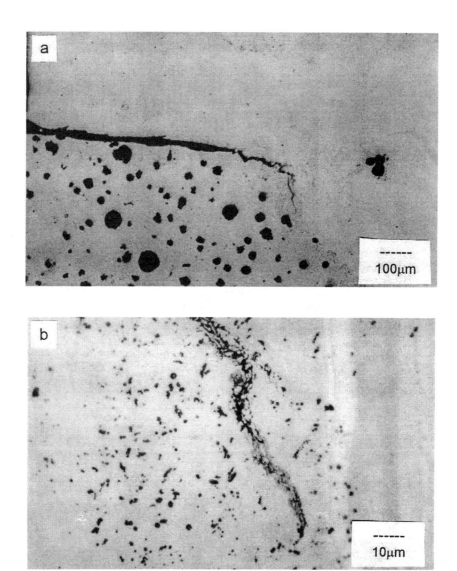

Figure 1. Photomicrographs showing Si-Mo ductile iron/NI-ROD filler metal 44 weld interface in part which joined a 409 stainless steel catalytic converter housing directly to a Si-Mo ductile iron exhaust manifold. The sample was exposed for 15-minutes in air at 870°C and rapidly cooled in ambient air. The observed crack has progressed from the toe of the weld along the heat-affected zone of the ductile iron. Photo b shows a magnified view at the tip of the crack shown in photo a. Samples were not etched.

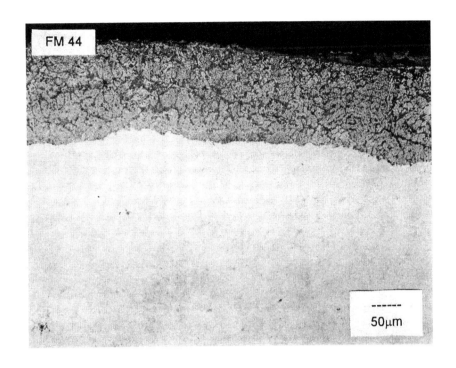

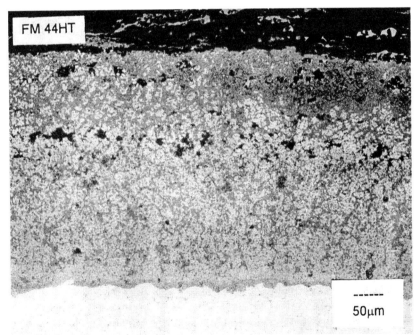

Figure 2. Photomicrographs showing surface oxide on NI-ROD filler metals 44 and 44HT weld deposits made onto Si-Mo ductile cast iron (cast iron not shown in photos), after a 100 hour isothermal exposure in air + 5% water vapor at 815°C. Samples were not etched.

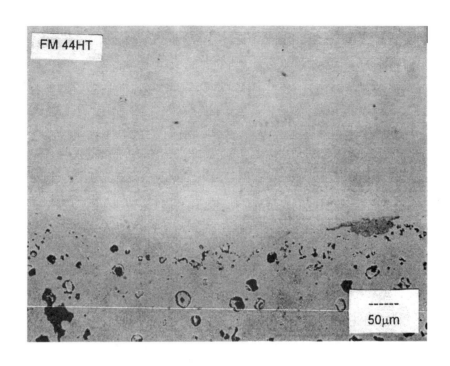

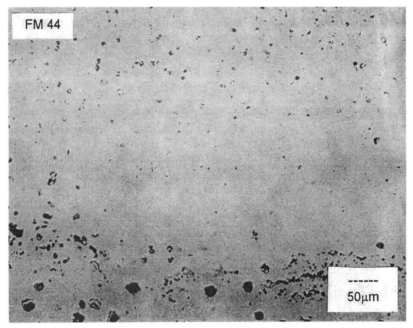

Figure 3. Photomicrographs showing the weld interface between Si-Mo ductile iron (bottom of each photo) and NI-ROD filler metals 44 and 44HT after 100 hours of cyclic exposure in air at 815°C. One cycle consisted of 15 minutes in the furnace followed by 5 minutes in ambient air. Samples were not etched.

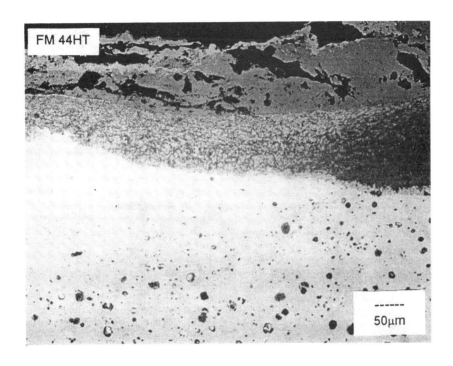

50μm

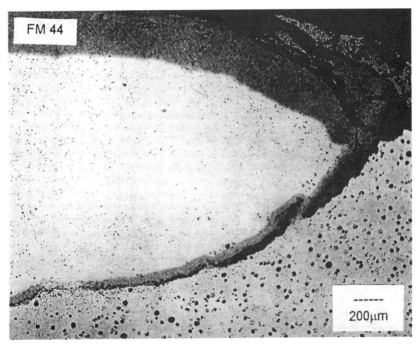

200μm

Figure 4. Photomicrographs showing the toe of weld deposits on Si-Mo ductile iron using NI-ROD filler metals 44 and 44HT, respectively, after 100 hours of cyclic exposure in air at 870°C. One cycle consisted of 15 minutes in the furnace followed by 5 minutes in ambient air. Note oxidation and cracking evident along the interface of the NI-ROD filler metal 44 weld. Samples were not etched.

Automotive Applications of Austempered Ductile Iron (ADI): A Critical Review

John R. Keoug and Kathy L. Hayrynen
Applied Process Inc., Technologies Div.

Copyright © 2000 Society of Automotive Engineers, Inc.

ABSTRACT

Austempered Ductile Iron was first commercially applied in 1972. By the mid 1970's it had found its way into Chinese Military trucks and into commercial truck applications in Europe. By 1978, austempered ductile iron had been applied to light cars and trucks in the US. Today, it is estimated that over 50,000 tons per year of austempered ductile iron components are installed in cars and trucks world-wide. That production appears to be growing at a rate of exceeding 10% per year.

As a family of materials, austempered ductile iron capably addresses the issues of weight, strength, stiffness, noise, cost and recyclability. From the first differential gear sets installed by General Motors in 1978, to light-weight truck-trailer wheel hubs, to high performance automobile suspensions, austempered ductile iron has found itself in many unique applications. This paper will review those applications, the reason(s) for the conversions, and the performance of those components.

INTRODUCTION

There have been numerous papers and works specifically related to Austempered Ductile Iron (ADI), its properties and its applications. This paper undertakes to critically review past, current and attempted automotive applications and discuss the results from a design fitness perspective. The authors begin by discussing the historical and technical background necessary for a reference basis. Then, applications, both successful and unsuccessful, are analyzed for the benefit of the reader to learn from precedent examples in the automotive industry.

HISTORY OF DUCTILE IRON / AUSTEMPERED DUCTILE IRON

The first commercial applications of Austempered Ductile Iron (ADI) occurred in 1972. However, the history of the development of ADI spans from the 1930's to the present. Pioneering heat treatment work with steel (1930's) and the discovery of ductile cast iron (1940's) are included among the important events which lead to the development of ADI.

In the 1930's, work was conducted by Bain et al on the isothermal transformation of steel. A new microconstituent was discovered that was described as "an acicular, dark etching aggregate." This new microstructure exhibited promising properties as it was found to be tougher, for the same hardness, than tempered martensite.

In the 1940's Keith Millis was assigned the task of investigating elements to substitute for chromium in the production of Ni Hard cast iron at the International Nickel Company (INCO). This investigation eventually lead to the treatment of gray cast iron with magnesium. On examination, spheroidal shaped graphite was found in this cast iron. The first magnesium treated ductile iron had been produced.

At the same time that Millis was conducting his experiments, Henton Morrogh et al were attempting to understand how to modify the shape of flake graphite in cast iron to a spheroidal form for the British Cast Iron Research Association. Morrogh presented a paper describing this work at the 1948 American Foundrymen's Society meeting. The announcement of ductile iron stated that "A cast material, possessing high strength, high elastic modulus and, in appropriate compositions, a substantial amount of ductility, has been developed." Until this time the work of Millis had been done in secrecy. A formal announcement of his work was soon made. 1948 marked the birth of ductile (spheroidal graphite) iron.

INCO patented the work of Millis and licensed the process to make ductile iron. When the patent expired in 1966, there were 651 licensees in 31 countries producing 2.1 million tons of ductile iron per year. The production of ductile iron continues to grow. By 1968, it had surpassed the production of malleable iron. In the year 2006, US shipments of ductile iron are forecasted to exceed 5 million tons per year. This would approach or possibly exceed gray iron shipment rates[1].

Although the knowledge about the austempering process had existed since the 1930's, the technology to accomplish it on an industrial scale lagged behind. It was not until the 1960's that the austempering process was widely applied to steel parts due to the improvements in the capacity and quality of commercial austempering equipment. Another decade would pass before the process was commercially applied to ductile iron.

In 1972 Tecumseh Products austempered a 0.5 kg ductile iron compressor crankshaft. In this instance, austempering was viewed to be a solution to a specific product problem. This first commercial application of ADI marked the beginning of many to follow. As of this writing, it is estimated that worldwide production of ADI is now exceeding 100,000 tons per year.

DEFINITION AND PROPERTIES OF ADI

Austempered ductile iron has a unique microstructure called ausferrite. This ausferrite microstructure sets ADI apart from as-cast ductile iron, quenched & tempered or surface hardened ductile iron. Excellent property combinations of strength, ductility, and toughness are produced from ausferrite.

The range of properties available for ADI are dependent on the choice of heat treatment parameters. In 1990 ASTM established five standard grades of ADI (ASTM 897-90 and 897M-90) which are listed in Table 1. An official European standard (EN-1564:1997) did not become available until 1997. Note Table 2.

When normal stresses are applied to an ADI part in service, a localized strain induced transformation which hardens the material can occur. As a result, ADI exhibits excellent abrasion resistance. ADI provides equivalent levels of abrasion resistance to both austempered and Q&T steels at lower hardness levels as shown in Figure 1.

The toughness of ADI is significantly better than that of conventional ductile iron. It is comparable to cast and forged steels, but the ductility of ADI can be lower.

Table 1- ASTM 897 / 897M: 1990 (USA)

THE FIVE ASTM STANDARD ADI GRADES (ASTM 897-90)

GRADE	TENSILE* STRENGTH (KSI)	YIELD* STRENGTH (KSI)	ELONGATION* (%)	IMPACT ENERGY** (FT-LBS)	TYPICAL HARDNESS (BHN)
1	125	80	10	75	269-321
2	150	100	7	60	302-363
3	175	125	4	45	341-444
4	200	155	1	25	388-477
5	230	185	N/A	N/A	444-555

*MINIMUM VALUES
**UN-NOTCHED CHARPY BARS TESTED AT 72 +/- 7F

THE FIVE ASTM STANDARD ADI GRADES (ASTM 897M-90)

GRADE	TENSILE* STRENGTH (MPa)	YIELD* STRENGTH (MPa)	ELONGATION* (%)	IMPACT ENERGY** (Joules)	TYPICAL HARDNESS (BHN)
1	850	550	10	100	269-321
2	1050	700	7	80	302-363
3	1200	850	4	60	341-444
4	1400	1100	1	35	388-477
5	1600	1300	N/A	N/A	444-555

*MINIMUM VALUES
**UN-NOTCHED CHARPY BARS TESTED AT 22 +/- 4C

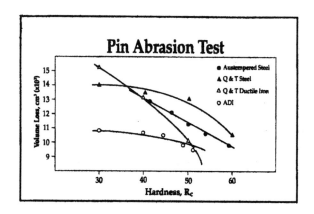

Figure 1- Relative abrasion resistance of ADI compared to other material/process combinations.

Table 2- EN 1564:1997 (Europe)

European standard for Austempered ductile cast irons.

The European standard EN 1564 :1997 "Austempered ductile cast irons" is a new standard first published in June 1997.
Before, in Europe there were no national standards available, only the USA standard ASTM A 897M-90.

Austempered ductile cast irons are spheroidal graphite cast irons which combine higher strenth and thoughness properties as the result of a special heat treatment.
This heat treatment, which is an integral part of the production process, consists of an austenitizing treatment at a temperature between 820 oC and 950 oC and an austempering treatment in the temperature range between 250 oC and 400 oC to form a predominantly austenitic-ferritic structure.
The method of manufacturing austempered ductile iron as well as its chemical composition and heat treatment, unless specified by the purchaser, shall be left to the discretion of the manufacturer.
Heat treatment parameters and chemical composition have to be chosen as a function of casting size (relevant wall thickness) and required grade.

The European standard EN 1564 defines the grades and the corresponding properties of austempered ductile irons and specifies a classification based om mechanical properties measured on machined test pieces prepared from:

- separately cast samples;
- cast-on samples;
- samples cut from a casting.

Table 1 gives the mechanical properties of austempered ductile iron for test pieces machined from separately cast samples.

Depending on the heat treatment, the Brinell hardness of this material (see table 2) is in general higher then the hardness of spheroidal graphite cast iron. The ranges of hardness for each grade reflect the effect of wall thickness.
Work hardening can cause a substantial surface hardness increase due to structural modification.

Impact resistance values measured on Charpy-notched test pieces machined from separately cast samples are given in table 3.

Mechanical properties measured on test pieces machined from separately cast samples

Material designation		Tensile strength R_m N/mm² min.	0.2% proof stress $R_{p0.2}$ N/mm² min.	Elongation A % min.
Symbol	Symbol			
EN-GJS-800-8	EN-JS1100	800	500	8
EN-GJS-1000-5	EN-JS1110	1000	700	5
EN-GJS-1200-2	EN-JS1120	1200	850	2
EN-GJS-1400-1	EN-JS1130	1400	1100	1

NOTE 1: The values for these materials apply to castings cast in sand moulds of comparable thermal diffusivity. Subject to amendments to be agreed upon in the order, they can apply to castings obtained by alternative methods.

NOTE 2: Whatever the method used for obtaining the castings, the grades are based on the mechanical properties measured on test pieces taken from samples separately cast in a sand mould or a mould of comparable thermal diffusivity.

NOTE 3: 1N/mm2 is equivalent to 1 Mpa.

NOTE 4: The material designation is in accordance with EN 1560

Hardness range

Material designation		Brinell hardness range HB
Symbol	Number	
EN-GJS-800-8	EN-JS1100	260 to 320
EN-GJS-1000-5	EN-JS1110	300 to 360
EN-GJS-1200-2	EN-JS1120	340 to 440
EN-GJS-1400-1	EN-JS1130	380 to 480

NOTE: the material designation is in accordance with EN 1560

Impact resistance values

Material designation		Minimum impact resistance values at room temperature (23 + 5) oC	
Symbol	Number	mean value of 3 tests	individual value
EN-GJS-800-8-RT	EN-JS1109	10	9

NOTE: the material designation is in accordance with EN 1560

The fatigue strength of ADI is equal to or greater than that of forged steel. ADI responds favorably to shot peening which can further increase the fatigue strength. It should be noted that ADI does not exhibit a true endurance limit for high cycle fatigue applications.

In the high cycle range, a slight drop-off occurs; however, this can be accommodated for in early design stages. In fact, ADI's fatigue curve is significantly higher and flatter than that of aluminum in the low load / high cycle region.

A component weight reduction of 10% can be realized by using ADI in place of a steel forging. Figure 2 shows the relative *weight per unit of yield strength* for a variety of materials. (For this analysis forged steel has been normalized to 1.)

Figure 2- Comparative weight per unit of yield strength.

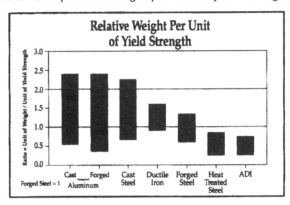

If weight per unit of yield strength is considered, ADI performs remarkably well. It is interesting to note that aluminum, which is perceived as a lightweight engineering material, is unable to match the weight per unit of yield strength of ADI in most instances.

Relative *cost per unit of yield strength* for aluminum, steel, ductile iron and ADI are given in Figure 3. (Ratios are based on steel forgings normalized to 1.) In most instances, ADI is the best buy per unit of yield strength.

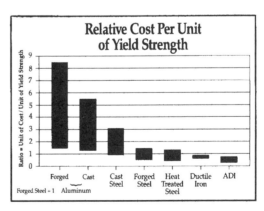

Figure 3- Comparative cost per unit of yield strength.

THE IMPLEMENTATION OF ADI IN AUTOMOTIVE APPLICATIONS

After the ground breaking application of ADI to compressor crankshafts by Tecumseh products in 1972, a flurry of engineering activity was undertaken. In those early years the process was not well quantified and ADI was met with only mixed success. However, in a project originally started in the 1960's, GM was methodically developing an ADI gear program. After a decade of design development, prototyping and testing, in 1977 GM released a hypoid ring and pinion gear set (Figure 4) in ADI for installation in all mid-sized vehicles produced at the Pontiac Motors complex in Pontiac, Michigan. This gear set ran successfully with no known warranty failures until rear wheel drive vehicle production ceased at Pontiac.

Figure 4- GM ADI hypoid differential gear set

The Pontiac process was unique and home-grown. It utilized a conventional high volume pusher-type furnace with a hot oil quench. The oil was limited in temperature to 243°C (470°F) so the resultant material matrix was a hybrid of austempered (ausferritic) and quenched and tempered (martensitic) structures. The 47Rc hardness gears performed as well as the 60Rc carburized and hardened gears that they replaced on durability tests for the load ranges used on the subject vehicles. In addition, the austempered gears could be quenched free standing, thus eliminating the need for expensive quench pressing. Additional savings were achieved in improved machinability of ductile iron as compared to forged 8620 steel. They were documented by Lottridge and Grindahl at GM[2] as follows:

Operation	Improvement
Pinion Blanking	
Center Press	30%
Drill	35%
Rough Lathes	70%
Finish Lathes	50%
Grind	20%
Ring Gear Bearing	
Bullard Turning	200%
Drilling	20%
Reaming	20%
Gleason Machining	
Rough Pinion	900%
Finishing Pinion	233%
Roughing Ring	962%
Finishing Ring	100%

It is important to note that these ADI gears were processed with the same equipment and used the same routing as the precedent steel gears. The press quenching was the only operation eliminated by switching to ADI.

These gears exhibited the ability to withstand contact loads at ten million cycles of over 1,680MPa (240 ksi). Today, with higher austempering temperatures and longer austempering times we can improve these allowable loads by at least 10%. However, in many current automotive applications even these contact strengths are acceptable.

When GM shifted from rear wheel drive to front wheel drive in 1980 the ADI ring and pinion gears were a casualty. But by 1979, the GM engineers had found another use for their Pontiac austempering operation. They began producing inboard constant velocity joints (Figure 5) for four wheel drive light trucks from ADI.

Figure 5- The original GM ADI inboard constant velocity joint.

162

These "tripot housings", as they are called, have today been re-engineered to reduce weight, (Figure 6), and are still produced by Delphi (Saginaw, Michigan) at a rate of over 8,000 per day.

Figure 6- GM's ADI constant velocity joint has been re-engineered to reduce weight for today's production.

They are cast in ferritic ductile iron at a nominal 150 BHN hardness, machined complete, austempered to about 450 BHN, cleaned and, (in some cases), seal ground and installed. Over the years these components have found their way into GM, Dodge, Jeep and Audi vehicles.

Meanwhile, in Europe, the Jot Companies had begun coordinating ADI developments for truck applications. By working with Oy Sis-Auto Ab (Finland), they developed a differential spider (Figure 7) that replaced carburized steel. Meehanite Metal Corp.[3] indicated that the manufacturing process was cut from ten steps to two. In-service testing of these components showed a measurable decrease in wear due to the improved sliding properties of ADI-to-steel as compared to steel-to-steel.

Figure 7- ADI differential cross (spider)

Jot also reported that ADI used in annular gears (Figure 8) yielded a peculiar benefit in addition to lower manufacturing cost. With its modulus of elasticity approximately 20% lower than that of steel, ADI showed a 5% lower contact stress for the same input torque due to the "conforming" of the ADI gear teeth. With their 10% graphite matrix, the ADI annular gears also ran quieter than the conventional gears. (Chrysler Corporation later produced millions of Austempered Malleable Iron (AMI) annular gears for the automatic transmissions in their popular mini-vans).

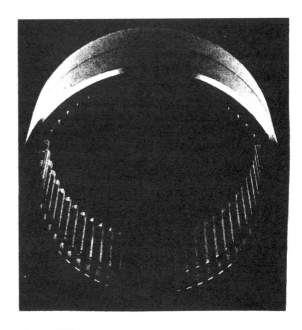

Figure 8- An ADI annular gear.

Further applications applied in Europe as early as the late 1970's included suspension spring seats and support brackets for Saab-Scania trucks. This technology has since been adopted for spring, torsion bar and engine brackets by other European truck manufacturers such as Iveco, Volvo and Daimler-Benz. (Figure 9). In fact today, the heavy truck and trailer industry world-wide uses ADI for hundreds of bracketry applications.

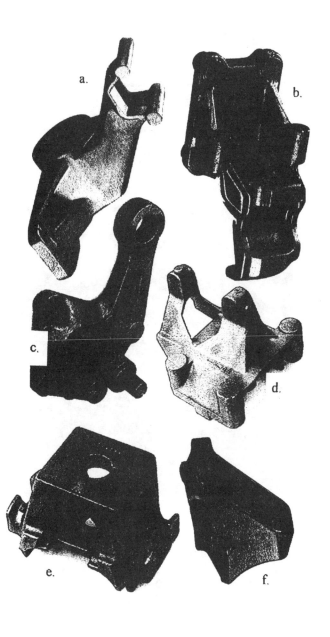

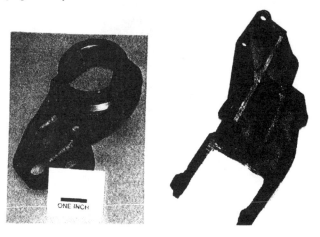

Figure 10 - a) Ford / Mazda engine bracket, b) Ford Taurus SHO engine bracket.

pitting. This camshaft was employed for the production life of the L-4 engine.

Soon ADI production in North America began to outstrip production in Europe and Asia combined. North American auto producers were no exception, employing ADI for engine brackets at GM, Ford and Mazda. (Figure 10).

By 1984 Cummins had employed ADI timing gears in its series B and C diesel engines (Figure 11). These gears, produced by Getrag, were produced using virtually the same process devised by GM for the hypoid ring and pinion gear sets in 1977. Although the process has gone through some modifications, Cummins is still a volume user of ADI timing gears for its diesel engines.

Figure 9- European applications of ADI in truck suspensions: a) rear axle swing bracket, b) torsion bar bracket, c) mounting bracket, d) torsion bar bracket, e) spring bracket, f) spring seat.

In the 1980's GM first applied ADI for an engine component. They chose the camshaft for the L-4 engine. This camshaft was produced for GM by Intermet Corporation and exceeded the requirement of 250ksi (1,750 MPa) contact stress at ten million cycles with no

Figure 11-ADI timing gear for a Cummins diesel engine.

In addition to the ADI timing gears, Cummins found another practical use for ADI in its engines. Shell cast, ADI injector clamps (Figure 12) turned out to be a weight and cost savings for the Cummins engine designers.

Figure 12- ADI diesel injector clamps for Cummins.

From its commercial birth in 1972, ADI had grown most quickly in the non-automotive sectors. Companies like International Harvister (now Navistar and Case), John Deere, Caterpillar and others had pushed the technology. In the middle to late 1980's with the understanding of ADI growing and commercial capacity for its production increasing, the pace quickened in the automotive sector. Trac-Tech found ADI to be the perfect component material for their popular Detroit Locker differential (Figure 13).

Figure 13- ADI differential case covers.

Aftermarket suppliers like Trailmaster began to offer ADI suspension lift kits for heavy duty off-road, four wheel drive trucks (Figure 14).

In the 1980's, Ford had successfully developed a high performance ADI crankshaft. (Figure 15). In fact, during the development of the ADI crank at Ford, as Bela Kovacs, the development engineer then at Ford commented, "the only thing we failed to do was to fail an ADI crankshaft". Unfortunately, the much awaited Thunderbird Super Coupe was coming in behind schedule and over budget so the ADI crank was dropped

in favor of a "known quantity"; an imported steel forging. Since that time, GM, Ford, Chrysler, Nissan and Toyota have all developed race-tested ADI crankshafts, but NONE are in production.

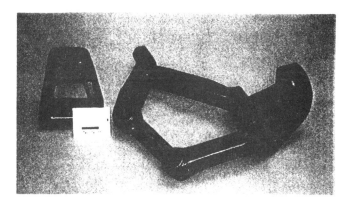

Figure 14- ADI aftermarket suspension lift kits.

Figure 15- Ford's ADI V-6 crankshaft

By the mid-1990's the Motor Industry Research Association (MIRA) had completed work on an ADI crankshaft development program[4]. That program produced the proper material, process and design characteristics necessary for a successful ADI crankshaft implementation except for one tiny detail. The coefficient of thermal expansion for ADI is about 20% greater than that of conventional ductile iron or steel. Therefore, when the ADI crank was put on test, once it heated to operating temperature it grew until there was negative oil clearance in the bearing areas and the engine seized. Unaware of this phenomenon, the MIRA work ended with no explanation for this failure. As of this writing, a new MIRA work is under consideration to resolve that mystery and prove out the design.

Today, to the knowledge of the authors, only tiny TVR Ltd., a sports car manufacturer in West Midlands, England is producing production automobiles with ADI crankshafts. These ADI cranks are used in their production V-8 and are being tested in their in-line six cylinder engines with good results.

By the 1990's Navistar, Freightliner, Kenworth, GM, Iveco, Volvo and other heavy truck manufacturers had adopted ADI as a high performance, low cost material for spring hanger brackets and u-bolt brackets, (Figure 16), accessory brackets, and shock absorber brackets (Figure 17). North American as well as various European suppliers, had adopted ADI for brake spiders (Figure 18), steering knuckles (Figure 19) and steering arms (Figure 20). Kenworth chose ADI for the heavy duty sway bar bushing shown in (Figure 21). Note that this part is machined completely before austempering and includes a precision spline and Acme threaded ID.

Figure 16- ADI truck spring bracket (top), spring stop (left) and u-bolt plates (middle,right).

Figure 17- ADI truck shock absorber brackets.

As outlined previously, ADI is not *always* the choice in the high stakes, competitive manufacturing world. When Ford contracted with Simpson Industries to produce a light-weight, low cost, one-piece knuckle/spindle (Figure 22) for one of its North American vehicles, ADI seemed to be the clear choice. The ADI spindle was about 10% lighter than its micro-alloyed, forged steel counterpart. The ADI

outperformed the steel in cold weather impact, yield strength and fatigue strength. The as-cast ductile iron machined much more readily than the micro-alloyed forging steel. However, the non-symmetrical nature of the part resulted in an unacceptable level of dimensional variation after austemper heat treatment. Before the dimensional variations could be resolved, the German forging producer reduced the price of the forging by something in excess of 20%, effectively killing any further development on that product. That product is, today, made from micro-alloyed forged steel.

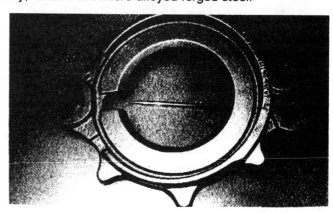

Figure 18- ADI truck brake spider.

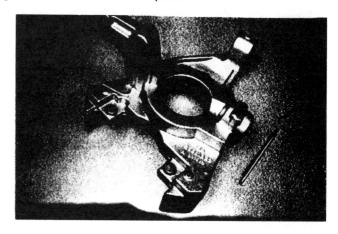

Figure 19- ADI truck steering knuckle.

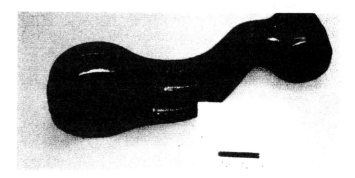

Figure 20- ADI truck steering arm.

Figure 21- ADI truck suspension sway bar bushing.

Figure 22- One piece ADI wheel spindle/knuckle.

Similarly, Caterpillar, a major user of ADI, attempted to produce ADI rocker arms for its diesel truck engines. The engine design was an existing design, thus the "envelope" for the part was prescribed. On paper the ADI should have been a good material in this application. However, fatigue testing proved otherwise. It so happened that at the common operating range of 2,000 to 3,000 rpms, the ADI, with its lower Young's Modulus, reached its natural frequency and failed in resonance. In a "clean sheet" design the engineer would have been able to address this issue by changing the section modulus. However, in this existing design that change was not possible, thus precluding the use of ADI as a cost effective alternative. Examples such as these are all illustrative of the issues that design engineers face when changing to new materials such as ADI.

The dynamic grades of ADI are more than three times stronger than the strongest grades of forged or cast aluminum. Furthermore, ADI's density is only 2.5 times that of aluminum and its stiffness is 2.3 times that of aluminum. Therefore, the opportunity exists for a properly designed ADI part to replace an aluminum part at an equal or lesser weight. With aluminum, on average costing roughly two to three times more per unit weight than ADI, the cost savings potential becomes

rather inviting. Of late, design engineers have begun to exploit that cost per unit of strength advantage.

Walther EMC a small, US manufacturing company, produces a product that they call the Duralite Wheel Hub (Figure 23). This hub, utilized on light weight truck trailers, is an ADI hub that is 2% lighter than its aluminum counterpart and costs roughly 30% less.

Figure 23- Lightweight ADI truck trailer wheel hub.

A major North American truck components manufacturer needed a tough, low cost material for a clutch collar and differential case to engage and disengage all wheel drive on heavy trucks. Two materials were tried. The first, a fully machined, carburized and hardened 8620 steel forging failed on a "dead skid", full load test. An ADI set with as-cast teeth (Figure 24) passed the test and is in production today as a "substantial" cost savings.

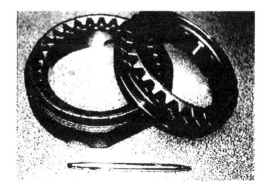

Figure 24- ADI truck differential case and clutch collar.

When GM switched to hydro-formed rails on their new light truck models, they created a need for a new design of tow hook. The precedent hook had been constructed of bent square steel wire. A new ADI design (Figure 25) allowed the engineers to slide the hook between the frame rails for attachment without the need for a second bracket. The ADI hooks passed all pull and crash testing requirements and are now in production.

Figure 25- ADI tow hooks for trucks and sport utility vehicles.

Truck and trailer engineers have aggressively employed ADI in their designs. Pintle hooks for multiple trailer truck rigs (Figure 26) have performed without failure for nearly ten years. ADI consumer trailer products like the load leveling hitch component shown in Figure 27 have proven to be safe, light-weight and cost effective.

Figure 26- ADI truck trailer pintle hook.

Figure 27- ADI load leveling hitch components

The "lost foam" casting technique is being used to produce the large, complex ADI truck suspension bracket shown in Figure 28. The shell casting process is being used to produce the ADI trailer jack stand gears with as-cast teeth shown in Figure 29.

Figure 28- A complex ADI Truck suspension bracket made using the "lost foam" casting process.

Figure 29- ADI truck trailer landing gears with "as-cast" teeth, made by the shell casting process.

A. T. systèmes, (France), did a direct comparison between aluminum and ADI for a next generation automotive engine bracket (Figure 30). The aluminum design was ultimately 10% lighter than the ADI design, but the cost and the acoustical performance of the ADI part made it the best selection in this application.

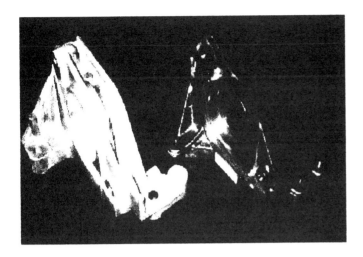

Figure 30- This ADI engine bracket for a next generation European passenger car proved to be the economical choice over aluminum.

Finally, in the area of passenger car suspensions, GM demonstrated the feasibility of using ADI suspension control arms (Figure 31) by successfully installing them on Cadillac Limousines since 1995. Recently, however, Bentler was contracted by Ford to produce a light-weight, cost effective, independent suspension system for its high performance Mustang Cobra sports car. ADI was chosen for the upper control arms (Figure 32) for its combination of low weight (approximately 3 kg finished), noise damping and low manufacturing cost.

Figure 31- ADI suspension control arms for Cadillac limousines.

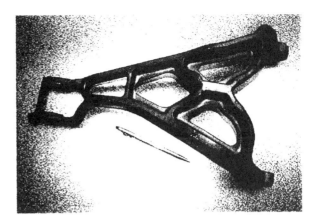

Figure 32- Lightweight ADI upper suspension control arms for the Ford Mustang Cobra.

SUMMARY

Like any material, ADI is not the answer for every difficult design. However, ADI offers the design engineer an intriguing new alternative to conventional materials.

The higher strength grades of ADI compete with carburized and hardened steels for wear resistance, while exhibiting better noise damping capabilities and a generally lower manufacturing cost.

The lower strength, "dynamic" grades of ADI compete favorably with forged steel as a cost and weight savings, although its lower stiffness needs to be addressed in the initial design phase.

Replacing aluminum with cast iron at equal weight is truly a new paradigm. As casting technology continues to improve, the range of applications for high strength, light weight ADI castings will increase.

Cast ADI components with three millimeter walls can compete at equal unit weight with aluminum sand and die castings, aluminum forgings and normalized and heat treated steel stampings, forgings and castings. Three millimeter wall, high integrity castings produced at automotive volumes represent the "next frontier" being explored by the casting industry.

In some automotive circles, cast iron has been "given up for dead". Meanwhile the average amount of ductile iron per vehicle is increasing and ADI is being found in new applications throughout the car and truck industry each year each year. Its high strength to weight ratio, low cost per unit of strength and 100% recyclability make this material difficult to ignore.

ACKNOWLEDGMENTS

The authors would like to gratefully acknowledge the contributions of the staffs of Applied Process Inc., AP Westshore Inc. and AP Southridge Inc. and our licensees ADI Engineering, Process and Heat Treatment Pty. Ltd, (Australia) and ADI Treatments (United Kingdom). We would like to thank Simon Day and Dr. Arron Rimmer for their assistance. Finally, we would like to thank all of the manufacturers who have contributed examples and information, but especially, Citation Corp., Waupaca Foundry, General Motors, Jot Components, Zanardi Fonderie De Globe, Intermet, Urick Foundry, Rio Tinto, Meritor, Vogel, Delphi, Navistar, Freightliner, Wells Manufacturing, Cummins, Getrag, Walther EMC, Ford, Volvo, Iveco, PSA and Daimler Chrysler.

Additionally, we would like to recognize the pioneering work, friendships and mentoring of Keith Millis, Dick Flinn, Bela Kovacs, Karl Rundman and Bob Keough.

Special thanks to Jerry Wurtsmith for his help in scanning the images and formatting this paper.

REFERENCES

1. Loper, C.R., "Ductile Iron - A Golden Anniversary," 1998 Keith Millis Symposium on Ductile Iron, Hilton Head, S.C., 1998, pp. 4-15.

2. Lottridge, N.M., Grindahl, R.B., "Nodular Iron Hypoid Gears," SAE 820696, SAE Fatigue Conference & Exposition, Dearborn, Michigan, USA 1982.

3. "Meehanite ADI- Guidelines for Designing and Machining Meehanite Austempered Ductile Iron Castings", Meehanite Metal Corporation publication B88/4/88.

4. Chatterley, T.C., Murrell, P., "ADI Crankshafts-An Appraisal of Their Production Potential", SAE 980686, SAE International Congress & Exposition, Detroit, Michigan, USA February 1998.

ADDITIONAL RESOURCES

+ "Ductile Iron Data for Design Engineers", Rio Tinto Iron and Titanium, revised 1998.

+ASTM 897(M) Austempered Ductile Iron Specification, 1990

+www.ductile.org, The Ductile Iron Society

CHASSIS APPLICATIONS FOR CAST COMPONENTS

Austempered Ductile Iron Castings for Chassis Applications

Robert J. Warrick, Paul Althoff, Alan P. Druschitz, Jeffrey P. Lemke and Kevin Zimmerman
Intermet Corporation

P. H. Mani
Research Consultant, Ductile Iron Society

Mitchell L. Rackers
Caterpillar Corporation

Copyright © 2000 Society of Automotive Engineers, Inc.

ABSTRACT

Austempered ductile iron (ADI) castings provide a unique combination of high strength and toughness coupled with excellent design flexibility for chassis applications.

This paper describes the development of the upper control arm for the 1999 Ford Mustang Cobra as an austempered ductile iron casting. The full service development process used is described from initial design through finite element analysis (FEA), design verification, casting production, heat treatment, nondestructive evaluation and machining. To achieve significant weight savings, an austempered ductile iron casting was chosen for this application instead of an as-cast SAE J434[1], Grade D4512 ductile iron casting or a steel forging.

This is believed to be the first application of an austempered ductile iron casting for a safety critical, automotive chassis application.

INTRODUCTION

For the 1999 Ford Mustang Cobra, the initial material candidates for the upper control arm (UCA) of the independent rear suspension (IRS) were an aluminum casting and a steel forging. A major challenge associated with the IRS Mustang was packaging the suspension within the existing body. The tight packaging requirements, which limited the cross section size, coupled with the load carrying requirements resulted in the elimination of aluminum as a material candidate. The packaging requirements also led to the demise of the steel forging. The available envelope required a relatively intricate part shape to satisfy the conflicting criteria of load carrying and weight requirements and clearance needs. The shape requirements clearly favored a casting over a forging.

Ford approached the Intermet Wagner Foundry regarding the design and production of an austempered ductile iron (ADI) upper control arm. After reviewing initial packaging and strength requirements and a number of ADI concerns (primarily cost related), the challenge was accepted.

The subsequent development of the 1999 Ford Mustang UCA as an austempered ductile iron casting is described in this paper. The full service development process used is described from initial design through machining. The selection of an ADI casting, instead of an SAE J434[1] D4512 ductile iron casting or a steel forging, was found to be highly beneficial by permitting significant component weight savings.

The use of ADI castings in vehicle applications has been remarkably slow as a result of reports of process inconsistency, from both a foundry and heat treating standpoint; machinability concerns; and cost unknowns (largely based on lack of production experience for automotive type volumes). For this program, responsibility for the ADI part from design through delivery of the assembled upper control arm was placed with a single supplier, greatly simplifying the development process. The results of this program demonstrate that austempered ductile iron castings can be successfully used for safety critical, automotive chassis applications.

SELECTION OF ADI FOR CHASSIS APPLICATIONS

Prime requirements for the upper control arm for the Mustang Cobra rear suspension were light weight coupled with strength and toughness.

One obvious reason for looking at a ductile iron component versus a steel design is that, because of the volume of graphite nodules present, a ductile iron casting will weigh approximately 10% less than a steel forging if both have exactly the same shape. In addition, the ductile iron casting will provide greater shape flexibility, as the result of reduced draft angle requirements and the ability to cast in features through the use of cores.

The geometric flexibility of a casting is too often understated. Beyond satisfying difficult clearance needs, one is often able to incorporate a number of intricate structural design elements (ribs, webbing, and windows) to maximize the amount of material in structural regions and reduce the amount of material in less structural regions.

DUCTILE & AUSTEMPERED DUCTILE IRON

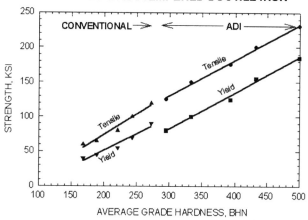

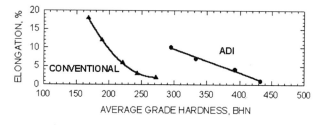

Figure 1. Minimum properties of conventional and austempered ductile irons as a function of the average hardness for each grade.

The density and design flexibility advantages would not be sufficient, particularly for light weight designs, if the material strength and toughness were inadequate. This is where the unique physical properties of austempered ductile iron come into the picture. While conventional ductile iron grades have long been used successfully for automotive safety components such as steering knuckles, lower control arms, brake calipers and

anchors, the high strength and toughness of austempered ductile iron offers even greater potential for weight reduced designs.

The relationships between hardness and yield strength, tensile strength, and elongation for conventional and austempered ductile are illustrated in Figure 1. In this figure, specification[1,2,3] minimum values of yield strength, tensile strength, and elongation are plotted against typical average grade hardness. As expected, for both conventional and austempered ductile irons, yield and tensile strength increase and elongation decreases, with increasing hardness. Of particular interest are two key factors for austempered ductile iron:

1. The magnitude of the yield strength of ADI starts approximately where the strength of the conventional ductile iron grades leaves off.

2. The elongation of the softest ADI grade is much higher than that of the harder and stronger conventional ductile iron grades.

The softest of the austempered ductile iron grades is the one normally considered for chassis applications as a result of its excellent strength and toughness. In addition to yield and tensile strength, the fatigue strength of ADI is much higher than that of the conventional ductile iron grades normally used for chassis applications. This is illustrated in Table 1. The endurance limit of a Grade 1 ADI is approximately twice as great as that of a conventional D4512 grade of ductile iron. Further, the fatigue strength of ADI can be greatly increased by mechanical working of the surface layers of the material through such processes as fillet rolling or shot peening. The major strengthening effect of fillet rolling is illustrated through the data in Table 1. The minimum specified unnotched Charpy impact strength for an ASTM 897 Grade 1 ADI is 100 Joules at 22°C +/- 4°C (75 foot-pounds force at 72°F +/- 7°F). Austempered ductile irons provide a unique combination of strength and toughness in a readily cast material.

Table 1
Approximate Endurance Limit Values for Ductile and Austempered Ductile Irons

Material	Hardness, Brinell	Endurance Limit, MPa(psi)
Ductile Iron	156	207 (30,000)
Ductile Iron	187	228 (33,000)
Ductile Iron	261	310 (45,000)
Ductile Iron, Fillet Rolled (Production)	187	317 (46,000)
Ductile Iron, Fillet Rolled (Lab)	187	372 (54,000)
ADI	302	414 (60,000)
ADI, Fillet Rolled (Crankshaft)	302	1,000 (145,000)

Based on properties, ADI should be widely used and, in fact, the rate of use is now increasing quite rapidly; primarily in lower volume non-automotive applications. However, the lack of positive production experience with

ADI in higher volume automotive applications has limited the acceptance of this material by the automotive industry. There are three major concerns:

1. Machinability. The lack of volume experience is a major factor. Best tools and tooling conditions are not well known. As a result, people have tended to shy away from the material because of cost and production rate unknowns.

2. Process Inconsistency Reports. Particularly early in ADI's history, there were a number of reports of material inconsistencies over time; for example, one lot machines fine and the next lot is almost impossible to machine.

3. Costs. ADI is produced by casting heat treatment, as will be discussed in more detail later in this report. Also, added alloy is typically required to insure that undesirable microstructure constituents don't develop during the quench from the austenitizing temperature to the austempering temperature. Both factors increase piece cost relative to conventional, non-heat treated ductile iron castings. However, the largest cost issue probably relates to uncertainty about machining, scrap, and process control costs.

Development work[6] has shown that ADI is quite machinable, can be produced consistently by a good, knowledgeable foundry and heat treater, and that costs are predictable.

THE APPLICATION

For 1999, Ford introduced a modular, independent rear suspension, initially available only on the limited-edition Special Vehicle Team (SVT) Cobra, to provide superior performance and handling relative to earlier versions. This new independent rear suspension features a wishbone-type, short and long arm suspension design. It is a self contained, bolt-in rear end that has been discussed in a number of recent articles[4,5]. It is built by Benteler Automotive and is illustrated in Figure 2.

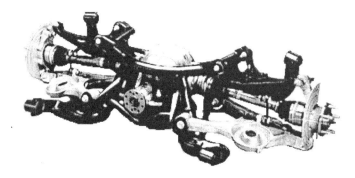

Figure 2. Photograph of the independent rear suspension for the 1999 Ford Mustang Cobra.

Adding an IRS would be expected to bring a relatively high weight penalty. This anticipation, along with the projected increase in vehicle performance, were the major driving forces for Ford SVT engineers in their quest for tough, high strength, light weight components, including the upper control arms.

The challenge was to design a minimum weight part that could be reliably produced under routine production conditions using a relatively untried material under volume production conditions. While Intermet had previously produced over 500,000 selectively austempered automotive camshafts and over a million austempered compressor crankshafts, this was the company's first production ADI venture for an automotive safety part.

THE APPROACH

Key advantages from the start of this program were the solid support of Ford SVT engineers and having full responsibility for the upper control arm from design through delivery of the assembled upper control arm. It's far easier to control product consistency when one has total responsibility for the design and all aspects of production of the component.

A team was brought together to handle various aspects of the program from component design through component delivery. All design, casting production, and the majority of the materials evaluation work were done internally at Intermet. Much of the component testing work was done at Defiance while Ford and Benteler handled module and vehicle testing. Applied Process, Inc was selected as the heat treat source for this program since there was not sufficient internal austempering capacity. Climate Control, Inc. an excellent and progressive machining source near the producing foundry in Decatur, Illinois was selected as the machining source. They worked closely with Wagner Foundry personnel to develop the machining strategy for the ADI upper control arm. This close interaction between designers, producing foundry, and machining source was highly beneficial.

It was this team, working together, that made the ADI Mustang upper control arm program a success.

COMPONENT DESIGN

The design information initially provided by Ford included wireframe and surface information for a cast design, which was the final iteration of earlier forged steel designs, and the initial load cases based on ADAMS results. Starting with this information, the designers went through four design phases.

Phase 1. This design is shown in Figure 3. It is essentially the last forging design modified to be an austempered ductile iron casting. While approximately 10% weight savings can be achieved simply by substitution of ductile iron for steel, this phase was necessitated by test casting timing requirements rather than by weight reduction goals. It also provided a starting point for analyses and design improvements. The Phase 1 casting met strength objectives but, as expected, was too heavy. The unmachined Phase 1 casting weight was 11.43 pounds.

Figure 3. Two views of the Phase 1 design.

Phase 2. The Phase 2 design, illustrated in Figure 4, is basically a weight reduced version of the Phase 1 design. While the casting weight was reduced by 1.4 pounds, the casting had insufficient strength. It weighed 9.94 pounds.

Phases 1 and 2 were workhorse phases. After these, the loading requirements were revised and additional clearance issues were identified which further restricted the design envelope. The upper control arm now needed to carry additional load with less section.

Figure 4. Two views of the Phase 2 design.

Phase 3. As a result of the increased loading requirements and the unsatisfactory overall strength-to-weight relationship for the Phase 2 design, a new shape approach was taken for Phase 3, as illustrated in Figure 5. Considerable enhancements were made to provide a more rigid structure with better overall stress distribution. (Note the webbing between the forward and aft legs and the somewhat parabolic shape approaches that of an ideal I-Beam or C-Channel with uniform stress distribution.) This design met the new component strength requirements while providing significantly reduced weight. Preliminary design verification studies were performed on the Phase 3 design with satisfactory results. At this point a final design was close but a few changes were deemed desirable to aid manufacturability and additional weight reduction opportunities were identified. The Phase 3 casting weighed 8.91 pounds.

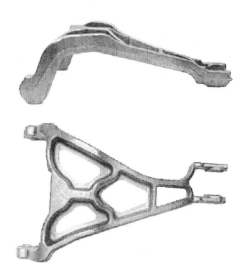

Figure 5. Two views of the Phase 3 design.

Phase 4. During Phase 3 prototype production, a despruing (gating and risering system removal) problem was identified that frequently caused excessive casting distortion. For the Phase 4 design, which is shown in Figure 6, a tie bar was added to prevent this problem. In addition, clamp pads were added at the ball joint end to provide greater part rigidity during machining. With these modifications for manufacturability, the design was ready for final verification and subsequent production verification studies. The Phase 4 casting weight is 8.53 pounds.

Initial design work was done using PDGS for the concept work, ARIES for pre- and post-processing, and NASTRAN for all finite element analysis work. At present, CATIA, UNIGRAPHICS, and SDRC are used internally for most design work along with PATRAN/NASTRAN for FEA analyses and MAGMA for casting process simulation studies.

176

Figure 6. Two views of the Phase 4 design.

DESIGN VALIDATION

Design verification responsibilities were split between Ford, Benteler, and Intermet. Ford and Benteler conducted all module and vehicle tests. Ford also handled the simulated vehicle durability and load vs. deflection tests. The latter were conducted to determine any possible interference between the upper control arm assembly and attaching components under maximum road load conditions. Intermet was responsible for the finite element analysis studies as well as all material tests, salt spray tests, component fatigue, cold impact, and spike stop tests, component tensile and compression tests, and bushing push-in and push-out tests. A number of the latter tests were performed at Defiance - STS. All design validation tests were passed satisfactorily. Ongoing In-Process tests for component fatigue, component ultimate tension, and bushing push-in and push-out are the responsibility of Intermet.

The design of the independent rear suspension is such that other components will fail before the upper control arm. The ability of the lightweight ADI upper control arm to readily pass 100,000 cycles at 115% of the peak one-event load is a testament to the design potential of ADI for chassis applications.

CASTING PRODUCTION

Molds for the Ford Mustang upper control arm castings are made on a DISA 2013 MK5 B machine. No cores are required. The ductile base iron for the castings is melted in coreless induction furnaces and magnesium treated using the Fischer converter process. Internally developed inoculation practices are used along with a pressure pour furnace for final metal treatment and pouring.

Keys to successful ADI production include excellent metal chemistry and inoculation control at the foundry. The amount of carbon in austenite at the time of the quench into molten salt has a significant effect on the properties developed in the austempered ductile iron. The carbon content of this austenite is controlled by both metal chemistry and austenitizing temperature. Since the castings will be heat treated in lots, consistent chemistry control within each lot is essential for consistent ADI characteristics. Also, lot-to-lot chemistry consistency is important to minimize the heat treat temperature adjustments that have to be made between lots. The effectiveness and consistency of the internally developed inoculation practice, coupled with the pouring temperature control resulting from pressure pouring, help produce castings with a consistent, relatively high nodule count. This reduces alloy segregation and thus improves microstructure homogeneity.

As a result of the intentional lack of heavy sections in the final upper control arm design, relatively little alloy is required to avoid the formation of any pearlite during the austempering quench operation. While some copper is added, additions of expensive alloy elements like nickel and/or molybdenum are not necessary.

Inspection operations following casting cleaning include x-ray audits for casting integrity and 100% ultrasonic velocity inspection for nodularity.

CASTING HEAT TREATMENT

A typical austempering heat treatment cycle is illustrated schematically in Figure 7. The casting is heated to a temperature, typically in the 870 to 900° C (1600 to 1650°F) range, and held at least long enough to be uniformly at temperature. This can be done in molten salt or in an atmosphere furnace. The latter, with an endothermic gas atmosphere, is used for the upper control arm. The part is next quenched in molten salt and held in the salt bath at a temperature, typically in the 260 to 371°C (500 to 700°F) range, for a time generally in the 1.5 to 2 hour range. The actual temperature is dependent on the casting properties desired. Lower temperatures give higher hardness and strength. Higher temperatures yield higher toughness and machinability. For the upper control arm, approximately 377 °C (710 °F) is used.

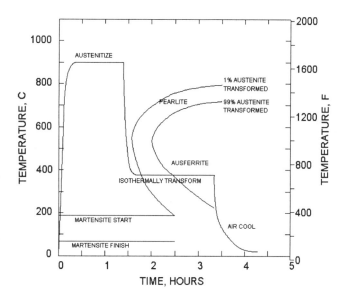

Figure 7. Schematic austempering heat treatment cycle.

Table 2
Comparison of Specification and Average ADI UCA Mechanical Properties

Property	Specification (ASTM A897/897M)	Average ADI UCA
Hardness, Brinell	269-321	301
Tensile Strength, MPa (psi)	850 min. (125,000 min.)	1,049 (152,100)
Yield Strength, MPa (psi)	550 min. (80,000 min.)	798 (115,700)
Elongation, %	10 min.	13.8
Impact Strength, Joules (ft-lbs)	100 min. (75 min.)	179 (132)

Since the optimum heat treat temperatures and times are chemistry dependent, relevant casting chemistry information is supplied to the heat treater along with the castings. However, casting chemistries are typically held tightly enough that heat treat cycle adjustments are not necessary.

AUSTEMPERED CASTING MATERIAL PROPERTIES

The bulk material properties of the casting are fully established after austempering. The surface properties can be further enhanced through subsequent operations such as shot peening or fillet rolling.

Average properties for test and production lots of castings cast over a twelve-month period are shown in Table 2. With excellent toughness, the yield and tensile strengths of the ADI are at least twice as large as those of a conventional SAE D4512 ductile iron. Studies[6] show that the endurance limit of a Grade 1 ADI is also approximately twice that of a conventional D4512 ductile iron.

The ability to achieve excellent strength and toughness, under routine production conditions, makes ADI an excellent material for chassis components.

POST HEAT TREATING/PRE-MACHINING OPERATIONS

Following the austempering heat treatment, the castings are shot peened to remove surface scale and discoloration caused by the heat treatment operation. This operation has the added benefit of significantly increasing the fatigue strength of unmachined casting surfaces. Almen strips were run with the pre-production approval samples to quantify the amount of peening that the castings were receiving. Almen strips will be run with future shot peening loads as an ongoing quality check.

After peening, the castings are 100% inspected using a multifrequency eddy current unit to verify that each casting was properly austempered. This procedure and the resulting correlations were developed and validated internally. At this stage, 100% casting inspection is being used to help insure that each casting was properly austempered and to look for variations that might relate to machining performance. It is important to insure that all process controls consistently do the necessary job. Also, the additional information being gathered should help in further optimizing quality and manufacturing performance.

MACHINING AND ASSEMBLY

Following heat treatment and painting with e-coat, the upper control arms are machined, gauged, and assembled at Climate Control. Figure 8 shows two views of a machined upper control arm with the bushings in place. The parts are machined on heavy duty, horizontal machining centers, as shown in Figure 9. After machining, the parts are 100% gauged in-cycle and the bushings are then pushed-in in a separate station. The 100% gauging currently being done was incorporated into the machining operation as part of the ongoing learning process.

178

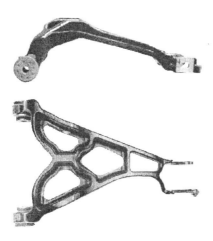

1. They have had no major problems machining the ADI upper control arms.

2. Tool usage is higher than for conventional grades of ductile iron (which are typically much softer).

3. They typically use slower and deeper cuts for ADI than for conventional ductile irons.

4. They are still evaluating alternate specialty insert grades to find the best insert for their machining conditions.

5. A key to successful ADI machining is a stable manufacturing process for the ADI castings (both foundry and heat treater).

There was an issue early on relating to ability to hold dimensions that was traced to casting distortion during heat treatment. This was resolved by modifying the casting stacking pattern in the heat treatment baskets.

Figure 8. Two views of a machined upper control arm casting with the bushings in place.

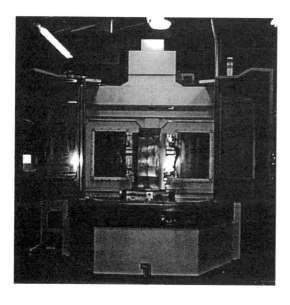

Figure 9. Photograph of a machining center with the doors open to show the fixture and casting orientation for machining.

Figure 10. Photograph of an upper control arm casting in the machining fixture.

The fixtures holding the casting during machining were deliberately designed to clamp the part solidly to a heavy base to minimize vibration during machining. A photograph of a casting in the machining fixture is presented in Figure 10. Climate Control personnel indicate that a solid setup which minimizes vibration during machining is key to successful ADI machining. They further indicate that:

The close, open minded, co-operative working relationship between foundry and machiner personnel and the proximity of the involved plants in Decatur, IL have been major assets in implementing and launching the Ford Mustang ADI upper control arm program.

179

SUMMARY

This program has demonstrated that austempered ductile iron is a suitable contender for chassis applications requiring lightweight, tough, high strength components. For the Ford Mustang upper control arm, it has proven superior to a steel forging. With good process control during casting production and heat treatment and with solid fixturing, ADI is readily machinable. It is clearly a material worthy of consideration for automotive applications

ACKNOWLEDGMENTS

We are grateful to all of the individuals at Ford, Benteler, Applied Process and Climate Control who supported us in this program. We would like to particularly recognize Cindy Jacob at Ford Motor Company for her numerous technical contributions to the program, and Monte Lange at Climate Control for his ongoing support, the time he spent with us in early phases of the development of this paper, and for the insights he provided regarding the machining of ADI. Other individuals deserving special recognition are Mitch Rackers for his handling of overall component design and design analysis, and Steve Braun for his development of the nondestructive test procedures used to confirm successful austempering of each casting.

CONTACT

Dr. Robert J Warrick received his degree in Metallurgical Engineering from the University of Michigan in 1963. His industrial career has been split between Ford Motor Company (first 14 years) and Intermet. He is currently Vice-President Materials R&D for Intermet Corporation and is located at the Intermet Product Design and Technical Center, 939 Airport Road, Lynchburg VA 24502. He can be reached by phone at (804) 237-8747 or at rwarrick@notes.intermet.com by email.

REFERENCES

1. SAE J434 Jun 86, 1998 SAE Handbook on CD-ROM, SAE International, Warrendale, PA.
2. ASTM A 536, 1999 Annual Book of ASTM Standards, Vol. 1.02, ASTM, West Conshohocken, PA, pp 310-314.
3. ASTM A897, 1999 Annual Book of ASTM Standards, Vol. 1.02, ASTM, West Conshohocken, PA, pp 570-575.
4. Natalie Neff, Mustang Cobra Gets Audited for 1999, WARD'S Auto World, February 1999, p 47
5. Norman Martin, Mustang Finally Gets An IRS, AI, March 1999, pp 63-64
6. Intermet internal studies.

2000-01-1291

Aluminum Alloys for Automotive Knuckle Castings

Gangalore Keshavaram, David Seiler and Dave DeWitt
Amcast Automotive

Copyright © 2000 Society of Automotive Engineers, Inc.

ABSTRACT

Knuckle castings for the automotive industry have traditionally been made from ductile iron, but engineers are now looking to aluminum castings as a lightweight alternative. Amcast Automotive has been involved in the development and manufacture of A206 aluminum knuckle castings since 1989 when it first supplied Aluminum castings for Ford Motor Co. (MN-12 platform). Recently, several new high volume automotive knuckle castings have been introduced using A356 aluminum alloy with T-6 temper.

This paper presents mechanical property information on both A206 and A356 aluminum alloys to assist engineers in the design of knuckle castings in aluminum. In addition to microstructural evaluation, mechanical properties will be obtained from test bars cut from actual heat-treated knuckle castings. Mechanical property information will include:

- Room temperature tensile, yield, and elongation values from mini-test bars (from knuckle castings)

- Elevated temperature tensile, yield, and elongation values from mini-test bars

- High frequency axial fatigue test data.

- Hardness

The A206 aluminum alloy is expected to exhibit superior mechanical properties compared to the A356 aluminum alloy. In A206 aluminum alloy higher strength is achieved both at room temperature and at elevated temperatures because of higher copper and lower silicon contents . Similarly, A206 alloy may show a fatigue advantage for the same reason. Regardless of the property values, both these aluminum alloys are suitable for automotive casting production usage and this this information is intended to assist suspension a knuckle designer in switching from iron to aluminum.

INTRODUCTION

Impact on energy savings is becoming increasingly important with time. This is because of depletion of fossil fuels and the increase of environmental pollution. In the automotive industry, the weight reduction of a vehicle addresses both the above issues. In recent years, materials research has put forward several exotic materials including composites which possess superior mechanical properties than conventional steel in addition to being light weight. High cost, difficulties in high volume production, and expensive cutting tools required for machining these advanced materials have prevented their use in passenger vehicles. Converting cast iron/ductile iron castings to aluminum alloy castings is a solution that may reduce the weight of passenger vehicles. It should be noted that ease of manufacture without compromising safety and comfort is the top priority. In this endeavor, the knuckle casting is one of the structural components which demands high tensile and fatigue properties. By replacing ferrous castings with aluminum castings, the designer will reduce the weight of suspension systems significantly (about 30%).

The choice of aluminum over ferrous alloys gives the distinct advantage of weight since the density of Iron is about three times that of aluminum. In aluminum knuckle castings weight reduction of 66% over ferrous casting is not realized since aluminum's elastic modulus is about 30% of cast iron. However, the actual weight reduction in aluminum casting over ferrous is about 40%. A comparison of a ferrous knuckle with an aluminum knuckle is given in Table 1.

Some of the design criteria for knuckle castings are as follows:

1) Static strength
2) Fatigue life.

Some of the performance criterions such as dimensional

181

of thin film network around solid grains during the solidification process. The region of solidification is designated as the semi-solidus zone. The zone is effected by the casting and alloy grain refinement and it is identified on the aluminum copper phase diagram in Figure 8.

The liquid film (A206 alloy has near eutectic liquid composition) can exist below equilibrium solidification temperature. The hot tear mechanism, therefore, occurs late in the solidification process. The mechanism of the hot tear involves the increased separation of the two solids by a thin liquid film. By definition, liquid has no shear stress resistance, the ability for the alloy to avoid separation at higher levels of fraction solid is critical to avoid the hot tear formation. Flemming indicates that a casting must be able to accommodate local strains at low fraction solids without formation of the defect.[1] The amount of local stresses within the casting as compared with its fraction solid will dictate the probability of a hot tear occurring.[2,3,5,6,8] The ability of the alloy for micro-liquid feeding is critical when a 'hot tear' take places at lower fraction solids. The separation tendencies of two solid fronts to accommodate solidification shrinkage and contraction stresses are lower when the micro-liquid feeding occurs. Liquid metal can easily flow into the area of separation. A hot tear anomaly will only occur when the alloy cannot recover or back fill the void region. This fluid flow is necessary until late in solidification to avoid the anomaly.

Therefore, The hot tear problem is based on the ability to withstand the stress build-up and the ability to feed metal into high stress areas at high fraction solids.

The hot tear phenomenon will occur in the A206 alloy primarily if no precautionary actions are taken to avoid it. The specific casting method discussed in this paper is the tilt pour permanent mold type casting process. The casting variable associated with this casting method must be examined before an in depth analysis of the local and general solidification hot tear phenomenon.

Three basic casting variables discussed are; 1) Tilt permanent mold, 2)-die material and coatings, and 3) the casting geometry.

TILT-POUR PERMANENT MOLD PROCESS

The tilt pour permanent mold casting process involves the introduction of the molten metal into the mold cavity by slowly tilting the mold. The metal flows into one part of the cavity initially, and to avoid metal turbulence, is slowly tilted to fill the entire mold. The tilting process allows solidification to initiate before the casting is completely filled. The casting is then "directionally" solidified toward the riser. Since the alloy solidifies as an equiaxed structure, the semi-liquid metal will constantly maintain the solidifying structure. The mold

must be preheated prior to casting. The mold must reach an equilibrium temperature when considering casting in high production facilities. Figure 9 gives a schematic diagram of the process.

DIE MATERIAL AND COATINGS

Permanent mold dies can be fabricated from a number of different materials; e.g. cast iron, tool steel (H-Series), beryllium copper, graphite, etc.[9,10] The base mold material that is covered by coatings is typically described as paints. Paint is necessary to prevent sticking (welding of the aluminum alloy to the mold material), provide a smooth casting surface, and assist in controlling the solidification.[10]

Coatings are typically applied as a water slurry of refractory coating. Each coating will have different thermal or lubrication properties, i.e. graphite is often used as a release agent. The thickness will also effect the solidification and is often employed to promote the directional solidification of the casting. During the production process, the coatings will wear off with each successive pour. This will impact how the casting solidifies.

CASTING GEOMETRY

Improperly designed castings can be thermally unstable and result in hot tears even in alloys that are not susceptible to hot tearing. It is especially critical, to have the best casting design obtainable when producing a product from a hot tear susceptible material like A206. Design consideration presented by Heine, Loper, & Rosenthal suggest the use of generous radii, slow transitions when changing casting section sizes, and eliminating pinning points.[9] Casting must be allowed to shrink without producing high stress regions.

MICRO-SOLIDIFICATION

Hot tearing theory, alloy composition, and casting considerations will each have an effect on the final casting. At any given point in the casting, solidification is the process of removal of heat, followed by nucleation of the alpha aluminum phase, its phase growth from 0% fraction solid to above 80% fraction solid. During phase growth, the eutectic composition (33 wt.% of Cu) is formed, and then the solidification is completed. The temperature drop as compared with the fraction solid for equilibrium solidification is given by the Schiel's Equation.[7] Figure 10 displays this equation graphically. The casting solidification process, however, is a non-equilibrium process. The 'real' process will differ from the 'Schiel's Equation' as a result of solid diffusion in the casting.[7] The amount of solid present at any time during solidification will provide a level of tensile strength.[12] The interaction of solidifying dendrites will determine this strength. The dendrites that weld together at rigidity, and part life under load are related to stiffness, freezing range (solidus liquidus range) and fatigue properties.

From Table 2, it is evident that both A206 and A356 aluminum alloys are candidate materials for the manufacture of 'rear knuckle castings' in high volumes using the gravity permanent mold-tilt pour technique.

VARIOUS PROCESS CONSIDERATIONS FOR PRODUCTION OF KNUCKLE CASTING

The green sand casting process may be less expensive. However, green sand castings generally have lower elongation, tensile strength, and fatigue properties in comparison to permanent mold casting. This is due to large secondary dendrite arm spacing (DAS). Hence, green sand castings are not recommended for safety critical automotive applications.

The die casting process was also not considered, although it has excellent surface finish, because of high gas porosity entrapment. Limited heat resistance, Poor mechanical properties are associated with the die casting process because alloys typically have higher iron content, which adversely affects elongation. Also, fatigue properties are typically poor due to the large number of pores.

From Table 3, it is evident that 'Gravity permanent mold tilt pour' technique has an advantage over other processes based on cost and repeatability of consistent quality castings.

Figures 1 to 5 shows various knuckles produced by permanent mold tilt pour process. Both A206 and A356 aluminum alloys were used in the above process. Porosity and other foundry anomalies were controlled by continuous improvement program and proper design of experiments.

A206 ALUMINUM ALLOY KNUCKLE CASTING DEVELOPMENT

At Amcast an A206 aluminum alloy knuckle casting was developed for Ford Motor Co. During the process development and subsequent production run some of the castability issues encountered will be discussed.

A201 and A206 are high strength - precipitation hardened structural aluminum alloys. These alloys were primarily developed in the 1970's for use in the aerospace industry. Recent applications include the use of A206 (Aluminum - 4-wt.% Cu) in the automotive industry. The casting alloy A201 is not economically desirable because of high silver content (0.40 wt.% to 1.00 wt.%). Although the A206 alloy has very beneficial mechanical properties, poor castability discouraged wide spread

development of this alloy. The tendency of this alloy to "Hot Tear" was the primary castability obstacle. A "Hot Tear" appears as a crack in the casting at the end of the casting process. Unlike a hot crack, however, the contraction and subsequent liquid separation of two solidifying fronts of the metal cause a hot tear. The anomaly rupture or split will occur before solidification is complete.[1] The alloy solidification characteristics and the method of casting process will primarily determine the tendency of an alloy to hot tear. However, casting design and alloy preparation must be considered in a complete study on hot tearing.

The mechanical properties of this A206 alloy were extensively evaluated as compared with the casting method (i.e. solidification rates) by A. Kearney in the 1970's.[2] The ASM Metals Handbook indicates that the minimum measured mechanical properties exceed most of the other common aluminum alloys.[3] Figure 6 illustrates the typical mechanical properties for the A206.0-T4 and other common aluminum alloys. The T4 temper condition is necessary to meet these mechanical properties. The A206 alloy can be represented in the study of the hot tearing phenomenon by an aluminum - 4 wt.% copper binary alloy.

Titanium (Titanium di-Borate) is typically used as a grain refiner necessary to improve the castability of this alloy.[4] Many researchers have indicated the effect of a grain refiner on the hot tearing phenomenon. The wide freezing range (112°C) and high thermal conductivity of the aluminum - 4 wt.% copper (A206) alloy will tend to promote equiaxed solidification grains instead of columnar grains. Typically, this reason is given as the cause of the high hot tear tendency of this alloy. The structural transition from columnar to equiaxed grains will take place at copper levels above 2.5 wt.%.[5] The 4.5 wt.% copper alloy has the most hot tear tendency of all the aluminum copper alloys, as seen by Figure 7.[5,6] However, hot tearing must be considered during the process development and design to eliminate the castability concerns of these alloys.

HOT TEAR PHENOMENON AL-4.5 CU ALLOY

Hot tear is a function of several casting variables. These variables include alloy composition, casting solidification rate, alloy grain refinement, alloy purity, type of mold, mold filling method, mold and alloy temperature, mold design, and type of casting removal (ejection, knock-out). Most of the research concentrates on the alloy variables rather than on the mold variables. These variables are discussed separately. 'Hot Tear' theory has been studied significantly in the past. Extensive work has been done by M.C. Flemmings et al at MIT. Flemmings presents the strain or thin film network theory of hot tearing.[1,5,6,7] This theory involves the development relatively low fraction solids will ultimately cause hot tearing. Conversely, the dendrites that do not interact until higher fraction solids will tend to avoid the hot tear anomaly. Grain refining will produce this effect on the solidifying alloy. Grain refining is necessary to limit the strength build up in the alloy.

Kubota indicates that the grain refining will reduce the temperature at which the first stresses will build-up from 640°C to 610°C (see Figure 11).[12] Kubota identifies those temperatures as the semi-solidus temperatures for the aluminum-4.5 wt.% copper alloy. The grain refining also will reduce contraction through the critical semi-solidus region and decreasing the local volume of eutectic liquid remaining prior to final solidification. However, the small amounts of eutectic fluid will remain the same.

The hot tear phenomenon occurrence will decrease as a result of suppressing the stress build-up until later in the solidification process. It will also reduce the micro--contraction of the solidifying solid. The liquid to solid phase change will decrease the volume required to feed the metal. Flemmings indicates that the grain refining makes the alloy weaker at a given fraction solid.[1] Kubota indicates that the stress build-up temperature (semi-solidus temperature) is decreased by grain refinement.[12] The grain refinement allows the solidification of independent grains to occur at higher fraction solid prior to any stress build-up. Therefore, the liquid to solid contraction is able to take place for a longer period with constant re-supply of liquid metal. The solidifying grains flow and slip during this solidification eliminating possible hot tear anomalies and then the alloy is able to rapidly gain strength after the semi-solidus temperature is reached. Grain refinement, however, is not the perfect hot tear solution. With adequate grain refinement, the defect may still occur. This problem must be addressed by further decreasing semi-solidus temperature as described by Kubota.[11] The grains must grow to a high fraction solid prior to any interaction (i.e. not strength build-up). This will result in adequate shrinkage feeding and minimize remaining liquid to 'hot tear'.

MACRO-SOLIDIFICATION

The macro-solidification case involves the entire casting solidification. Casting process and design variables have an effect on macro-solidification. Ideally, the micro-solidification would take place over the entire casting, however, in the actual practice this will not happen. Some of the variables which needs to be considered include casting geometry, macro shrinkage (risering), consistency of heat transfer, and consistency of the mold coatings. The casting geometry is identified as a key point in the prevention of the hot tear defect in a casting. As solidification progresses through the casting during the semi-solidus temperature (as described earlier) the local stress levels will increase. Further,

stress increase can be the result of unfavorable geometry. Sharp corners produce hot spots, hence, some of the casting areas will result in high stress levels.[2] The combination of these two factors often leads to a hot tear anomaly. Fundamental casting design gating and risering must be followed to have any chance of reducing the hot tear tendency of a casting. Inadequate risering and/or gating practices will lead to hot tearing from starvation of feed metal during solidification in the region.[5] Areas of metal shrinkage are very susceptible to the formation of the hot tear anomaly.

The removal of heat from the metal is a fundamental process of solidification. It is critical that the heat flow be consistent to maintain appropriate solidification. Generally, a steady state production process is developed for the mass production of these castings. The optimal steady state process will involve repeatable cycles or casting shots that are able to maintain the solidification as presented in the micro-solidification considerations section.[9] In the ideal process, the die will reach a steady state range of temperatures from the cycle of cast, solidification, casting removal, and followed by subsequent casting process where the defect will not occur. Deviation from this "standard" cycle will often lead to the formation of hot tear anomaly (other types of anomalies can also occur) from inconsistent heat transfer. The ideal rate of heat transfer must be determined for the best casting results. However, the ability to produce tear free castings when slight thermal deviations are present is necessary for a robust process. The condition of the painted surface will lead to inconsistent heat transfer and ultimately to the hot tear anomalies. As castings are produced in the gravity tilt permanent mold, the paint will actually wear away with every pour. The die surface will appear and will produce a isolated chilling effect causing the stress to increase at lower fraction solids leading to the hot tear anomaly as described earlier.

The macro-solidification considerations are important because of their effect on the micro-solidification process as earlier discussed. The engineering solutions necessary to resolve the hot tear anomaly phenomenon need to be worked out by addressing the unsolved variables as described in the preceding discussion. The two 'hot tear unknowns' are 1) the additional process changes necessary to produce high fraction solids prior to any dendritic interaction and 2) maintain the die cavity at constant heat transfer rates (steady state process).

CHEMISTRY OF 206 AND A356 ALUMINUM ALLOYS

The primary difference between A206 and A356 alloy is the higher copper content, low silicon, low magnesium, and low iron in A206 alloy. Low silicon in A206 will reduce casting fluidity and makes the alloy prone for hot tear. Also, in A206 alloy, the copper suppresses the eutectic changing to liquidus. In addition, copper increases the density of A206 alloy by about 4% when compared to the A356 alloy. Literature indicates that the A206 alloy may exhibit less resistance to corrosion than A356 alloy. However, A206 alloy showed no deterioration in mechanical properties when knuckle castings were tested after 5 years in actual service.

MICROSTRUCTURAL EVALUATION OF A206 AND A356 ALUMINUM ALLOYS

Cut sections from the knuckle castings from several different cross sections were mounted, polished, and inspected using a metallographic microscope. The findings were as follows:

A206 aluminum alloy structure shows some intermetallics such as $CuAl_2$. However, structure was very similar to a typical A206 aluminum alloy given in the handbook as given in Figure 12.

A356 aluminum alloy specimen has a well-modified eutectic Si phase. The Si phase was spheroidized to a maximum of 10 microns in diameter. The specimen exhibited regions of Si eutectic structure as given in Figure 12.

No secondary phases were present. A356.2 ingot was used to produce castings with low Fe levels. Combined heat-treating, the A356.2 alloy did not form additional inter-metallic compounds. In general, magnesium compounds were successfully distributed in the solutionizing and quenching process. Very few Mg_2Si (dark portions in the micro structure) were seen. No needles were seen throughout the microstructure.

No intermetallic compounds were found on the polished surface of the specimen at X750 even after etching shown in figure 12.

Both A206 and A356 aluminum alloys show good microstructure and no intermetallics were found as shown in Figures 13 and 14.

MECHANICAL PROPERTIES

Tensile tests were conducted on both A206 and A356 alloys at room temperature per ASTM E-8 and at high temperature per ASTM E-21. Test samples were taken from the area between upper control arm attachment and wheel bearing for MN-12 platform Ford Motor Co knuckle casting made with a T-4 tempered A206 aluminum alloy. Additional samples were taken from the McPerson strut area for the W-Car platform DELPHI knuckles made of T-6 tempered A356 knuckle castings.

In actual service, it is less likely that knuckle castings would be subjected to elevated temperatures. However, a part of the knuckle from the caliper attachment could be subjected to higher temperatures. Hence, it was relevant to measure elevated temperature mechanical properties.

One slug was cut from each casting and tested at elevated temperatures 250F and 400F. Tests were conducted with a soak time of 30 minutes. The average of five readings are given in Figures 14 and 15.

Variation in tensile, yield, and elongation of both A206 and A356 aluminum alloys is given in Figure 15, and percentage variation in the properties is similar for both the alloys. At elevated temperatures, percentage variation is higher than at room temperature. This is probably due to artificial aging at elevated temperatures.

As shown in Figure 14 and 15 elevated temperature elongation decreases at 400^0F when compared with 250^0F. This was attributed to artificial aging of the sample during soaking time (30 minutes) before testing. This trend was found in both (A206 and A356) the alloys.

The dimensions of the mini-bars test specimens for tensile test and fatigue test are shown in Figures 17 and 18 respectively. The test parameters are defined in Table 7.

Fatigue tests on A206 and A356 alloys were conducted in accordance to ASTM E-466, and the test conditions are given in Table 7.

S-N curves for both alloys are given in Figures 19 and 20. It is seen that both A206 and A356 alloy shows similar fatigue endurance limits (maximum stress at 10^7 cycles) of approximately 100MPa. However, maximum stress at 10^4 and 10^6 cycles are higher for A206 than A356. Both of these alloys were well above the minimum endurance required by designers of 70 MPa (10 ksi) at 10^7 cycles.

An A206 aluminum alloy knuckle castings used on a car assembled at MN-12 platform shows no visible corrosion on the surface after 5 years of service. Literature indicates that the A206 alloy is susceptible to stress corrosion cracking.[1] Mechanical tests from knuckle casting after 5 years of service (minibars) showed no indications of property deterioration as given in Table 6.

HARDNESS

The Hardness was measured at the surface of castings of both A206 and A356 alloys at various positions of casting. The average of five Brinell hardness readings were taken on five castings, and the data is presented in Table 8.

CONCLUSIONS

- Both A206 and A356 aluminum alloys are appropriate for the manufacture of knuckle castings.

- Both alloys have produced high volume knuckle castings successfully in the 'Gravity Permanent mold-Tilt Pour' process.

- The Gravity Permanent Mold (GPM) tilt pour-technique was found to be the most competitive choice to produce high quality rear knuckle castings.

- A206 aluminum alloy exhibited a higher tendency to hot tear where as A356 alloy showed little hot tearing behavior in the normal operating temperatures.

- To cast A206 alloy, one or more of the following is recommended to control hot tear;

    1. Increase Grain Refinement

    2. Keep Titanium values as high as possible in the melt.

    3. Vibrating the die cavity during the solidification of the casting to promote better liquid mixing and break dendrites.

    4. Provide extra heat to the specific die locations to reduce paint wear .

- The A206 aluminum alloy tensile properties, at both room temperature and at elevated temperature, are higher than A356. Both of the alloys exhibited tensile strength, yield, and elongation well above the minimum design requirements.

- The average room temperature Brinell hardness numbers for A206 and A356 were 97.82 and 97.33, respectively (average of 150 readings).

- The endurance limit (maximum stress at 10^7 cycles) for both A206 and A356 aluminum alloys were measured to be about 100 MPa. A206 alloy showed higher stress values at lower cycles. However, both the alloys exhibited fatigue properties well above the specification from a design point of view.

- There was no degradation of properties for A206 alloy after 5 years of service, which indicates corrosion may not be as big a issue in A206 aluminum alloy as far as mechanical properties are concerned.

- Machinability ratings for both the alloys are similar and both of the alloys possess good machinability ratings.

- Microstructure showed good casting integrity and no secondary phases, which are detrimental to properties.

- A206 alloy is more expensive alloy and has a higher density, and is more difficult to process as compared to A356 alloy.

ACKNOWLEDGMENTS

The authors wish to thank Dr. Jim Van Wert Jr. for his editorial comments and suggestions.

REFERENCES

1. M. C. Flemmings (1974) Solidification Processes. New York: McGraw-Hill, pp. 156-167.
2. A. L. Kearney and J. Raffin (1977). "2X206.0-T4 and XA206.0-T7 vs. Comparable Alloys at Various Cooling Rates." American Foundrymen's Society Transactions, Volume 85, pp. 559-570.
3. L.A Willey (1980). "Aerospace Material Specification 4236, 7-15-80." , pp. 1234-1321
4. D. G. McCartney (1988, February). "Discussion of The role of Boron in the Grain Refinement of Aluminum with Titanium." Metallurgical Transactions, Volume 19A, pp. 385-387.
5. M. C. Flemmings and S. A. Metz (1970). "A Fundamental Study of Hot Tearing." American Foundrymen's Society Transactions, Volume 78, pp. 456-460.
6. M. C. Flemmings, R. A. Rosenberg, and H F. Taylor (1960). "Nonferrous Binary Alloys Hot Tearing." American Foundrymen's Society Transactions, Volume 68, pp. 518-524.
7. M. C. Flemmings and S. A.. Metz (1969). "Hot Tearing in Cast Metals." American Foundrymen's Society Transactions, Volume 77, pp. 329-334.

1. C. H. Yeh, T. S. Chen, and Y. L. Lin (1988). "The Effect of HIP on A206 Aluminum Castings." American Foundrymen's Society Transactions, Volume 96, pp. 719- 724.
2. R. W. Heine, C. R. Loper, and P. C. Rosenthal (1967). Principles of Metal Casting. New York: McGraw-Hill, pp. 285 and 307-309.
3. N. S. Mahadevan, K. S. Sreenivasa, and M. R. Seshadri (1968). "Influences of Solidification Gradients on the Casting Soundness of Aluminum-4.5% Copper Alloy." American Foundrymen's Society Transactions, Volume 76, pp. 77-84.
4. M. Kubota and S. Kitaoka (1973). "Solidification Behavior and Hot Tearing Tendency of Aluminum Casting Alloys." American Foundrymen's Society Transactions, Volume 81, pp. 424--427.

TABLE 1: COMPARISON OF IRON AND ALUMINUM KNUCKLE CASTINGS		
Factors	**Comparison 'Rear Knuckle Casting'.**	
	Ferrous	Aluminum
Weight	7.9 density	2.7 density (about 1/3 of ferrous)
Properties	High Tensile and high modulus	Moderate tensile, high elongation and moderate elastic modulus
Part size	Small	Larger than ferrous casting
Overall weight savings	1 Unit	40% weight savings over ferrous
Corrosion	Prone to Rust	Good corrosion resistance.
Unsprung mass	High-Less ride comfort	Low-More ride comfort
Fuel consumed over 100,000 miles	1unit	0.78 units
Initial cost	Less expensive	More expensive

TABLE 2: VARIOUS ALUMINUM ALLOYS CONSIDERED TO PRODUCE KNUCKLE CASTINGS BY GRAVITY PERMANENT MOLD TILT POUR PROCESS	
Alloys	**Remarks**
A206	Good choice from property stand point of view. However, alloy is about 4% heavier than A356. Higher melt temperature than A356 (about 120 F). This alloy is very hot short and is prone to hot tear due to long solidification range.
354	Good tensile and yield properties, good flow charecterstics. Good machinability. However, 1% heavier than A356. Also, poor elongation. Hence not recommended.
A356	Good choice from a machinability and mold filling point of view. Good tensile properties and fatigue properties. Hence strongly recommended.
A201	Good mechanical properties. Expensive because of silver content. Hence not recommended.
319	Less expensive alloy. Good fluidity. High copper content results in higher density. Poor elongation, poor fatigue properties. Not recommended for knuckle casting.
357	Good choice both from a property as well as from a machinability view point. High corrosion resistance. Good flow characteristics and lower density. Poor elongation and hence not recommended for knuckle casting production.

TABLE 3: PRODUCTION OF 'KNUCKLE CASTINGS' CHOICE OF VARIOUS PROCESSES

Various processes of permanent mold

Gravity tilt pour (GPM)	Low pressure (LPPM)	Squeeze casting (HiCast)
Castability of Various Alloys		
Alloys with silicon over 4%.	A 356 or other aluminum alloys with Si above 6%.	A 356 or other aluminum alloys with Si above 6%.
General Characteristics of castings		
Low gas porosity. Medium surface finish. Good mechanical properties	Low gas porosity. Medium surface finish. Good mechanical properties	Low gas porosity. Superior surface finish. Superior mechanical properties
Fatigue Property of castings		
Good	Good	Very Good
Typical DAS value in microns (μm)		
25 to40	25 to38	22 to 35

TABLE 4 : CHEMISTRY FOR A206 ALLOY AND A356 ALUMINUM ALLOYS

AA Alloy No	Si	Fe	Cu	Mn	Mg	Cr	Ni	Zn	Sn	Ti	Others	
											Each	Total
A206	0.05	0.10	4.2-5.0	0.05-0.2	0.05-0.20	0.05	0.05	0.1	0.05	0.15-0.3	0.05	0.15
A356	6.5-7.5	0.2	0.2	0.1	0.25-0.45	0.05	0.05	0.1	0.05	0.2	0.05	0.15

TABLE 5: SUMMARY OF MICROSTRUCTURES OF A206 AND A356 KNUCKLE CASTINGS (MICROSTRUCTURES ARE GIVEN IN FIGURES 11,12 and 13)

customer	Microstructure	Comments
Ford	Typical of A206 aluminum Alloy after T-4 heat-treat	No anomalies are seen in the entire cross section of the polished specimen. Very few micro pores of less than 15 microns. DAS varied from 28 to 38
Delphi	Typical Heat treated T-6 A356 Aluminum alloy	No anomalies are found in the entire cross section of the polished specimen. Very few micro pores of less than 15 microns. DAS varied from 25 to 35

TABLE 6: THE PROPERTIES OF FORD KNUCKLE CASTING AFTER 5 YEARS OF SERVICE.

Test sample	Tensile MPa	Yield MPa	Elongation	Hardness (Brinell)	Remarks
1	398	246	14.4	100	No property deterioration in 5 years
2	406	257	16.2	96	
3	401	260	15.5	100	
4	389	244	12.6	100	

TABLE 7: TEST CONDITIONS OF TENSILE AND FATIGUE TESTING

Type of test	Test conditions	Remarks
Tensile room temperature per ASTM E8	Extensometer Gage Length 0.5 inch. Test Temperature 75 F Strain through 0.2% yield: 0.005 in/in/Min Head rate thence to failure: 0.05 in.	All the samples failed within the gage length. Fracture was ductile for both A206 and A356 alloy
Tensile elevated temperature per ASTM E-21 (250F and 400F)	Extensometer Gage Length 1.0 inch. Test Temperature 300 F and 400 F Strain through 0.2% yield: 0.005 in/in/Min Head rate thence to failure: 0.05 in.	All the samples failed within the gage length. Fracture was more ductile at 250F than at 400F. Ductility was more for A206 than for A356
High cycle fatigue per ASTM E466 (room temperature)	Mode: Axial load control Temperature: 75 F Stress ratio: R=-1 Frequency: 90 Hz Waveform: Sinusoidal Test Machine: Closed loop controlled system of 89 KN capacity	Most of the samples failed within the gage length. Fracture was typical of fatigue test.

TABLE 8: HARDNESS OF 354 AND 357 ALLOYS

Load	Alloy	Location	Hardness (Brinell)	Remarks
500 Kg	A206	Disc brake pad and top end of lower control arm attachment	97.8	Not much variation between castings or locations.
500 Kg	A356	Lateral link (end)	98.2	

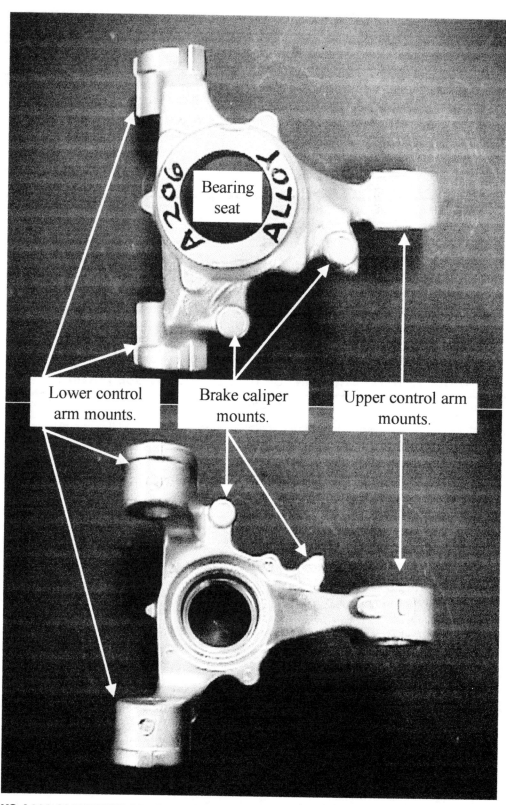

FIGURE 1 SHOWS A206 ALUMINUM ALLOY KNUCKLE CASTING PRODUCED FOR MN-12 PLATFORM -'FORD MOTOR CO.' BY AMCAST AUTOMOTIVE CEDARBURG PLANT.

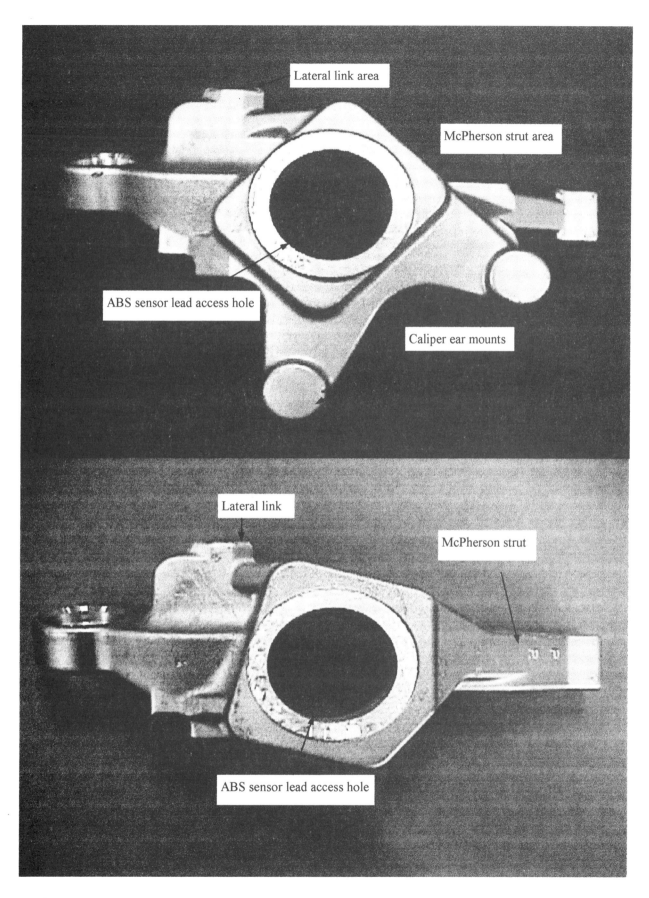

FIGURE 2 GMX 130 (TOP) AND FIGURE 3 P 90 BOTTOM SHOWS A356 ALUMINUM ALLOY KNUCKLE CASTINGS PRODUCED FOR 'DELPHI CHASSIS SYSTEM' BY AMCAST AUTOMOTIVE RICHMOND PLANT.

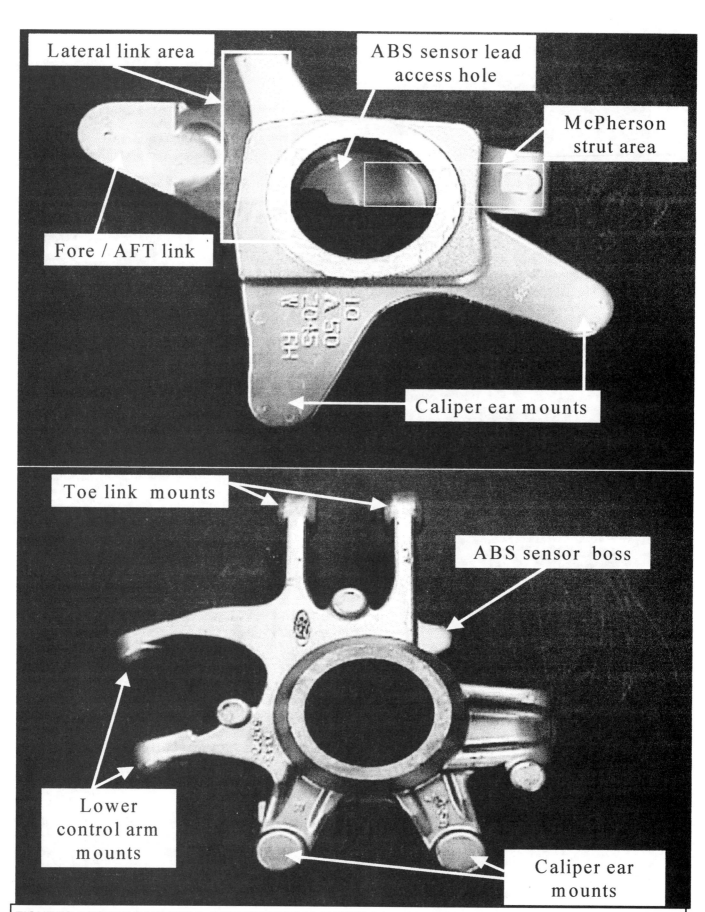

Lateral link area

ABS sensor lead access hole

McPherson strut area

Fore / AFT link

Caliper ear mounts

Toe link mounts

ABS sensor boss

Lower control arm mounts

Caliper ear mounts

FIGURES 4 TOP W CAR AND 5 BOTTOM DEW 98 SHOWS A356 ALUMINUM ALLOY KNUCKLE CASTINGS PRODUCED FOR 'DELPHI CHASSIS SYSTEM' AND 'FORD MOTOR CO' RESPECTIVELY BY AMCAST AUTOMOTIVE RICHMOND PLANT.

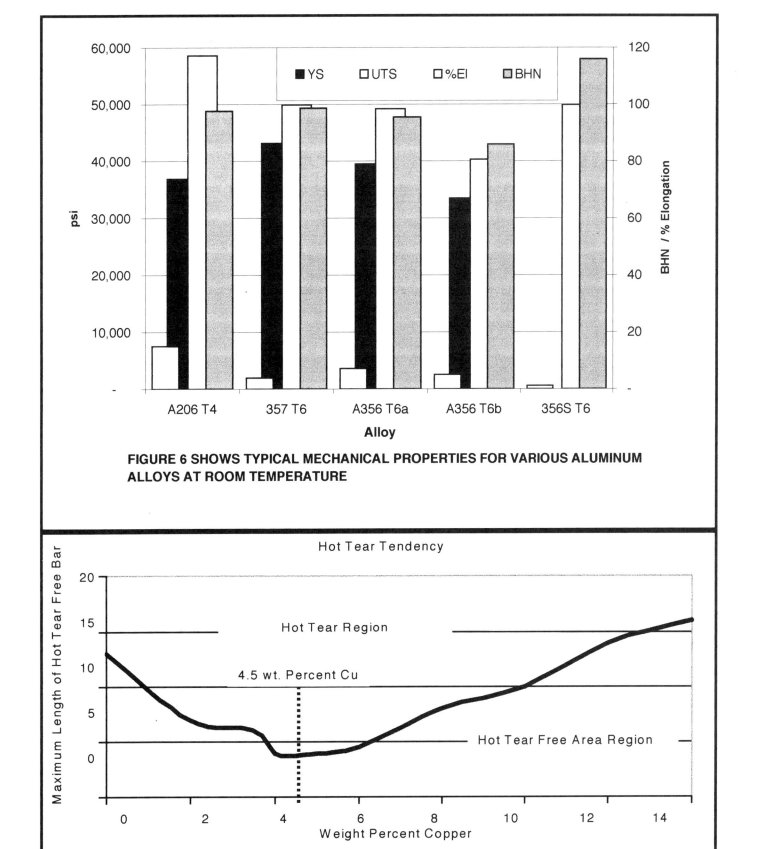

FIGURE 6 SHOWS TYPICAL MECHANICAL PROPERTIES FOR VARIOUS ALUMINUM ALLOYS AT ROOM TEMPERATURE

FIGURE 7 SHOWS MAXIMUM LENGTH OF HOT TEAR FREE ZONE IS MINIMUM FOR Al-4.5%Cu ALLOY

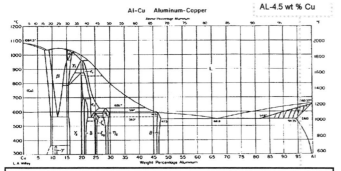

FIGURE 8 PHASE DIAGRAM OF Al –Cu SYSTEM ASM METALS HANDBOOK 8TH EDITION; VOLUME 8, 1973, PAGE 259.

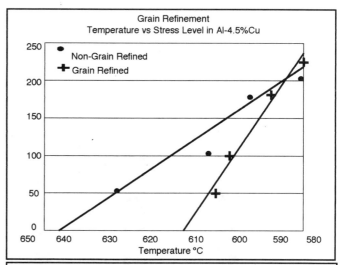

FIGURE 11 GRAIN REFINEMENT TEMPERATURE VS STRESS LEVEL IN Al-4.5%Cu ALLOY

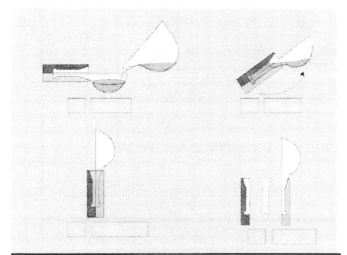

FIGURE 9 SHOWS A SCHEMATIC DIAGRAM OF 'TILT POUR GRAVITY PERMANENT MOLD ' PROCESS

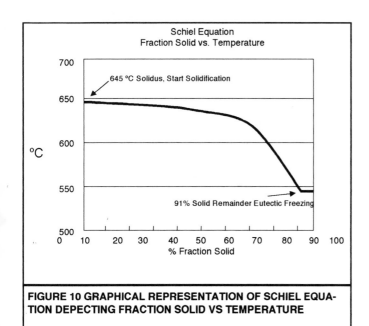

FIGURE 10 GRAPHICAL REPRESENTATION OF SCHIEL EQUATION DEPECTING FRACTION SOLID VS TEMPERATURE

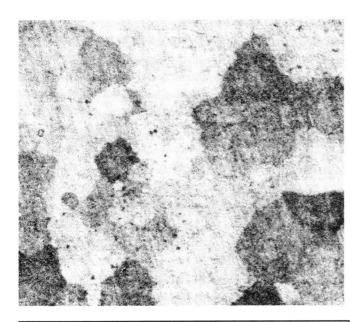

A. A206 aluminum alloy etched with 0.5% HF for 35 seconds shows grains X50

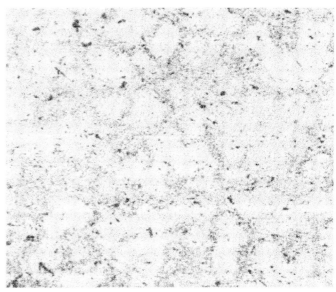

B. A206 aluminum alloy dendrites are seen DAS 30 microns X150

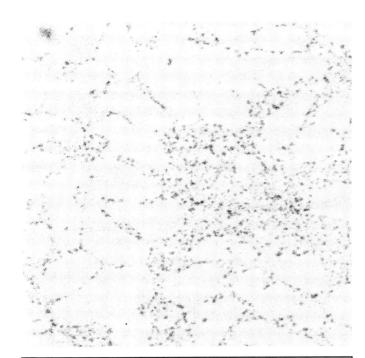

C. A356 aluminum alloy shows Silicon eutectic region DAS 28 microns X200

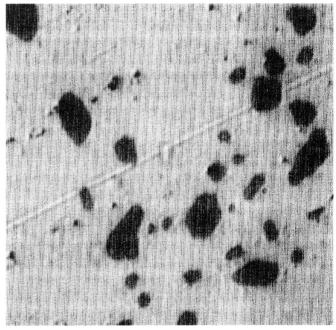

D. A356 aluminum alloy Si eutectic modified and near spherical morphology to a size of 10 microns

FIGURE 12 OPTICAL PHOTOMICROGRAPHS OF A206 AND A356 ALUMINUM ALLOYS

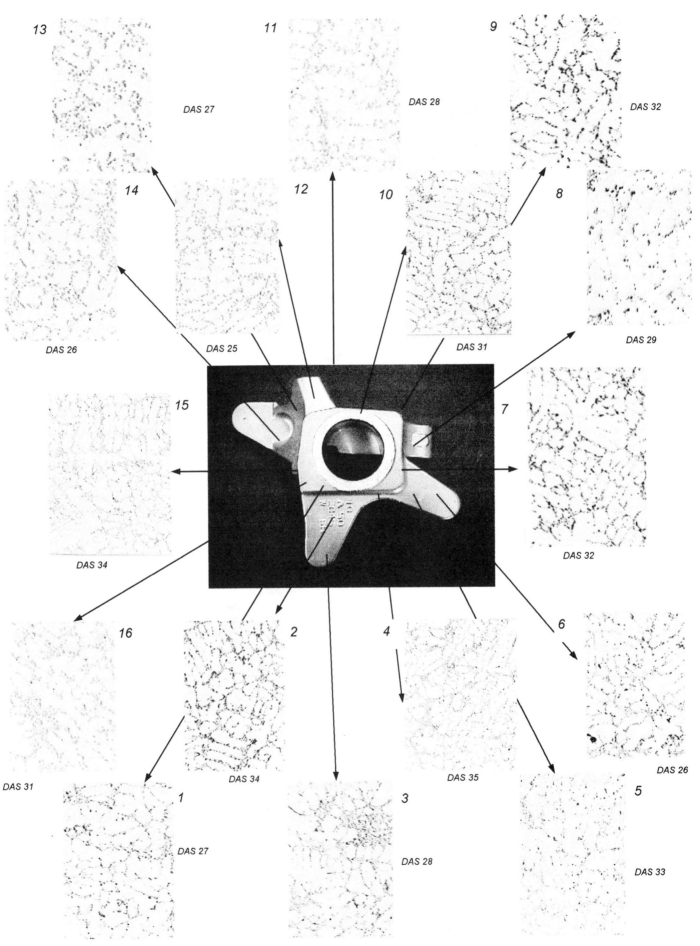

13 — DAS 27

11 — DAS 28

9 — DAS 32

14 — DAS 26

12 — DAS 25

10 — DAS 31

8 — DAS 29

15 — DAS 34

7 — DAS 32

16 — DAS 31

2 — DAS 34

1 — DAS 27

3 — DAS 28

4 — DAS 35

6 — DAS 26

5 — DAS 33

Fig 13: Microstructures of A356 aluminum alloy (X75—X200) at various sections of W-CAR knuckle casting (DAS in microns)

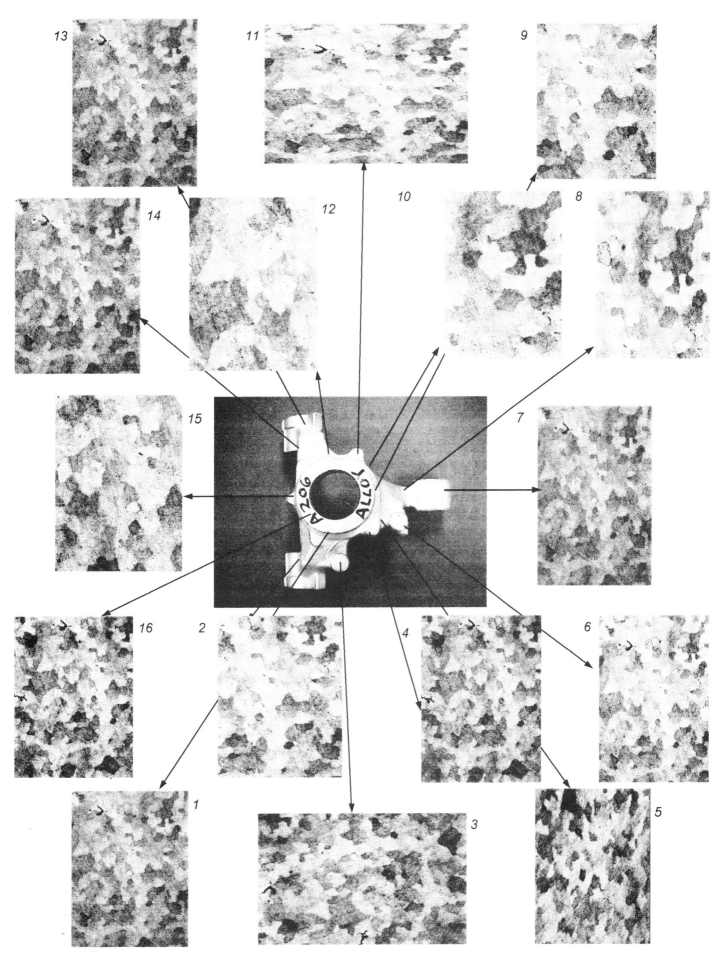

Fig 14 : Microstructures of A206 aluminum alloy (X50-X75) at various sections of MN-12 Knuckle casting after etching with 0.5%HF.

197

Mechanical properties at Elevated temperature

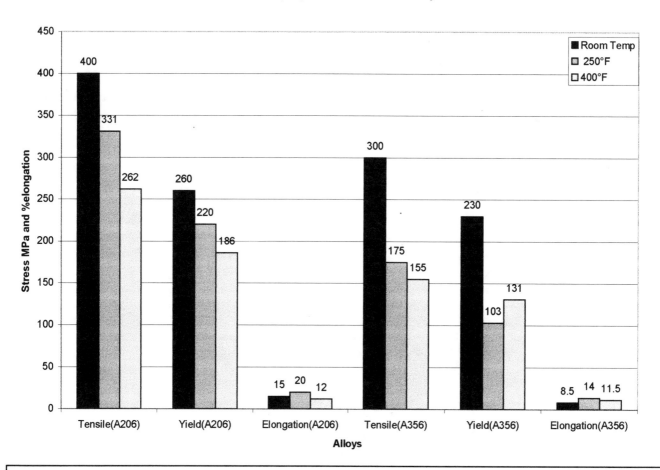

FIGURE 15 OVER VIEW OF MECHANICAL PROPERTIES (BOTH A206 AND A356 ALUMINUM ALLOYS) BOTH AT ROOM TEMPERATURE AND AT ELEVATED TEMPERATURES

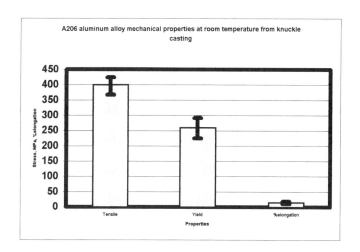

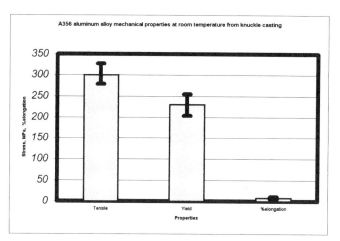

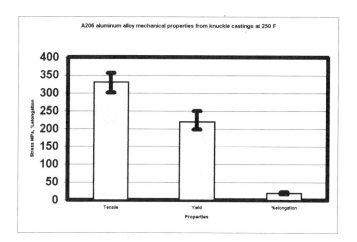

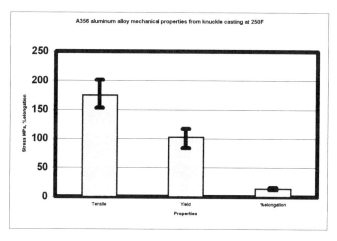

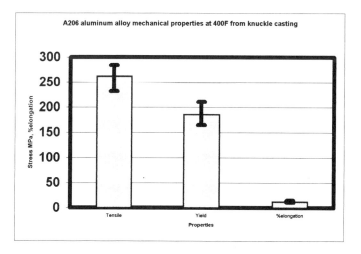

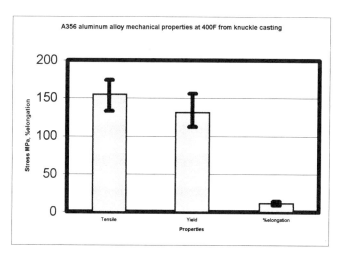

Figure 16 compares mechanical properties of A206 and A356 aluminum alloys both at room temperature as well as at elevated temperatures

19

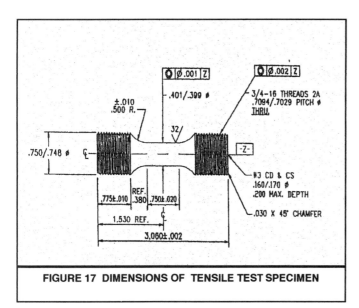

FIGURE 17 DIMENSIONS OF TENSILE TEST SPECIMEN

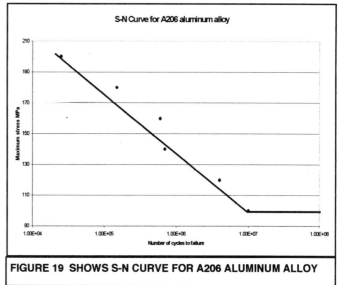

FIGURE 19 SHOWS S-N CURVE FOR A206 ALUMINUM ALLOY

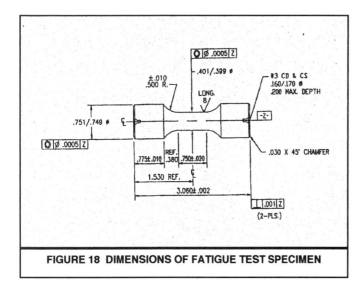

FIGURE 18 DIMENSIONS OF FATIGUE TEST SPECIMEN

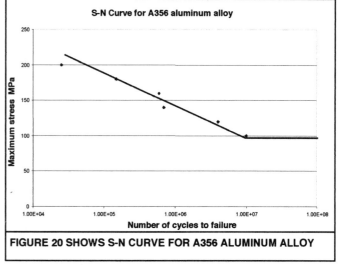

FIGURE 20 SHOWS S-N CURVE FOR A356 ALUMINUM ALLOY

CASTING INDUSTRY RESOURCES

Metalcasting Technology Nomenclature

Michael J. Lessiter and Ross Foti

The American Foundrymen's Association

Reprinted from Engineered Casting Solutions Spring/Summer 1999 Issue

GLOSSARY OF METAL CASTING TERMS

This Glossary of Metalcasting Terms provides the automotive product engineer, casting designer, and purchasing representative with practical definitions of common metalcasting phrases and terms.

AQL Acceptable Quality Level. A quality level established on a prearranged system of inspection using samples selected at random.

As-cast condition Casting without subsequent heat treatment.

Backing sand The bulk of the sand in the flask. The sand compacted on top of the facing sand that covers the pattern.

Binder The bonding agent used as an additive to mold or core sand to impart strength or plasticity in a "green" or dry state.

Burn-on sand Sand adhering to the surface of the casting that is extremely difficult to remove.

Chaplet A small metal insert or spacer used in molds to provide core support during the casting process.

Charge A given weight of metal introduced into the furnace.

Chill A metal insert in the sand mold used to produce local chilling and equalize rate of solidification throughout the casting.

Cleaning Removal of runners, risers, flash, surplus metal and sand from a casting.

Cold shut A surface imperfection due to unsatisfactory fusion of metal.

Cope The top half of a horizontally parted mold.

Core A sand or metal insert in a mold to shape the interior of the casting or that part of the casting that cannot be shaped by the pattern.

Core assembly An assembly made from a number of cores.

Corebox The wooden, metal or plastic tool used to produce cores.

Coreprint A projection on a pattern that leaves an impression in the mold for supporting the core.

Core wash A liquid suspension of a refractory material applied to cores and dried (intended to improve surface of casting).

Crush The displacement of sand at mold joints.

Cupola A cylindrical, straight shaft furnace (usually lined with refractories) for melting metal in direct contact with coke by forcing air under pressure through openings near its base.

Cure To harden.

Die A metal form used as a permanent mold for die casting or for a wax pattern in investment casting.

Dowel A pin of various types used in the parting surface of parted patterns or dies to assure correct registry.

Draft Taper on the vertical sides of a pattern or corebox that permits the core or sand mold to be removed without distorting or tearing of the sand.

Drag The bottom half of a horizontally parted mold.

Ejector pins Movable pins in pattern dies that help remove patterns from the die.

Facing sand The sand used to surround the pattern that produces the surface in contact with the molten metal.

Feeder Sometimes referred to as a "riser," it is part of the gating system that forms the reservoir of molten metal necessary to compensate for losses due to shrinkage as the metal solidifies.

Finish allowance The amount of stock left on the surface of a casting for machining.

Finish mark A symbol (f, fl, f2, etc.) appearing on the line of a drawing that represents the edge of the surface of the casting to be machined or otherwise finished.

Flask A rigid metal or wood frame used to hold the sand of which a mold is formed and usually consisting of two parts, cope and drag.

Foundry returns Metal (of known composition) in the form of gates, sprues, runners, risers and scrapped castings returned to the furnace for remelting.

Gas porosity A condition existing in a casting caused by the trapping of gas in the molten metal or by mold gases evolved during the pouring of the casting.

Gate (ingate) The portion of the runner where the molten metal enters the mold cavity.

Green sand Moist clay-bonded molding sand.

Heat A single furnace charge of metal.

Heat treatment A combination of heating and cooling operations timed and applied to a metal or alloy in the solid state in a manner that will produce desired mechanical properties.

Hotbox process A resin-based process that uses heated metal coreboxes to produce cores.

Hot tear Irregularly shaped fracture in a casting resulting from stresses set up by steep thermal gradients within the casting during solidification.

Inclusions Particles of slag, refractory materials, sand or deoxidation products trapped in the casting during pouring solidification.

Investment casting A pattern casting process in which a wax or thermoplastic pattern is used. The pattern is invested (surrounded) by a refractory slurry. After the mold is dry, the pattern is melted or burned out of the mold cavity, and molten metal is poured into the resulting cavity.

Ladle A container used to transfer molten metal from the furnace to the mold.

Locating pad A projection on a casting that helps maintain alignment of the casting for machining operations.

Locating surface A casting surface to be used as a basis for measurement in making secondary machining operations.

Master pattern The object from which a die can be made; generally a metal model of the part to be cast with process shrinkage added.

Mechanical properties Those properties of a material that reveal the elastic and inelastic properties when force is applied. This term should not be used interchangeably with "physical properties."

Metal lot A master heat that has been approved for casting and given a sequential number by the foundry.

Mold Normally consists of a top and bottom form, made of sand, metal or any other investment material. It contains the cavity into which molten metal is poured to produce a casting of definite shape.

Mold cavity The impression in a mold produced by removal of the pattern. It is filled with molten metal to form the casting.

Mold coating (See core wash.)

Nobake process Molds/cores produced with a resin-bonded air-setting sand. Also known as the airset process because molds are left to harden under normal atmospheric conditions.

Parting line The line showing the separation of the two halves of the mold.

Pattern The wood, metal, foam or plastic shape used to form the cavity in the sand. A pattern may consist of one or many impressions and would normally be mounted on a board or plate complete with a runner system.

Pattern draft The taper allowed on the vertical faces of a pattern to permit easy withdrawal of the pattern from the mold or die. (See draft.)

Pattern layout Full-sized drawing of a pattern showing its arrangement and structural features.

Patternmaker's shrinkage The shrinkage allowance made on all patterns to compensate for the change in dimensions as the solidified casting cools in the mold from freezing temperature of the metal to room temperature. The pattern is made larger by the amount of shrinkage characteristic of the particular metal in the casting and the amount of resulting contraction to be encountered.

Permeability The property of a mold material to allow passage of mold/core gases during the pouring of molten metal.

Physical properties Properties of matter such as density, electrical and thermal conductivity, expansion and specific heat. This term should not be used interchangeably with "mechanical properties."

Pig iron Blocks of iron to a known metal chemical analysis that are used for melting (with suitable additions of scrap, etc.) for the production of ferrous castings.

Pilot or sample casting A casting made from a pattern produced in a production die to check the accuracy of dimensions and quality of castings that will be made.

Porosity Holes in the casting due to: gases trapped in the mold, the reaction of molten metal with moisture in the molding sand, or the imperfect fusion of chaplets with molten metal.

Recovery rate Ratio of the number of saleable parts to the total number of parts manufactured, expressed as a percentage.

Refractory Heat-resistant ceramic material.

Reject rate Ratio of the number of parts scrapped to the total number of parts manufactured, expressed as a percentage.

Riser (See feeder.)

Runner system or gating The set of channels in a mold through which molten metal is poured to fill the mold cavity. The system normally consists of a vertical section (downgate or sprue) to the point where it joins the mold cavity (gate) and leads from the mold cavity through vertical channels (risers or feeders) (Fig. 3).

Sand inclusions Cavities or surface imperfections on a casting caused by sand washing into the mold cavity.

Scrap (a) Any scrap metal melted (usually with suitable additions of pig iron or ingots) to produce castings; (b) reject castings.

Shakeout The process of separating the solidified casting from the mold material.

Shrinkage Contraction of metal in the mold during solidification. The term also is used to describe the casting defect, such as shrinkage cavity, which results

from poor design, insufficient metal feed or inadequate feeding.

Slag A fused nonmetallic material that protects molten metal from the air and extracts certain impurities from the melt.

Slag inclusions Casting surface imperfections similar to sand inclusions but containing impurities from the charge materials, silica and clay eroded from the refractory lining, and ash from the fuel during the melting process. May also originate from metal-refractory reactions occurring in the ladle during pouring of the casting.

Slurry A flowable mixture of refractory particles suspended in a liquid.

Sodium silicate/CO2 process Molding sand is mixed with sodium silicate and the mold is gassed with CO_2 gas to produce a hard mold or core.

Sprue (downsprue-downgate) The channel, usually vertical, that the molten metal enters.

Test bar Standard specimen bar designed to permit determination of mechanical properties of the metal from which it was poured.

Test lug A lug cast as a part of the casting and later removed for testing purposes.

Vent An opening or passage in a mold or core to facilitate escape of gases when the mold is poured.

ACKNOWLEDGMENTS

This section has been reprinted with the permission of the American Foundrymen's Society. This glossary is available on the Engineered Casting Solutions website at www.castsolution

Metalcasting Industry Organizations
Michael J. Lessiter and Ross Foti
The American Foundrymen's Society

Reprinted from Engineered Casting Solutions Spring/Summer 1999 Issue

GLOSSARY OF METAL CASTING TERMS

This listing of technical organizations is intended to be a resource to automotive product engineers, casting designers, and purchasing representatives.

The Aluminum Assn., Inc.
9–00 19th St., NW
Washington, DC 20006-7168
202/862-5100
Fax: 202/862-5164
Website: www. alum.org
   A subcommittee—the Technical Committee on Castings—is responsible for producing a major casting publication, "Standards for Aluminum Sand and Permanent Mold Castings." Publications: Special Reports on Mechanical Properties of Sand and Permanent Mold Aluminum Alloy Test Castings.

American Foundrymen's Society, Inc.
505 State St.
Des Plaines, IL 60016-8399
800/537-4237; 847/824-0181
Fax: 847/824-7848
Website: www.afsinc.org
Charles H. Jones, Executive Vice President
   Services offered by the Society include: more than 200 technical publications; computer programs for the foundry industry; technical and management committee participation; annual Casting Congress and triennial CastExpo; reference library with information retrieval and abstract service; technical field services; insurance programs; industry research; environmental testing for airborne contaminants and leachates; in-plant assistance for contract negotiation, grievance handling and arbitration; supervisory training; marketing assistance; organization of grass-roots lobbying efforts; and annual issues/action conferences. Publications: modern casting; Engineered Casting Solutions/Casting Source Directory, Transactions of Casting Congresses; Annual Forecast of Casting Demand; Hourly Wage and Benefit Survey; Salary Survey; Benefits Cost Survey; Human Resources Report; Labor Case Comments; catalog of publications, software and services.

ASM International
9639 Kinsman Rd.
Materials Park, OH 44073
440/338-5151
Fax: 440/338-4634
E-Mail: mem-serv@po.asm-intl.org
Website: www.asm-intl.org
   The organization gathers, processes, disseminates and publishes information on metals, metalworking and engineered materials. ASM's goal is to promote the understanding and application of engineered materials and their research, design, reliable manufacture, use, and economic and social benefits.

Canadian Foundry Assn.
1 Nicholas St.
Ste. 1500
Ottawa, Ontario K1N 7B7
Canada
613/789-4894
Fax: 613/789-5957
Judith Arbour, Executive Director
   Assists and represents the membership in dealing with government on industry-specific issues

and other areas of interest. Communicates information to the industry to assist members in strengthening their own competitive position, thus ensuring a strong Canadian foundry industry.

Casting Industry Suppliers Assn.
223 West Jackson Blvd.
Suite 800
Chicago, IL 60606
312/957-1701
Fax: 312/957-1702
www.cisa.org
info@cisa.org
Darla Boudjenah, Executive Director
CISA is an association of manufacturers of equipment and consumable supplies for the metalcasting industry. Founded in 1919, it provides information, education and opportunities for its members, including such services as collecting, analyzing and disseminating industry statistics relevant to members; providing a forum for direct contact between its members, their customers, distributors, industry associations, government agencies and educators in the foundry industry; and developing ties with international associations that have common objectives.

Cast Metals Institute, Inc. of AFS
505 State St.
Des Plaines, IL 60016-8399
800/537-4237 847/824-0181
Fax: 847/824-7848
Website: www.castmetals.com
Wayne M. Rasmussen, Executive Director
The Cast Metals Institute is the continuing education department of the American Foundrymen's Society, Inc. Courses dealing with metalcasting technology to upgrade foundry and design personnel are conducted at the Institute's facilities, as well as at various locations in the U.S., Canada and Mexico. Professional certification in seven areas of foundry operations can be obtained.

Copper Development Assn. Inc.
260 Madison Ave.
New York, NY 10016
212/251-7200
Fax: 212/251-7234
CDA serves as the advanced market development and engineering development services arm of the copper and brass industry in the U.S. The association has three major objectives: to create business opportunities for its members by expanding the markets and applications for copper and its alloys; to defend existing copper markets; and to provide technical support to customer industries in their use of copper metals.

Diecasting Development Council
9701 W. Higgins Rd.
Suite 855
Rosemont, IL 60018-7421
847/292-3625
Fax: 847/292-3613
Website: www.diecasting.org/ddc
Leo J. Baran, Executive Director
The DDC is the OEM technical communications affiliate of the North American Die Casting Assn. Services: facilitates design planning, die casting and casting production through its members and the toll free "DDC Design Information Line." Literature: distributes design, specification and sourcing documents. Seminars: sponsors regional "Design for Die Casting" seminars.

Ductile Iron Society
28900 Office Park
28938 Lorain Rd./Suite 202
North Olmsted, OH 44070
440/734-8040
Fax: 440/734-8182
Website: www.ductile.org

DIS concentrates its efforts on ductile iron technology pertaining to production, properties and applications. DIS sponsors research and keeps members informed through a system of meetings and publications of new technology. Publications: Ductile Iron News.

The Ferroalloys Assn.
1505 Crystal Dr.
Arlington, VA 22202
202/842-0292
Fax: 202/842-4840
Services of the association include technology, international trade matters, environmental affairs, safety, legislative matters and government relations.

Foundry Educational Foundation
484 E. Northwest Highway
Des Plaines, IL 60016-2202
847/299-1776
Fax: 847/299-1789
E-Mail: FEFoffice@aol.com
Website: www.FEFoffice.org
Bill W. Sorensen, Executive Director
FEF provides the cast metals industry with an adequate supply of college-degreed, technical manpower; develops a favorable climate for casting research by directing the interest of a larger number of professors and students to the casting field; and promotes knowledgeable teaching staffs and practical cast metals courses at colleges and technical institutes. Publications: University staff directory listing all the FEF schools with key university personnel.

Institute of Scrap Recycling Industries, Inc.
1325 G St. NW
Washington, DC 20005
202/737-1770
Fax: 202/626-0900
Robin Wiener, Executive Director
ISRI is the trade association representing processors, brokers and consumers of ferrous and nonferrous metals, paper, glass, plastics and textiles. Its 1800 member companies, operating at more than 5000 locations, annually return more than 95 million tons of recovered materials to the economic mainstream.

International Lead Zinc Research Organization, Inc.
PO Box 12036
2525 Meridian Parkway
Research Triangle Park, NC 27709
919/361-4647
Fax: 919/361-1957
Research and technology services for all lead and zinc castings, both gravity and pressure cast. Database on alloy processing and properties. Publications: manuals and reports on lead and zinc alloy casting technology.

International Magnesium Assn.
1303 Vincent Place
Suite 1
McLean, VA 22101
703/442-8888
Fax: 703/821-1824
Website: www.intlmag.org
IMA promotes the general welfare of the magnesium industry by collecting and disseminating information, encouraging research and publicizing innovative uses of the metal. Publications: technical papers, books, videos and informational brochures.

International Titanium Assn.
1871 Folsom St.
Ste. 200
Boulder, CO 80302-5714
303/443-7515
Fax: 303/443-4406

Services available through the association include the distribution of various technical publications (see below), as well as the promotion of titanium in industrial, commercial and aerospace applications. Publications: Titanium the Choice...; Titanium Technology; Present Status and Future Trends, Proceedings; 1990 Conference on Titanium. Products and Applications; Titanium Statistics; How to Weld Titanium (Video).

Investment Casting Institute
8350 N. Central Expwy.
Suite M1110
Dallas, TX 75206-1602
214/368-8896
Fax: 214/368-8852
Website: www.investmentcasting.org

The Institute is a trade association representing investment casters in 16 countries. It acts as the statistical, promotional, educational and communication voice of the industry. The Institute holds annual management and technical meetings, and sponsors industry trade shows and numerous training seminars. Publications: Conference proceedings; Industry Newsmagazine, INCAST; training manuals; video tapes; industry surveys; and handbook.

Iron Casting Research Institute
2802 Fisher Rd.
Suite B
Columbus, OH 43204-3574
614/275-4201; 614/275-4202
Fax: 614/275-4203
E-mail: icri@csi.com
Website: www.ironcasting.org

Provides technology transfer and application of known technology into member companies' operations and the development of new technical/operating features. Objectives are accomplished through committees, topical meetings and workshops, and plant and lab service for members and casting users, as well as complementary involvement by staff and members in other industry groups. Publications: technical reports, surveys and extracts—principally for member companies.

Lead Industries Assn.
13 Main St.
Sparta, NJ 07871
973/726-5323
Fax: 973/726-4484

Services include market development, technology transfer, publicity, advertising, audio/visuals, publications and technical literature. Publications: Directory of Lead Casters; Properties of Lead and Lead Alloys; Lead for Corrosion Resistant Applications: A Guide.

Non-Ferrous Founders' Society
1480 Renaissance Drive
Suite 310
Park Ridge, IL 60068
847/299-0950
Fax: 847/299-3598
E-Mail: staff@nffs.org
Website: www.nffs.org
James L. Mallory, CAE, Executive Director

The only national foundry trade association exclusively representing the concerns and interests of brass, bronze and aluminum foundries. Conducts surveys and seminars on important industry issues. Annual meeting offers informative and educational presentations on industry and management topics. Monitors government regulations affecting nonferrous foundries. ISO-compliant quality documentation system NQS 9000. Publications: Crucible magazine and Directory of Non-Ferrous Foundries (computer disk and book versions); monthly newsletter; bimonthly safety/regulatory newsletter; government affairs bulletins. Casting design reference manuals for aluminum and copper-base alloys.

North American Die Casting Association
9701 W. Higgins Rd.
Suite 880
Rosemont, IL 60018-4721
847/292-3600

Fax: 847/292-3620
Faxback information system: 847/292-3622
E-mail: nadca@diecasting.org
Website: www.diecasting.org
Daniel L. Twarog, Executive Vice President

Services of NADCA include: education and training courses; develop product standards; publish magazine, text and reference books; Washington Affairs; business indicators; industry surveys produce biennial exposition and congress and technical conferences; maintain reference library; manage industry R&D projects and all matters of diecasting industry interest. Publications: Diecasting Engineer; Transactions of each biennial Congress; variety of diecasting text and reference books.

Society of Manufacturing Engineers

One SME Dr.
PO Box 930
Dearborn, MI 48121-0930
313/271-1500
Fax: 313/271-2861

Educational activities and materials available for manufacturing engineers and managers include local chapters, expositions, conferences, in-plant courses, periodicals, books, newsletters, videotapes, etc. Also, certification for engineers and technologists; education foundation; and related membership associations in robotics, machine vision, computer and automated manufacturing systems, composites, electronics manufacturing, finishing and research. Publications: Manufacturing Engineering (monthly magazine); Forming Fabrication, Integrated Design-Manufacturing, Plastics, Rapid Prototyping, Machining, Technology, Forming, Journal of Mfg. Research; Tool & Mfg. Engineers handbook; SME News (newspaper); and technology quarterlies on robotics, machine vision, composites, electronics manufacturing and finishing.

Steel Founders' Society of America

205 Park Avenue
Barrington, IL 60010
847/382-8240
Fax: 847/382-8287
Website: www.sfsa.org
Raymond W. Monroe, Executive Vice President

Steel casting technical information development and exchange, including technical research projects, regional and national technical conferences, is the driving force of SFSA. The Society represents the steel foundry industry in development of product specifications by ASTM, ISO, etc. Regional and national management meetings, collection of industry statistics and production of collateral material for steel foundry sales personnel are also part of SFSA's program. Publications: Steel Castings Handbook and Supplements; Directory of Steel Foundries; and Buyers' Guide.

ACKNOWLEDGMENTS

This section has been reprinted with the permission of the American Foundrymen's Society. More information is available on the Engineered Casting Solutions website at www.castsolution.com.

Metalcasting University Programs
Bill W. Sorenson, Executive Director
The Foundry Education Foundation

FOUNDRY EDUCATIONAL FOUNDATION SCHOOLS

This listing of Foundry Educational Foundation Schools and Contact Information is intended to be a resource to automotive product engineers, casting designers, and purchasing representatives.

ALABAMA, UNIVERSITY OF
205/348-1748 (Fax 205/348-8574) P.O. Box 870202, Tuscaloosa, AL 35487-0202
- Andrew Sorensen, President
- Timothy J. Greene, Dean, College of Engineering
- Richard Bradt, Professor and Head, Metallurgical and Materials Engineering
- Doru M. Stefanescu, Professor, Metallurgical and Materials Engineering
- E-Mail: doru@coe.eng.ua.edu
- Nagy H. El-Kaddah, Associate Professor, Metallurgical and Materials Engineering
- Thomas S. Piwonka, Director, Metal Casting Technology Center
- Darrell Hobson, Director, Engineering Placement

BRADLEY UNIVERSITY
309/677-2982 (Fax 309/677-2853)
Department of Industrial Mfg. Engineering & Tech., Peoria, IL 61625
- Dr. Alexey Sverdlin, Associate Professor, IMET Department
- E-Mail: sverdlin@bradley.bradley.edu

CALIFORNIA STATE UNIVERSITY, CHICO
916/898-5097 or 5346 (Fax 916/898-4675)
Department of Mechanical Engineering and Manufacturing, Chico, CA 95929-0789
- Manuel Esteban, President
- Kenneth Derucher, Dean, College of Engineering, Computer Science, and Technology
- Michael Waid, Chairman, Department of Mechanical Engineering and Manufacturing
- W. Ray Rummell, Professor and Coordinator of Manufacturing Systems Management
- E-Mail: rrummell@csuchico.edu
- Noele M. Winans, Director of Placement

CALIFORNIA STATE POLYTECHNIC UNIVERSITY, POMONA
909/869-2571 (Fax 909/869-2564)
3801 W. Temple Ave., Pomona, CA 91768
- Bob Suzuki, President
- Dr. Edward C. Hohmann, Dean, College of Engineering
- George Matulich, Professor, Industrial & Manufacturing Engineering
- E-Mail: gamatulich@csupomona.edu
- Don Zook, Professor, Department of Industrial and Manufacturing Engineering
- Manuel Perez, Placement

CALIFORNIA POLYTECHNIC STATE UNIVERSITY, SAN LUIS OBISPO
805/756-2131 (Fax 805/756-6503)
College of Engineering, San Luis Obispo, CA 93407
- Warren J. Baker, President
- Peter Y. Lee, Dean, College of Engineering
- H. JoAnne Freeman, Chair, Department of Industrial and Manufacturing Engineering
- Robert Heidersbach, Head, Department of Material Engineering
- Paul E. Rainey, Professor, Department of Material Engineering, and Associate Dean, College of Engineering
- E-Mail: prainey@calpoly.edu
- Richard Strahl, Associate Professor, Department of Industrial and Manufacturing Engineering
- Martin Koch, Lecturer, Department of Industrial and Manufacturing Engineering

- E-Mail: mkoch@calpoly.edu
- Richard Equinoa, Director of Placement

CASE WESTERN RESERVE UNIVERSITY
216/368-4221 (Fax 216/368-3209)
10900 Euclid Ave. 506 White Building, Department of Materials Science and Engineering Cleveland, OH 44106-7204
- Agnar Pytte, President
- Richard A. Zdanis, Provost
- Tom Kicher, Dean of Engineering
- John F. Wallace, LTV Professor Emeritus
- Gary M. Michal, Associate Professor of Metallurgy
- E-Mail: gmm3@po.cwru.edu
- Clayton T. Barnard, Director of Career Planning and Placement

CENTRAL WASHINGTON UNIVERSITY
509/963-1191 (Fax 509/963-1795)
Industrial and Engineering Technology, Ellensburg, WA 98926
- Dr. Ivory Nelson, President
- Dr. Lin Douglas, Dean, College of Education & Professional Studies
- Dr. Tim Ytheimer, Department Chairman of Industrial and Engineering and Technology
- Dr. G. W.(Bo) Beed, Professor of Industrial and Engineering Technology
- E-Mail: beedg@cwu.edu
- Dr. Walter Kaminski, Associate Professor of Industrial Engineering Technology
- Robert Malde, Interim Director of Career Planning and Placement

CINCINNATI, UNIVERSITY OF
513/556-6580 (Fax 513/556-5056)
College of Applied Science, Cincinnati, OH 45206-2839
- Joseph A. Steger, President
- Allen Arthur, Interim Dean, College of Applied Science
- Laura Caldwell, Head, Department of Mechanical Engineering Technology
- Dick Able, Department Head, Department of Professional Practice
- Allen Arthur, Interim Dean, College of Applied Science
- E-Mail: allen.arthur@uc.edu
- Richard J. Abel, Dept. Head/Faculty, Professional Practice

KENT STATE UNIVERSITY
330/672-2892 (Fax 330/672-2894)
P.O. Box 5190, School of Technology Kent, OH 44242-0001
- Carol Cartwright, President
- Dr. A. Raj Chowdhury, Dean
- Scott W. Layman, Associate Professor, School of Technology
- E-Mail: slayman@tech.kent.edu
- John Rowe, Associate Professor, School of Technology
- Thomas Cobett, Part-Time Instructor, School of Technology
- Vasko Popovsky, Part-Time Instructor
- David Baumgarner, Director of Career Planning and Placement

KETTERING UNIVERSITY
810/762-7875 (Fax 810/762-9924)
1700 W. Third Ave., Flint, MI 48504-4898
- James E.A. John, President
- John D. Lorenz, Vice President for Academic Affairs
- B. Lee Tuttle, Professor, Industrial & Mfg. Engineering
- E-Mail: btuttle@kettering.edu
- Charles V. White, Professor
- Robert Nichols, V.P.-Recruitment, Retention & Placement

MASSACHUSETTS INSTITUTE OF TECHNOLOGY

617/253-3233 (Fax 617/258-6886)
77 Massachusetts Ave. Building 8, Room 407 Cambridge, MA 02139
- Charles Vest, President
- Thomas L. Magnanti, Acting Dean of Engineering
- Samuel Allen, Department of Materials Science & Engineering
- E-Mail: smallen@mit.edu
- Toby Bashaw, Professor, Department of Materials Science & Engineering
- E-Mail: trbashaw@mit.edu
- Douglas Matson, Dept. of Materials Science & Engr.
- Christopher Pratt, Director, Office of Career Services

MICHIGAN TECHNOLOGICAL UNIVERSITY
906/487-2632 (Fax 906/487-2934)
Department of Metallurgical & Materials Engineering 1400 Townsend Drive Houghton, MI 49931
- Curtis J. Tompkins, President
- Fredrick J. Dobney, Executive Vice President and Provost
- Robert Warrington, Dean, College of Engineering
- Calvin L, White, Professor and Chair, Department of Metallurgical and Materials Engineering
- Karl B. Rundman, Professor, Metallurgical and Materials Engineering
- E-Mail: krundman@mtu.edu
- Donald E. Mikkola, Professor, Metallurgical and Materials Engineering
- Dennis Moore, Engineer/Scientist
- Joseph A. Galleto, Director, University Career Center

MICHIGAN, UNIVERSITY OF
734/764-7489 or 734/936-0248 (Fax 734/763-4788)
2300 Hayward Street 2146B Dow Building North Campus Ann Arbor, MI 48109-2136
- Lee C. Bollinger, President
- Stephen W. Director, Dean, College of Engineering
- Albert Yee, Head, Materials Science and Engineering
- Robert D. Pehlke, Professor, Materials Science and Engineering
- E-Mail: bob_pehlke@mse.engin.umich.edu
- Paul K. Trojan, Professor, Metallurgical Engineering - Dearborn
- C. Dootz, Placement Service

MISSOURI-ROLLA, UNIVERSITY OF
573/341-4711 or 4730 (Fax 573/341-6934)
223 McNutt Hall, School of Mines and Metallurgy Rolla, MO 65409
- John T. Park, Chancellor
- Lee Saperstein, Dean, School of Mines and Metallurgy
- John L Watson, Professor, Chairman, Department of Metallurgical Engineering
- Don R. Askeland, Professor, Metallurgical Engineering
- E-Mail: askeland@umr.edu
- Chris Ramsay, Associate Professor, Metallurgical Engineering
- David VanAken, Associate Professor, Metallurgical Engineering
- Robert Wolf, Professor Emeritus, Metallurgical Engineering
- Kent Peaslee, Assistant Professor, Metallurgical Engineering
- Jamie Archer, Director, Career Placement & Co-op

NORTHERN IOWA, UNIVERSITY OF
319/273-2590 (Fax 319/273-5818)
Department of Industrial Technology Cedar Falls, IA 50614
- Robert D. Koob, President
- Dr. Gerald Intermann, Dean, College of Natural Science
- Dr. Mohammed F. Fahmy, Professor & Head, Dept. of Industrial Technology
- Dr. Yury Lerner, Professor
- E-Mail: yury.lerner@uni.edu
- Douglas H. Miller, Director, Metal Casting Center
- Allan Stamberg, Cooperative Education Director

- Muriel Stone, Director, Counseling, Placement and Career Services

THE OHIO STATE UNIVERSITY
614/292-5770 (Fax 614/292-8186)
Department of Metallurgical Engineering, 2041 College Rd., Columbus, OH 43210
- William Kirwan, President
- Dr. David B. Ashley, Dean, College of Engineering
- Robert Snyder, Chairman, Department of Materials Science and Engineering
- Carroll E. Mobley, Professor, Materials Science and Engineering
- E-Mail: mobley.1@osu.edu
- A. Miller, Chairman, Department of Industrial Systems Engineering
- Jerry Brevick, Associate Professor,Industrial, Welding & Systems Engineering
- Taylan Altan, Director, NSF Engineering Research Center for Net Shaping Manufacturing
- Marianne Mueller, Placement Director, College of Engineering

PENNSYLVANIA STATE UNIVERSITY
814/863-7290 (Fax 814/863-4745)
Department of Industrial and Manufacturing Engineering, 207 Hammond Building, University Park, PA 16802
- Graham Spanier, President
- David N. Wormley, Dean, College of Engineering
- Robert C. Voigt, Professor, Department of Industrial Engineering
- E-Mail: rcv2@psu.edu
- Donald A. Koss, Chairman, Metal Science and Engineering
- J. Kim, Program Manager
- Joseph L.Platt, Metalcasting Technician
- Robert Haefner, Metalcasting Research Manager
- Richard G Swails, Director of Development

PITTSBURGH STATE UNIVERSITY
316/235-4375 (Fax 316/235-4004)
Department of Engineering Technology Pittsburgh, KS 66762-7565
- John R. Darling, President
- Thomas R. Baldwin, Dean, College of Technology
- James L. Otter, Chairman, Department of Engineering Technology
- William L. Williamson, Professor, Department of Engineering Technology
- Phil McNew, Associate Professor, Department of Engineering Technology
- Russell L. Rosmait, Professor, Department of Engineering Technology
- E-Mail: rrosmait@pittstate.edu
- J. Don Book, Assistant Professor, Department of Engineering Technology
- Pamela I. Ehlers, Director of Career Services

PURDUE UNIVERSITY - INDIANAPOLIS
317/274-7377 (Fax 317/278-3669)
799 West Michigan Street Department of Manufacturing Technology Indianapolis, IN 46202
- Dr. H. Oner Yurtseven, Dean, School of Engineering and Technology
- Ken Rennels, Chairman, Department of Mechanical Engineering Technology
- Jamie Workman, Assistant Professor, Mechanical Engineering Technology
- E-Mail workman@engr.iupui.edu

PURDUE UNIVERSITY -WEST LAFAYETTE
765/494-5866 (765/494-6219)
Knoy Building, Room 117 West Lafayette, IN 47907
- Steven Beering, President
- Don Gentry, Dean, School of Technology
- Mark Pagano, Head, Department of Mechanical Engineering Technology
- Mileta M. Tomovic, Associate Professor, Department Mechanical Engineering Technology
- E-Mail: mmtomovic@tech.purdue.edu
- R. A. Stewart, Director, University Placement Services

SOUTHWEST TEXAS STATE UNIVERSITY
512/245-2137 (Fax 512/245-3052)
Department of Technology San Marcos, TX 78666
- Jerome Supple, President
- Robert Gratz, Vice President of Academic Affairs
- Gene Martin, Dean, Applied Arts and Technology
- Robert Habingreither, CMfgE, Chair, Department of Technology
- E-Mail: rh03@a1.swt.edu
- Gary Winek, Associate Professor, Materials Quality Assurance
- Vedaramin Sriraman, Assistant Professor Manufacturing Technology
- Curt Schafer, Director of Placement

TENNESSEE TECHNOLOGICAL UNIVERSITY
931/372-3527 (Fax 931/372-6172)
Department of Industrial Technology Cookeville, TN 38505
- Dr. Angelo Volpe, President
- Dr. Glen E. Johnson, Dean, College of Engineering
- Dr. L. Fred Vondra, Assistant Professor, Industrial Technology Department
- E-Mail: fvondra@tntech.edu
- Dr. Robert Craighead, Career Services

TRI STATE UNIVERSITY
219/665-4235 or 800/347-4878 (Fax 219/665-4188)
Aerospace and Mechanical Engineering P. O. Box 307 Angola, IN 46703-0307
- Dr. R. John Reynolds, President
- Paul Barker, Chairman, Cast Metals Industrial Advisory Committee
- Dr. Tom Enneking, Vice President of Academic Affairs
- Von L. Richards, Associate Professor, Mechanical Engineering Department
- E-Mail: richardsv@alpha.tristate.edu
- Jane L. Mitchell, Career Center Director

VIRGINIA POLYTECHNIC INSTITUTE AND STATE UNIVERSITY
540/231-6825 (Fax 540/231-8919)
Department of Materials Science and Engineering Blacksburg, VA 24061-0237
- Dr. Paul Torgerson, President
- F. W. Stephenson, Dean, College of Engineering
- Ronald S. Gordon, Head, Department of Materials Engineering
- William T. Reynolds, Jr., Associate Professor, Materials and Engineering
- E-Mail Bill Reynolds at: reynolds@vt.edu
- J. H. Malone, Director, Placement Services

WESTERN MICHIGAN UNIVERSITY
616/387-4046 (Fax 616/387-4075)
Department of Industrial and Manufacturing Engineering Kalamazoo, MI 49008
- Dr. Elson Floyd, President
- Leonard Lamberson, Dean, College of Engineering and Applied Science
- Phillip Guichelaar, Associate Professor, Mechanical Engineering
- Sam N. Ramrattan, Professor, Industrial and Manufacturing Engineering
- E-Mail: ramrattan@wmich.edu
- Larry Williams, Coordinator, Cooperative Education
- Marsha Bernhart, Director of Placement

WINDSOR, UNIVERSITY OF
519/253-3000 Ext. 3588 (Fax 519/561-1405)
Mechanical and Materials Engineering Prog., 209 Essex Hall 401 Sunset Ave. Windsor, Ontario, Canada N9B 3P4
- Dr. Norm Wilson, Interim Dean, Faculty of Engineering
- Phil Alexander, Associate Dean, Faculty of Engineering
- Dr. Jerry Sokolowski, Ph.D, Engineer, Senior Industrial Research Chair and Associate Professor
- E-Mail: moosber@uwindsor.ca

WISCONSIN - MADISON, UNIVERSITY OF

608/262-2562 (Fax 608/262-8353)

Department of Materials Science and Engineering 1509 University Avenue, Madison, WI 53706

- Dr. Paul Peercy, Dean, College of Engineering
- Eric E. Hellstrom, Professor & Chairman, Dept. of Materials Science & Engineering
- Kenneth W. Ragland, Professor and Chairman, Department of Mechanical Engineering
- Fred J. Bradley, Assistant Professor, Department of Materials Science and Engineering
- Richard W. Heine, Emeritus Professor, Department of Materials Science and Engineering
- Jay Samuel, Senior Lecturer, Department of Materials Science and Engineering Mechanical Engineering
- Carl R. Loper, Jr., Professor, Department of Materials Science and Engineering
- E-Mail: loper@engr.wisc.edu
- Kyle E. Metzloff, Teaching Assistant, Department of Materials Science and Engineering
- Sandra Amn, Director, Career Planning and Placement

WISCONSIN - MILWAUKEE, UNIVERSITY OF

414/229-4987 (Fax 4l4/229-6958)

Materials Department, 3200 North Cramer Street, EMS Building, Milwaukee, WI 53211

- Dr. S.H. Chan, Dean, College of Engineering
- Devarajan Venugopalan, Professor and Chairman, Materials Department
- Pradeep K. Rohatgi, Wisconsin Distinguished Professor and Director Foundry and Composites Laboratory, Materials Department
- E-Mail: prohatgi@csd.uwm.edu
- Hugo F. Lopez, Associate Professor, Materials Department
- Devarajan Venugopalan, Associate Professor, Materials Department
- Robert D. Borchelt, Assistant Professor, Department of Industrial and Manufacturing

WISCONSIN - PLATTEVILLE, UNIVERSITY OF

608/342-1141 (Fax 608/342-1254)

Department of Industrial Studies, 1 University Plaza, Platteville, W1 538l8-3099

- Dr. David Markee, Chancellor
- Dean, College of Business, Industry, Life Science and Agriculture
- Joseph F. Thomas, Head, Department of Industrial Studies, Industrial Internship Coordinator
- Roger E. Hauser, Professor, Department of Industrial Studies
- E-Mail: hauserr@uwplatt.edu
- Roger L. Hoover, Professor, Department of Industrial Studies
- Majid Tabrizi, Associate Professor, Department of Industrial Studies
- Sandra Stacy, Placement Director

WORCESTER POLYTECHNIC INSTITUTE

508/831-5647 (Fax 508/831-5178)

Department of Mechanical Engineering,100 Institute Road, Worcester, MA 01609

- Edward A. Parish, President
- John Carney, Provost and Howmet Professor of Engineering
- Mohammad Noori Professor and Department Head, Mechanical Engineering
- Richard D. Sisson, Jr., Professor, Mechanical Engineering, Section Head-Materials Engineering
- Makhlouf Makhlouf, Associate Professor, Mechanical Engineering
- E-Mail: mmm@wpi.edu
- Yvonne Harrison, Career Development

ACKNOWLEDGMENTS

This section has been reprinted with the permission of the American Foundrymen's Society. More information is available on the Engineered Casting Solutions website at www.castsolution.com.